LLOYD'S OF LONDON

RAYMOND FLOWER · MICHAEL WYNN JONES
LLOYD'S OF LONDON
AN ILLUSTRATED HISTORY

LLOYD'S OF LONDON PRESS LTD

Cover: *View of Richard Roger's new Lloyd's building looking over Leadenhall Market.*
Inset: *Salvage in space of the Westar satellite by US astronauts from the shuttle Discovery.*

First published in 1974
Revised edition 1981 published by Lloyd's of London Press Limited
Sheepen Place, Colchester, Essex CO3 3LP
Reprinted 1983
Third edition 1987

USA and Canada
Lloyds of London Press Inc
611 Broadway
New York, NY 10012, USA

Germany
Lloyd's of London Press (Germany) GmbH
PO Box 1123 47, Deichstrasse 41
2000 Hamburg 11
West Germany

South-East Asia
Lloyd's of London Press (Far East) Ltd
903 Chung Nam Building
1 Lockhart Road, Wanchai
Hong Kong

The authors gratefully acknowledge the assistance given by the following picture sources

Lloyd's Library
Radio Times Hulton Picture Library
Mary Evans Picture Library
Mansell Collection
Greenwich Maritime Museum
British Museum: Crace Collection
U.S. Information Service
Bateman Cartoon by courtesy of Mr. G. J. Stewart of Stewart, Smith
Associated Press

Designed and produced by Nicholas Enterprises Limited
70 Old Compton Street, London W1V 5PA

British Library Cataloguing in Publication Data

Flower, Raymond
    Lloyd's of London : an illustrated history.
    1. Lloyd's of London—History   2. Insurance
    —Great Britain—History
    I. Title   II. Wynn Jones, Michael
    368'.012'094212   HG8039

ISBN 1-85044-121-9

Printed in Belgium

TO
AGML
WITH GRATITUDE

WAITING FOR BAD NEWS.

"One of the most important local objects in the commerce of this enterprising country and indeed of the globe itself, is Lloyd's Coffee House, a name which it derived from the first person who kept it, and who little imagined that it would progressively acquire a celebrity as great in the annals of the commercial world as that of any sovereign in the history of courts."

The Percy Anecdotes Vol. XVIII p. 175 (1823)

CONTENTS

MODERN LLOYD'S 129

IMPORTANT DATES IN LLOYD'S HISTORY   186

FOREWORD
By the Chairman of Lloyd's

Since this illustrated history of Lloyd's was first published in 1974 there have been several reprints, and a second edition in 1981. Only six years later it has been found necessary to produce a third edition because those few years have seen momentous changes at Lloyds: the passing of the Lloyd's Act, the setting up of a new Council and regulatory structure, the advent of computerised information to assist underwriting, and the opening by Her Majesty the Queen of the new headquarters in Lime Street. Like other sectors of the City, Lloyd's has also had its share of problems and controversies in this period, but on the eve of its three hundredth anniversary in 1988 its future has rarely looked brighter. Membership stands at an all-time high of more than 31,000, and Lloyd's premium income capacity is in excess of £10,000 million.

It is instructive to see Lloyd's in a worldwide context, to see how it affects the daily lives of people all over the globe, and how the members of the Society have sought to extend the frontiers of risk-taking—and continue to do so, for instance in the brilliant salvage of errant satellites in space. *Lloyd's of London*, by Michael Wynn Jones and Raymond Flower, offers just that perspective, and explains how Lloyd's has evolved into a unique and important British institution.

Peter Miller

AUTHORS' PREFACE

THIS IS NOW the third edition of *Lloyd's of London* and it brings the story of this great institution right up to date. Since the book was first published in 1974 the Society has suffered mixed fortunes; but the intervening years have been a period of very significant change, during which membership has grown from under 8,000 to over 31,000 Names. In a sense, therefore, Lloyd's is entering a new era as it prepares to celebrate its tercentenary.

The story of Lloyd's has been told before, but most previous publications have tended to be specialised and are now out of print. So there seemed to be a need not simply for an up-dated account of how an ordinary London coffee-house grew into the acknowledged world centre of risk insurance, but rather – since it touches the daily lives of business concerns and private individuals everywhere – for this remarkable British organisation to be presented as graphically as possible and in its widest historical context.

Although this book is now published by Lloyd's of London Press it was not originally commissioned by the Corporation or indeed anyone else. Yet from the moment the idea was first suggested we have received a greater and kinder support from everyone concerned, from the Chairman downwards, than we could have hoped for. In particular we would express our gratitude to Mr. Paul Dixey and the Committee of Lloyd's for having backed the project from the start, and to the present Chairman, Mr. Peter Miller, for having inspired this new edition. We also wish to thank Mr. Clifford Welch and successive members of the Information Department, Leonard Kirby and Terry Atkins who so enthusiastically threw open the dustiest of archives and answered our most outlandish queries in the beginning, and to Peter Hill who helped us to take the story up to 1987.

Once again it is a pleasure to dedicate the book to our good friend Mark Loveday, without whose constant and heart-warming encouragement it would surely never have seen the light of day. That is the least we can do.

Raymond Flower
Michael Wynn Jones

THE BEGINNINGS OF LLOYD'S

Previous page: *one of the earliest merchant vessels, a Greek trireme of the sixth century BC as depicted on an Attic cup, found at Vulci.*

THE ORIGINS OF INSURANCE

EVEN AS MAN gropes out towards the stars, he makes prudently sure of being protected on earth; and Lloyd's, to no one's great surprise, has already given cover for a car on the moon. So timeless, indeed, is this desire to hedge the risks that the origins of insurance are buried in the earliest dawn of antiquity. While evidence may lack that the ancient Egyptians underwrote their long "double-ended" vessels against disaster, an engraved stele unearthed in Mesopotamia, known as the Code of Khammurabi (who was a king of Babylon around 2300 BC) proves that the Babylonians did. For inscribed on the black diorite stone are some 282 clauses which testify that over four millenia ago these early businessmen practised, among other things, a form of insurance known as "bottomry".

Basically a mortgage on the hull, bottomry simply meant that the ship-owner would be indemnified if the vessel were lost, but paid over a substantial share of the profits if it reached its destination safely. This way of covering risks was a current practice with the Phoenicians and the Rhodians, and George Clayton of Sheffield University reckons that the Greeks perfected it "to such an extent that a number of very notable 19th century lawyers have claimed that Greek contracts of bottomry, similar to the one quoted by Demosthenes in a speech against Lacritus, were so nearly identical with those in vogue in London in 1860 that *mutatis mutandis* they could have been used at that date".

The Romans had a similar system, which they probably inherited from the Etruscans. Plutarch records somewhat caustically that Marcus Cato, Cato the Censor (234–149 BC), was a great money-lender and "used to loan money in what is surely the most disreputable form of speculation, that is the underwriting of ships". (Cato, he adds, also invested in the slave trade, but this seems to have worried Plutarch less.) He explains that "those who wished to borrow money from him were obliged to form a large association, and when there were fifty partners, and as many ships for his security, he took one share in the company himself and was represented by Quintio, a freedman of his who accompanied his clients on all their ventures. In this way his security was not imperilled, but only a small part of it, and his profits were large".

Bottomry, known as *Foenus Nauticum*, was developed by the Romans into insurance as it is understood today. Livy describes a guarantee by the government in 215 BC, and Cicero wrote to Sallust in 50 BC asking him to underwrite some cash in transit from Laodicia to Rome (at the prevailing premium in specie no doubt). The earlier Roman emperors experimented with a state scheme of marine insurance, and according to Suetonius the Emperor Claudius, in an attempt to boost the corn trade, went so far as to accept personal responsibility for merchants' losses which were caused by storms.

This marine insurance practised by the Romans found an echo in the 8th century guilds in Flanders and in England – which, according to Cornelius Walford, were "very much in the nature of an insurance association" – but above all in the Italian city-states of the Middle Ages.

For undoubtedly from the Crusades until the discovery of America, Italy was the dominant economic power in the western world. The Italians were not only the principal merchants, but they had a near monopoly in banking. First and foremost, they were financiers and business-agents to the Church. As such, the vast taxes and dues levied by Rome throughout western Europe passed through their hands, it being their particular responsibility to ensure that the money and merchandise due to the Church were channelled safely back to the Vatican. To achieve this they created partnerships and a network of branch offices managed by remote control, and in so doing to a very large extent laid the foundations for most of our modern business institutions. (The Medici Bank, for instance, foreshadowed in many respects the holding company of today.) They invented the draft bill of exchange, developed double-entry book-keeping, and were undoubtedly exponents of marine insurance which, according to Villani, originated in Lombardy in 1182. Arnauld has left a clear definition of what was meant: "One party, for a stipulated sum, undertakes to indemnify the other against loss arising from certain sea perils or sea risks to which his ship, merchandise or other interest may be exposed during a certain voyage or a certain period of time."

Among the documents of a Florentine merchant, Francesco di Marco Datini – assembled by Professor F. Melis at San Casciano and brought so vividly to life by Iris Origo in the *Merchant of Prato* – are some 400 insurance policies which indicate how widespread marine insurance was in the 14th century, even if, as Francesco wrote irritably to his wife, underwriters were not always trustworthy: "For when they insure it is sweet to them to take the monies; but when disaster comes it is otherwise and each man draws his rump back and strives not to pay."

The goods Datini insured included shipments of wool from Barcelona to Pisa; of silk in the reverse direction; and of fortified wines to Southampton, at premiums which varied from 3.5 percent to 5 percent, but 8 percent for the wine. (The crafty Florentine did not, in fact, do so badly, since Giovanni da Uzzano, writing at the same period, states that the normal premiums on such shipments ran from 12 percent to 15 percent.)

Above: *medieval merchantmen in Venice, from a painting by Carpaccio. The Italian city-states were the originators of our modern form of insurance: from the Italian 'polizza' is derived the word policy.*

Left: *one of the Merchants of the Steelyard – painted by Holbein the Younger (from the Royal Collection) – who ruled English trade while London was a Hansa League city.*

Others soon followed the Italian lead. Over in the Low Countries, Bruges was not only an important centre in the wool trade, it was the first northern sea-port to have a Chamber of Insurance. (It also had a stock exchange: traders met at the house of a certain Van der Buerse – the origin, probably, of the *Bourse*.) The records say that: "On the demand of the inhabitants of Bruges, the Count of Flanders permitted in the year 1310 the establishment in the town of a Chamber of Assurance, by means of which the merchants could insure their goods exposed to the risks of the sea, or elsewhere, in payment of a stipulated percentage." In the city archives there is, indeed, a document dated 12 April 1377 which speaks of an insurance policy on a consignment of silk and stuffs.

London, with its curious mercantile community of the Steelyard living in monk-like seclusion on the banks of the Thames (in a building only demolished in 1863 to make way for Cannon Street Station) was itself a Hansa League city in the late Middle Ages. But it was probably the "Pope's merchants" or Lombards – those Italians after whom the famous street is named – who first introduced insurance to England. In fact it is not until the 16th century that records exist of any specific marine insurance contracted by English merchants. The earliest English policies followed the wording of the Ordinance of Florence of 1523, and even today the wording of Lloyd's policies reflects this Italian derivation: "And it is agreed by us, the Insurers, that this writing of Policy of Assurance shall be of as much Force and Effect as the surest Writing heretofore made in Lombard Street or in the Royal Exchange or elsewhere in London." The word policy itself is derived from the Italian *polizza*, a promise or undertaking, and the earliest one in the Admiralty archives (dated 20 September 1547) was, indeed, written in Italian.

In Tudor days there were no insurance offices and marine insurances were private transactions between individuals. The Royal Exchange, founded in 1570 by Sir Thomas Gresham, gave merchants a centre at which to meet instead of congregating, as they had hitherto done, in Lombard Street – rather like Birmingham businessmen still tend to do in New Street. Finally in 1601 Francis Bacon introduced a Bill "touching Policies Assurancies used among merchants", and the earliest English Act dealing with insurance reached the Statute Book. Although the preamble states that it has been "tyme out of mynde an usuage amonste merchantes, both of this realme and of forraine nacyons", only slight progress was actually made in the organisation of marine insurance business, and up until the time of the Great Fire the writing of risks was still carried on as a sideline by merchants, bankers and even money-lenders in their private offices.

Oddly enough, it was the introduction of coffee in the middle of the 17th century that brought the first great leap forward. Before long, coffee-houses had opened up all over London; and the one destined to become the most famous of them all was founded in 1687 by a man called Edward Lloyd.

COFFEE AND THE COFFEE-HOUSES

YET COFFEE, THAT unlikely midwife at the birth of Lloyd's, was a relatively recent innovation. "It is said that the discovery of the refreshing beverage afforded by the berry of the coffee-plant was made in the latter part of the Seventh Century of the Flight (or of the 13th Century of the Christian era) by a certain devotee named Sheikh Omar who, driven by persecution to a mountain of El-Yemen, with a few of his disciples, was induced by the lack of provisions to make an experiment of the decoction of coffee-berries; the coffee-plant being there a spontaneous production." Thus wrote Edward Lane 150 years ago in *The Manners and Customs of the Modern Egyptians*. He went on to say that its use only became common in the Yemen two centuries later, and that coffee was first imported into Egypt at the end of the 15th or the beginning of the 16th century (about a hundred years before the introduction of tobacco to the East) where it was apparently drunk at the Mosque-University of Al Azhar by "the fakirs of El-Yemen and Mekkeh and El-Medieneh, who found it very refreshing while engaged in their exercises of reciting prayers". Some decades later, according to De Sacy's *Christomathic Arabe*, it was introduced into Constantinople. Certainly Bacon was writing in 1626 that: "They have in Turkey a drink called Coffee, made of a berry of the same name, as Black as Soot, and of a strong scent, but not aromatical; which they take beaten in Pouder, in Water, as Hot as they can drink it; and they take it and sit at it in the Coffee-houses, which are like our Taverns. The drink comforteth the Brain, the Heart, and helpeth Digestion".

Archbishop Laud, a gastronome whose two inaugural banquets for the new part of St John's College, Oxford, cost half as much as the buildings themselves, is always credited with having introduced coffee into England. While this prickly prelate had no qualms in turning down James Shirley, the dramatist, because of the mole on his left cheek (which obviously denoted contact with the Devil), he was always prepared to give a helping hand to any Christians who were suffering from Moslem oppression, and as Chancellor of Oxford University he secured the admittance to Balliol of a Cretan scholar named Canopius. There, it seems, his protégé followed the Mediterranean custom of confecting strong coffee in small cups. Evelyn the Diarist, who went up in 1637, remarked that: "There came in my time to the College one Nathanial Canopius, out of Greece . . . he was the first I ever saw drink coffee. . . ."

Nathanial was eventually sent down from the university, but he had sowed the seed, and Oxford had the distinction of having the first coffee-house in England. Anthony à Wood, the Merton antiquarian, relates that in 1650 "Jacob, a Jew opened a Coffey-house at the Angel . . . and there it was by some, who delighted in noveltie, drunk. In 1654 Jacques Jobson, a Jew and a Jacobite . . . sold coffey in Oxford; and in 1655 Arch. Tillyard, apothecary, sold coffey publicly in his house against All Soul's College".

A plaque in the cooperative grocery store in the High between University College and the Examination Schools now marks the spot where Jacob's coffee-house in the Angel once stood, and if Bernard Darwin is right it was at Oxford that the term "Club" was first applied, somewhat loosely, to those who met for coffee and gossip at Tillyard's. (Entering into the spirit John Houghton, a Cambridge don, declared that a man might pick up more useful knowledge in a coffee-house than by applying himself to his books for a month.)

It was not until two years later that the earliest London coffee-house was opened in St Michael's Alley, Cornhill, close to the Royal Exchange. In 1652 in the heyday of the Levant Company (when the British Consul in Smyrna was endowing the Sibthorpian Professorship at Oxford) a certain David Saunders brought home a Ragusian servant named Pasqua Rosée (sic) who made coffee for his master's breakfast each morning. The story goes that this exotic beverage attracted such an inconvenient number of early callers at his house that Saunders, with a good nose for business no doubt, set his servant up in an establishment specialising in the sale of coffee.

Pasqua Rosée's venture was so immediately successful that innumerable competitors jumped in to follow his example. Coffee-drinking became a fashion and coffee-houses mushroomed up all over London. They were quieter and cheaper than the taverns; for a penny the customer could have a cup of "kauffee", sit by the fire, read the newspapers, and talk to his heart's content. But not surprisingly in Puritan England, these establishments had their detractors, and in 1657 James Farr, the proprietor of the famous Rainbow Coffee-house in Fleet Street, was prosecuted at the Wardmote for creating a public nuisance with the smell of his roasting coffee. All sorts of complaints were brought up before the Wardmote, or City of London court. The inhabitants of Lime Street, for instance, where Lloyd's now stands, complained of "a very serious deprivation of rest they experienced by the barking and yelling of the various dogs that drew the butchers' carts at a very early hour in the morning".

Since the Danish invasion – and perhaps, it must be confessed, even earlier – drunkenness had been an English characteristic, and although the coffee-houses were obviously more sober than the taverns and the inns, a good many of them were probably not too fussy about their customers' behaviour. In a monologue of sometimes stunning scurrility, they were described in 1673 as being: "The rendez-vous of idle pamphlets and persons more idly employed to read them; a High Court of Justice where every little fellow in a Chamelot-cloak takes upon him to transpose affairs both in church and state and show reason against Acts of Parliament and condemn the Decree of the General Councils".

The company was often mixed: ". . . You may see a silly *Fop*, and a worshipful *Justice*, a griping *Rock*, and a grave *Citizen*, a worthy *Lawyer*, and an errant *Pickpocket*, a Reverend *Nonconformist* and a canting *Mountebank*; all blended together, to compose an *Oglio* of Impertinence". And not just the patrons, but the setting itself was a target for the writer's scorn: "The room stinks of tobacco worse than Hell of Brimstone, and is as full of Smoak as their heads that frequent it, whose humours are as various as those of Bedlam, and their discourse of times as heathenish and dull as their liquor".

Narkiness apart, there was probably more than a germ of truth in what he wrote. For while notices and letters of general interest were invariably posted up in the coffee-houses, in an age unblessed with mass-media it was the news brought in by the customers themselves which made them such an important part of the political and commercial life of London. They were a buzz of rumours and conjectures, so much so that the government itself was not above using them for propaganda purposes. Pepys, for instance, tells how, in order to stir people up into a war-like frame of mind, he was asked to put around a story of Englishmen in Dutch handcuffs "at the coffee-houses, where it will spread like leprosy". In fact, Charles II, in 1675, considered that the coffee-houses had become such hot-beds of sedition that he ordered them to be shut down.

But Londoners did not take kindly to this royal ordinance, which provoked such an uproar that it had to be revoked only sixteen days later, on condition that the owners should "prevent all scandalous papers, books and libels from being read in them, and hinder every person from declaring, uttering or divulging all manner of false and scandalous reports against the government or the ministers thereof". (A significant ruling, since by placing the onus so squarely on the shoulders of the "Masters", who were thus made responsible for the conduct and even the opinions of their guests, it gave them a standing they had never enjoyed before.)

From the reign of the Merry Monarch to the early

Above: *the Fire of London 1666. The flames approach St Pauls, having already engulfed Tower Street (where twenty years later Edward Lloyd was to set up his coffee shop in the newly-built area). The fire, which devastated half the city, turned many people's attention to insurance against fire and provided an incentive to the first private fire insurer, Nicholas Barbon, (and later, to the first fire insurance company, the Phoenix).*

Georges, the London Coffee-house was the centre of social life. The Wits and the *beau-monde* congregated at Man's, the Royal Coffee-house at Charing Cross, or at Will's in Bow Street, where Dryden was to be found on the balcony in summer or by the fire in winter. Scholars debated the doctrinal controversies of the day at the Grecian; doctors and clergymen swapped their respective anecdotes at Child's; soldiers held forth at Young Man's and stock-jobbers at Old Man's. As public establishments the coffee-houses, like the taverns, were naturally open to all-comers, but it did not take long for a definite specialisation to begin, particularly after the Plague and the Great Fire had left so many Londoners homeless. It was obvious that men with the same interests would tend to foregather at those coffee-houses where they were most likely to meet their friends, and for business folk the ones near the Royal Exchange, such as Garraway's (where later Pickwick was to write his letter to Mrs Bardell about chops and tomato sauce) Jonathan's and Bridge's became a natural focal point. In fact, as time wore on, they developed into accepted addresses for many merchants, brokers and underwriters who even conducted the bulk of their business around the coffee table. This was particularly true of shipping people, even before the disasters of 1664-6, and Pepys relates how by pure chance at the coffee-house he learnt of the safe arrival of a hemp ship in which he was interested: "Nov 23rd 1663. Up and to Alderman Backewell's where Sir W. Rider, by appointment, met to consult about the insuring of our hemp ship from Archangell. . . ." (The Admiralty, it would seem, only began to think about insuring a vessel when it was already overdue.) ". . . . Back to the Coffee-house and then to the 'Change', where Sir W. Rider and I did 15 percent, and nobody will take it under 20 percent, and 15 percent more to be abated in case of losse, which we did not think fit without order to give. . . . called at the Coffee-house and there by great accident hear that a letter is come that our ship is safe come to Newcastle." Along with this glimpse of how insurance was transacted in those days, Pepys slips in a very human little comment: "With this news I went like an asse, presently to Alderman Backewell and told him of it. . . . Now what an opportunity had I to have concealed this and seemed to have made an insurance and got £100 with the least trouble and danger in the whole world. This troubles me to think that I should be so oversoon."

Pepys' coffee-house in this case was probably Garraway's, which thrived until the middle of the 19th century, and is usually considered to have been the origin of the Stock-Exchange. Edward Lloyd himself was only a youth of about fifteen at the time, and would not be opening his own establishment for another twenty-five years. But this, on

Above: *The Coffee House Politicians, another 18th century satirical print. Just as Lloyd's became a centre for news of shipping, other establishments were frequented for the latest gossip from Court or Parliament.*

Opposite: *The CoffeHous Mob* [sic], *an early 18th century satire on the clientele of London's coffee shops 'whose humours are as various as those of Bedlam'.*

the whole, is incidental. For the grass-roots of Lloyd's stretch back not only to the coffee-house from which the great and intricate corporation draws its name, but further still to those even earlier establishments where men met who were willing to stake their money underwriting adventures on the high seas.

LLOYD'S COFFEE-HOUSE: THE EARLY DAYS

FIGURING IN THE official list of "victuallers" for the year 1687–8 was to be found the name of Lloyd, frame-work knitter, but a casual advertisement in the London Gazette of 18 February 1688 is the earliest existing reference to a coffee-house owned by Edward Lloyd. Some watches had been stolen from a man called Bransby, who offered a reward of one guinea to anyone who could supply information about them to his address in Derby or to "Mr Edward Lloyd's Coffee-House in Tower Street".

> STolen the 10th Inftant, from Edward Bransby in Darby, five Watches; one was a Pin Cafe, and a Silver Box, with a Silver Dyal Plate, hours cut upon Harts, it was a five Wheel Chain, the Watch-Makers Name was Wilkins of Leicefter; The fecond was a plain Silver Box, with a Glafs, the Dyal had a Pot of Flowers, the Makers Name was William Corder in Darby; The third had a Silver Box with a clofe Silver Cafe, a Pearlf Dyal Plate, with the day of the Month; The fourth had a Silver Box and Pin Cafe, many of the Pins being come out, fo that the Brafs was feen, The fifth Watch had a Silver Box and Pin Cafe, long hours of the Dyal Plate, and frotted, it was a 5 Wheel Chain Watch: Suppofed to be taken by a middle fized Man, having black curled Hair, Pockholes in his Face, wearing an old brown Riding Coat, and a black Bever Hat Whoever gives notice of them at Mr Edward Loyd's Coffee Houfe in Tower-ftreet, or to Mr. Edward Bransby in Darby as above, fhall have a Guinea Reward.
>
> LOft the 16th Inftant, from the Right Honourable the Lord Vifcount Cholmondley's Houfe by St James's, a little Italian Bitch, with a white Ring round her Neck, white under her Belly, white on the end of her Tail, her Body toward a dunnifh Whoever will bring her to the above-mentioned Houfe, fhall have a Guinea Reward.

At this period Tower Street was the main thoroughfare between Wapping and the Thames-side. Described by Stowe in his Survey of London as "a spacious street, well built and inhabited by able tradesmen", it was a favourite haunt of sailors landing at St Katherine's and "Galley Key" who easily found their way down to the coffee-house at the western end, and undoubtedly Lloyd's early clientele must have been largely composed of sea-faring persons, including captains and "ships husbands" who met there to transact their day-to-day business.

At all events Lloyd prospered well enough in Tower Street to be able to move in 1691 to a larger and more central location at the corner of Lombard Street and Abchurch Lane, a few doors from the Post Office and strategically close to such well

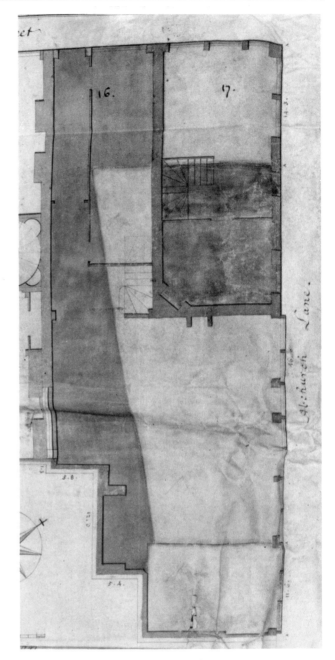

Above: *the ground plan of Lloyd's Coffee House at 16, Lombard Street, found attached to a deed of 1773.*

Opposite: top: *anonymous 18th century drawing of a city establishment (questionably Lloyd's).*

Opposite below: *artist's sketches, based on the plan above, of the interior and exterior of Lloyd's—for a reconstruction of the coffee-house exhibited at the Festival of Britain.*

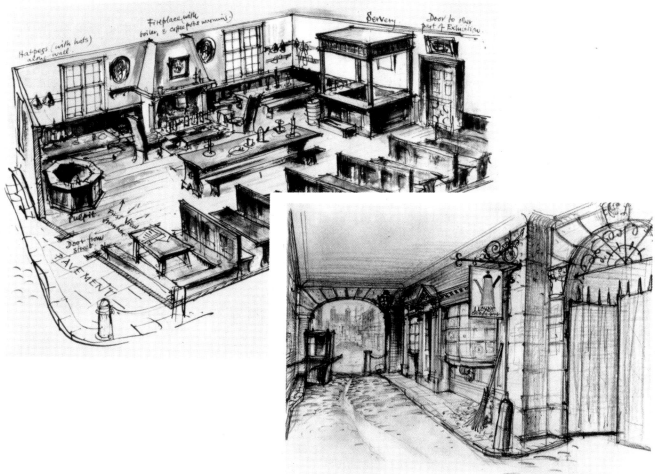

known coffee-houses as Garraway's, Jonathan's and John's. As Frederick Martin has pointed out, this was "a decidedly progressive step, calculated to make his establishment, more than could otherwise have been the case, the meeting place of merchants of the highest class", and Lloyd's growing success is shown by an advertisement a year later in the *London Gazette* for the sale by auction of three ships and their contents at Plymouth, prospective bidders being advised that "the inventories thereof can be seen at Lloyd's Coffee-House in Lombard Street".

As part of a drive to attract businessmen of substance to his rooms, Lloyd began to build up a network of correspondents in the principal ports at home and on the continent who could send in news of the movements of vessels and other information likely to interest the shipping world. Then in 1696 he embarked on an even more enterprising piece of public relations. He began to publish a newssheet of his own called *Lloyd's News*. Like other contemporary papers, it was printed in italics both sides of a single sheet (in this case containing $10\frac{1}{2} \times 5\frac{1}{4}$ inches of letterpress, neater and easier to read than the *Protestant Mercury* and the *Post-Man*) and carried regular messages from nearby ports in the British Isles, as well as periodic items from an astonishing range of far-away places in Italy, Greece, Turkey, and even Egypt.

A complete file of *Lloyd's News* from the eighth to the last is conserved at the Bodleian in Oxford, (Bodleian ref: Nichols newspapers m q London 1696 sm.fol. Pre-1920 catalogue, vol. 43, p. 2710). and it is clear from a study of them that Lloyd aimed above all at producing a specialised trade paper. But as it happens, his brave venture into journalism was short-lived. The final issue, No. 76 dated 23 February 1697, carried what seems like an innocuous little paragraph:

"Yesterday the Lords passed the Bill to restrain the wearing of all wrought silks from India, with this amendment, to prohibit the importation of them from all Parts, which they sent to the Commons for their concurrence. They also received a Petition from the Quakers that they be freed from all Offices."

Censorship – and the ban on reporting governmental affairs – had only been relaxed in 1693, and this reference to a petition from the Quakers provoked the authorities sufficiently for Lloyd to be summoned to the Bar of the House of Lords, told what he had published was "groundless and a mistake", and ordered to "rectifie it in his next". According to the *Protestant Mercury* of 26 February 1697, Lloyd answered that the offending paragraph had been added by his printer, and that he would "print no more at present". His motives for ceasing publication can only be surmised. Possibly he resented being admonished for a mistake that was

Above: *Samuel Pepys, whose Admiralty business presented him with easy opportunities to make quick profits on ship insurance: a temptation which, he relates, he nobly resisted.*

Opposite: *Old East India wharf at the end of the 17th century, painted by Peter Monamy.*

not his own. Conceivably he feared a more serious repetition in the future. But more likely he had already begun to find that there was not enough regular shipping intelligence to justify the trouble and cost of producing a paper two or three times a week, and that his method of sending round what material he had available and leaving the printer to fill up both sides of the sheet with miscellaneous news items was simply not good enough. For the needs of his patrons, it was sufficient to circulate a handwritten sheet which could be read in the coffee-house. He did, in fact, continue to publish printed lists of ships' movements.

Yet for all this, *Lloyd's News* had done its job. By drawing the public's attention to Lloyd's as a nerve-centre of shipping news it had attracted merchants and ship-owners to the coffee-house; and since the insurance business in due course grew out of this connection it substantiates Edward Lloyd's place in history as the inspirer, if not the actual founder, of present-day Lloyd's.

For there is no doubt that in a relatively short time he succeeded in establishing his rooms as a focal point for the shipping business, and from 1698 onwards auction sales were regularly conducted on the premises. Nat Ward (an author who kept a pub and, as Pope said, exported vile rhymes to the colonies in exchange for bad tobacco) made a reference to them in a doggerel called *The Wealthy Shopkeeper*:

"Now to Lloyd's Coffee-House he never fails to read the letters and attend the Sales."

Steele and Addison both left their first-hand accounts of the premises, which make it clear that by the beginning of the 18th century the auction pulpit at Edward Lloyd's establishment had become a well known feature of London life.

CONTEMPORARY DESCRIPTIONS

By the end of the 17th century, marine insurance was coming into its own – even if it was still the mark of a substantial trader to save money by carrying the risk himself (just as some of the Saudi magnates often do today). But there was very little specialisation and merchants tended to insure their own risks at one moment and underwrite those of their friends the next. This cosy arrangement was made possible by the close relationship of the men who met daily at the coffee-house. Sitting there in the boxes, each in his favourite pew, with the latest shipping information posted up on the board or brought round by the waiters, these "regulars" were the prototypes of the modern underwriter with his computers and photocopiers in the great marble palace which even today, in its general plan, shows traces of Edward Lloyd's coffee-house.

From the title deeds can be seen that the property which he leased had a double frontage: a narrow one at No 16 Lombard Street, and a wider one of about forty feet, in Abchurch Lane. Edward Lloyd took it over from the "Pontack's Head" – one of London's most fashionable and expensive eating houses, famed for its choice clarets which the owner, Monsieur Le Roche, brought over from Bordeaux – which had now moved a few doors down the street. The coffee-house itself was on the first floor, a big rather bare room with chairs around the fireplace, a line of tables and a bar at the end. As in similar establishments the tables were "very Neat, and shined with Rubbing, like the upper leather of an Alderman's shoes. . . ." (Nat Ward observed) ". . . of as brown a colour as the top of a country housewife's cupboard". To look after his customers' needs, Lloyd employed a staff of five; a waiter or "mayd" took round the refreshments (coffee, tea or sherbet, or something stronger if required, as well as food) and provided paper and ink for those who had business to transact, while others sat "smoking their nasty puffing engines", presumably to the disgust of non-smokers, and passed the time of day gossiping, joking, and reading the papers. The place remained open practically round the clock – Steele used to go to his favourite coffee-house near the Inns of Court at around six in the morning – and served as a communal centre for getting things done; at certain times of day it would become so crowded with people making so much hubbub that Lloyd or a waiter would have to go to the "pulpit" to read out some titbit of news that had just been received. Between one coffee-house and another, there was probably not much to choose, but Steele's and Addison's descriptions of Lloyd's, which remained true for a generation or two, are reproduced here:

The TATLER.

By Isaac Bickerstaff Esq;

—— O te, Bollane, Cerebri
Felicem ! Aiebam tacitus, cum quidlibet ille
Garriret. —— Hor.

From *Saturday December* 23. to *Tuesday December* 26, 1710.

From my own Apartment;

AT my coming Home last Night, I found upon my Table the following Petition or Project, sent me from *Lloyd's* Coffee-house in the City, with a Present of *Port* Wine, which had been bought at a late Auction held in that Place.

To Isaac Bickerstaff *Esq;* Censor *of* Great Britain.

Lloyd's Coffee-house, Lombard-street, Dec. 23.

WE the Customers of this Coffee-house, observing that you have taken into your Consideration the great Mischiefs daily done in this City by Coffee-house Orators, do humbly beg Leave to represent to you, That this Coffee-house being provided with a Pulpit for the Benefit of such Auctions that are frequently made in this Place, it is our Custom, upon the first coming in of the News, to order a Youth, who officiates as the Kidney of the Coffee-house, to get into the Pulpit, and read every Paper with a loud and distinct Voice, while the whole Audience are sipping their respective Liquors. We do therefore, Sir, humbly propose, That there be a Pulpit erected within every Coffee-house of this City and the adjacent Parts; That one of the Waiters of the Coffee-house be nominated as Reader to the said Pulpit; That after the News of the Day has been published by the said Lecturer, some Politician of good Note do ascend into the said Pulpit; and after having chosen for his Text any Article of the said News, that he do establish the Authority of such Article, clear the Doubts that may arise thereupon, compare it with parallel Texts in other Papers, advance upon it wholesome Points of Doctrine, and draw from it salutary Conclusions for the Benefit and Edification of all that hear him. We do likewise humbly propose, That upon any such Politician's quitting the Pulpit, he shall be succeeded by any other Orator that finds himself moved by the same publick Spirit, who shall be at full Liberty either to enforce or overthrow what the other has said before him; and may in the same Manner be succeeded by any other Politician, who shall with the same Liberty confirm or impugn his Reasons, strengthen or invalidate his Conjectures, enlarge upon his Schemes, or erect new ones of his own. We do likewise further propose, That if any Person, of what Age or Rank soever, do presume to cavil at any Paper that has been read, or to hold forth upon it longer than the Space of one Minute, that he be immediately ordered up into the Pulpit, there to make good any Thing that he has suggested upon the Floor. We do likewise further propose, That if any one plays the Orator in the ordinary Coffee-house Conversation, whether it be upon Peace or War, on Plays or Sermons, Business or Poetry, that he be forthwith desired to take his Place in the Pulpit.

'This, Sir, we humbly presume may in a great Measure put a Stop to those superficial Statesmen who would not dare to stand up in this Manner before a whole Congregation of Politicians, notwithstanding the long and tedious Harangues and Dissertations which they Daily utter in private Circles, to the breaking of many honest Tradesmen, the seducing of several eminent Citizens, the making of numberless Malecontents, and to the great Detriment and Disquiet of Her Majesty's Subjects.

I do heartily concur with my ingenious Friends of the above-mentioned Coffee-house in these their Proposals; and because I apprehend there may be Reasons to put an immediate Stop to the Grievance complained of, it is my Intention, That till such Time as the aforesaid Pulpits can be erected, every Orator do place himself within the Bar, and from thence dictate whatsoever he shall think necessary for the publick Good.

And further, because I am very desirous that proper Ways and Means should be found out for the suppressing of Story-Tellers and fine Talkers in all ordinary Conversation whatsoever, I do insist, that in every private Club, Company, or Meeting over a Bottle, there be always an Elbow-Chair placed at the Table; and that as soon as any one begins a long Story, or extends his Discourse beyond the Space of one Minute, he be forthwith thrust into the said Elbow-Chair, unless upon any of the Company's calling out *to the Chair*, he breaks off abruptly, and holds his Tongue.

There are Two Species of Men, notwithstanding any Thing that has been here said, whom I would exempt from the Disgrace of the Elbow-Chair. The First are those Buffoons that have a Talent of mimicking the Speech and Behaviour of other Persons, and turning all their Patrons, Friends and Acquaintance, into Ridicule. I look upon your *Pantomime* as a Legion in a Man, or at least to be like *Virgil's* Moutser, with an Hundred Mouths and as many Tongues.

—— Lingua centum sunt, Oraqu: centum.

And therefore would give him as much Time to talk in, as would be allowed to the whole Body of Persons he represents, were they actually in the Company which they divert by Proxy. Provided however, That the said *Pantomime* do not, upon any Pretence whatsoever, utter any Thing in his own particular Opinion, Language or Character.

I would likewise in the Second Place grant an Exemption from the Elbow-Chair to any Person who treats the Company, and by that Means, may be supposed to pay for his Audience. A Guest cannot take it ill if he be not allowed to talk in his Turn by a Person who puts his Mouth to a better Employment, and stops it with good Beef and Mutton. In this Case the Guest is very agreeably silenced, and seems to hold his Tongue under that Kind of Bribery which the Ancients called, *Bos in Lingua.*

If I can once extirpate the Race of solid and substantial Hum-drums, I hope, by my wholsome

and

The SPECTATOR.

Non bene junctarum discordia semina rerum. Ovid.

Monday, April 23. 1711.

WHEN I want Materials for this Paper, it is my Custom to go abroad in quest of Game; and when I meet any proper Subject, I take the first Opportunity of setting down an Hint of it upon Paper. At the same Time I look into the Letters of my Correspondents, and if I find any thing suggested in them that may afford Matter of Speculation, I likewise enter a Minute of it in my Collection of Materials. By this Means I frequently carry about me a whole Sheet full of Hints, that would look like a Rapsody of Nonsense to any Body but my self: There is nothing in them but Obscurity and Confusion, Raving and Inconsistency. In short, they are my Speculations in the first Principles, that (like the World in its Chaos) are void of all Light, Distinction, and Order.

About a Week since, there happened to me a very odd Accident, by Reason of one of these my Papers of Minutes which I had accidentally dropped at *Lloyd's* Coffee-house, where the Auctions are usually kept. Before I missed it, there were a Cluster of People who had found it, and were diverting themselves with it at one End of the Coffee-house: It had raised so much Laughter among them before I had observed what they were about, that I had not the Courage to own it. The Boy of the Coffee-house, when they had done with it, carried it about in his Hand, asking every Body if they had dropped a written Paper; but no Body challenging it, he was ordered by those merry Gentlemen who had before perused it, to get up into the Auction Pulpit and read it to the whole Room, that if any one would own it they might. The Boy accordingly mounted the Pulpit, and with a very audible Voice read as follows.

MINUTES.

Sir Roger de Coverly's Country-Seat—— Yes, for I hate long Speeches—— Query, if a good Christian may be a Conjuror—— *Childermas-day,* Saltseller, House-Dog, Screech-Owl, Cricket,—— Mr. *Thomas Inkle* of *London,* in the good Ship called the *Achilles. Yarico*—— *Egrescitque medendo*—— Ghosts—— The Lady's Library—— *Lion* by Trade a Taylor—— Dromedary called *Bucephalus*—— Equipage the Lady's *summum bonum*

——*Charles Lillie* to be taken Notice of—— Short Face a Relief to Envy—— Redundancies in the three Professions—— King *Latinus* a Recruit—— Jew devouring an Ham of Bacon—— *Westminster-Abby*—— *Grand Cairo*—— Procrastination—— *April Fools*—— Blue Boars, Red Lyons, Hogs in Armour—— Enter a King and two Fidlers *solus*—— Admission into the Ugly Club—— Beauty, how improveable—— Families of true and false Humour—— The Parrot's School-Mistress—— Face half *Pict* half *British*—— No Man to be an Hero of a Tragedy under six Foot—— Club of Sighers—— Letters from Flower-Pots, Elbow-Chairs, Tapestry-Figures, Lion, Thunder—— The Bell rings to the Puppet-Show—— Old Woman with a Beard married to a smock-faced Boy—— My next Coat to be turn'd up with Blue—— Fable of Tongs and Gridiron—— Flower Dyers—— The Soldier's Prayer——Thank ye for nothing says the Gally-Pot ——*Pactolus* in Stockings, with golden Clocks to them—— Bamboos, Cudgels, Drum-sticks—— Slip of my Land-lady's eldest Daughter—— The black Mare with a Star in her Forehead—— The Barber's Pole—— *Will. Honeycombe's* Coat-pocket—— *Cæsar's* Behaviour and my own in Parallel Circumstances—— Poem in Patch-work—— *Nulli gravis est percussus Achilles*—— The Female Conventicler ——The Ogle-Master.

The reading of this Paper made the whole Coffee-house very merry; some of them concluded it was written by a Madman, and others by some Body that had been taking Notes out of the *Spectator.* One who had the Appearance of a very substantial Citizen, told us with several politick Winks and Nods, that he wished there was no more in the Paper than what was expressed in it: That for his Part, he looked upon the Dromedary, the Gridiron, and the Barber's Pole, to signify something more than what is usually meant by those Words; and that he thought the Coffee-man could not do better, than to carry the Paper to one of the Secretaries of State. He further added, that he did not like the Name of the outlandish Man with the Golden Clock in his Stockings. A young *Oxonian,* who

THE AUCTION PULPIT AT LLOYD'S

As STEELE OBSERVED, the "auction pulpit" from which the "kidney" read Addison's notes was a speciality of Edward Lloyd's coffee-house, and was used for the sale of a large variety of goods.

The auction sales of the period were normally conducted by "inch of candle", just as they continued to be by the Church authorities in France and Italy until very recent times. The method was as follows: a pin was stuck into a candle about an inch from the top, and bidding went on until the candle was burnt down to the pin; the last bidder before the pin dropped into the candlestick was declared the purchaser. Sometimes this was varied by simply lighting an inch of candle, the final bid which had been made before the flame went out being successful.

Describing one of these auctions, Pepys noted in his Diary on 6 November 1660: "To our office, where we met all, for the sale of two ships by an inch of candle (the first time that I ever saw any of this kind) where I observed how they do invite one another, and at last how they all do cry, and we have much to do to tell who did cry last. The ships were the *Indian* sold for £1300, and the *Half Moone* sold for £830".

Five months later he was recording a visit to Chatham, where some surplus stores from the dockyard were being sold: "After dinner we went to fit books and things . . . for the sale, by an inch of candle, and very good sport we and the ladies that stood by had to see the people bid".

In another entry (3 September 1662) Pepys explains the trick of how to make a successful bid: "After dinner by water to the office and there we met and sold the *Weymouth, Successe,* and *Fellowship* hulkes; t'were pleasant to see how backward Men are at first bid; and yet when the candle is going out how they bawl and dispute afterwards who bid the most first. And I observed one man cunninger than the rest that was sure to bid the last man, and to carry it; and enquiring the reason he told me that just as the flame goes out the smoke descends, which is a thing I never observed before, and by that does he know the instant when to bid last, which is very pretty".

When compiling his history of Lloyd's a hundred years ago, Frederick Martin went through the London newspapers from 1698 to 1712 looking for advertisements for the auction sales at Lloyd's coffee-house. Samples taken at random from the long list which he compiled show that they were a regular occurrence, and that a multiplicity of different items were put on offer:

Protestant Mercury No 241: "At Lloyd's Coffee-house in Lombard Street, near the General Post Office, will be sold by auction, or who bids most, a catalogue of

Above: *a City merchant on his way to a candle auction, from an anonymous contemporary print.*

FOR
SALE
BY THE
CANDLE,

At NEW LLOYD's COFFEE-HOUSE, CORNHILL,

On FRIDAY, *the* 15*th Day of* JULY, 1796,
at Two o'Clock precisely,

THE GOOD GALLIOT

CATHARINE,

Round Stern, Dutch built, and free, 140 Tons Register
Tonnage; is well calculated for the Coal or Coasting
Trade, shifts without Ballast, draws little Water, and
takes the Ground well; is well found in Stores, and
may be sent to Sea at a small Expence.   Now lying
at King James's *Edward* Stairs.

INVENTORY.

Hull, Masts, Yards, standing and running Rigging, with all Faults, as they now lie.

ANCHORS.		
1 sheet anchor	2 warps	2 steering sails
1 best bower	1 towline quite new	1 square sail
1 small ditto		1 save all
1 kedge	—	1 boat's sail
	SAILS.	
CABLES.	2 main sails	—
	1 fore sail	CARPENTER's and BOATSWAIN's
	4 jibs	STORES.
1 best bower	1 top sail	3 hand dogs
1 small ditto	1 mizen	1 iron ditto

choice English books etc on Wednesday 23 February 1698"

Postman No 1134: "At Lloyd's Coffee-house in Lombard Street next Friday (4 June 1703) will be sold 53 Hogsheads of extraordinary neat French Wines at 3 o'clock precisely"

Postman No 1191: "On Wednesday 6 of this instant (October 1703) will ve exposed to sale a parcel of coffee at Lloyd's Coffee-house in Lombard Street at three o'clock in the afternoon"

Tatler No 25: "At Lloyd's Coffee-House in Lombard Street to Morrow, being 8th instant (Wednesday 8 June 1709) at 3 o'clock, will be on Sale a fine fresh Stone-horse, first come out of Yorkshire, 60 Guineas value to be thrown for by Dice, each lot a Guinea, to be paid to Mr Lloyd when subscribed"

But Lloyd was not just specialising in auction sales. Business of all descriptions was transacted in his rooms. In 1701 the *London Gazette* summoned creditors of the Transport Debts to a meeting at Lloyd's and in 1706 the Spanish stockholders were called together for a meeting there.

Indeed some 200 advertisements over a period of fifteen years indicate the progressive development of Lloyd's coffee-house during the reign of Queen Anne from a general meeting place of merchants and ships' captains into London's principal auction rooms; and in the following decade, during which the sale of ships and cargoes – a vast number advertised as "sold by order of the Court of Admiralty" – kept constantly increasing, the direction in which the coffee-house was heading became ever more apparent. In 1710 Lloyd's was already considered to be "the chief commercial Saleroom in London", and by the time Lloyd died in 1713 at the age of sixty-five his establishment could safely be described as the acknowledged headquarters of maritime affairs – if not yet specifically of marine insurance.

EDWARD LLOYD

FOR ALL THIS, remarkably little is known about the man who gave his name to the world's most prestigious mercantile organisation – and yet who was not, strictly speaking, the founder of modern Lloyd's at all. Despite the dedicated research of scholars and antiquarians, hardly more than the bare facts of his life have so far come to light.

In the allegation for his second marriage in 1698, for instance, he was described as "of the age of about fifty years", which would date his birth at around 1648. Like his father, he became a member of the Framework-knitters Company (he described himself in his will as "Citizen and Framework-

Above: *the entry in the Rating-book of Tower Ward. Edward Lloyd's household is rated at six shillings per annum.*

Opposite: *advertisement for a candle auction at the end of the 18th century.*

29

DEED, dated 22nd January, 1712, by EDWARD LLOYD.

An Assignem^t of an Order for an Annuity of £10:-s:- Annu for 99 yeares. 22: *January*, 1712.

TO ALL PEOPLE to whom these pñts shall come I EDWARD LLOYD of St Mary Woolnoth London Coffeeman Adm^r of all & Singular ye Rights Creditts Goods & Chattells of my late wife Eliza Lloyd als Mashborne late of ye P'ish of St Mary Woolnoth London deced Send Greeting WHEREAS by an Order N^o (3314) dated ye 1st day of Novr 1706 by vertue & in pursuance of an Act of Parliam^t made & passed in ye 4th yeare of her p'sent Maj^{ties} Reign (Entituled an Act for continuing an addiconall Subsidy of Tonnage & poundage & certaine dutyes upon Coals Culme & Cynders & addiconall dutyes of Excise & for Settling and establishing a ffund thereby and by other wayes & meanes for payment of Annuityes to be sold for Raising a further Supply to her Maj^{ty} for ye Service of ye yeare 1706 & other uses y^{r}in menconed) & in cons^n of ye sume of 155^{li} of lts paid into ye Receipt of her Maj^{ties} Excheq^r by ye s^d Eliz Lloyd as in ye s^d Order is menconed at 4 seuerall times as by 4 seuerall Tallys of ye same dates appeares There is ordered to be satisfyed & pd unto ye s^d Eliz Lloyd or her ass^t an Annuity or Yearely sume of 10^{li} for & during & untill ye full terme & expiracon of Ninety nine yeares to comence from ye 25th day of March 1706 As by ye s^d rec^d Ord^r more plainely appeares NOW KNOW YEE That I ye s^d E. Lloyd in cons^n of 5^s of lawfull &c to me in hand pd at or before ye sealing hereof by Richard Elford Cs & Merch^t Taylor of London ye receipt whereof I do hereby acknowleg accordingly & also for divers other good causes and valuable consideracons me hereunto moving HAVE Assigned transferred & sett over And by these pñts Do Assigne transferr & sett over unto ye s^d R. Elford ye said Order & Tallyes And ye said Annuity or Annuall Sume of £10: & all arreares thereof & also all ye right tytle interest property claime & demand w^{t}soever of me ye said E. Lloyd of it & to ye same TO HOLD to ye s^d R. Elford his ex^rs ad^rs & ass^t from henceforth for & during all ye rest & residue of ye s^d terme of 99 yeares which is yet to come & unexpired In trust Nevery^{e}less To & for ye sole Use & benefitt of me ye said E. Lloyd my ex^rs ad^rs & ass^t & to & for no other use intent or purpose w^{t}soever IN WITNES whereof I ye s^d E. Lloyd have hereunto set my hand & Seale ye 22^d day of Janry Anno Dni 1712 in ye 11th Queen Anne &c.

Indorsed on ye margin.

Intrat' in Officio Audit. Recept. Scij XXVIII° die Januarij 1712

E. LLOYD.

London Ss.

Benj^a Manning of ye Parish of St Mary Woolnoth London maketh Oath That on or about ye 22^d day of January 1712 Edwd Lloyd late Cs & ffameworke knitter of London deced Did in ye p'sence of this Deponent Signe Seale publish & declare as & for his last Will & testam^t a certaine Writing bearing date ye s^d 22^d of Janry 1712 wherein & whereby ye said Testators wife Martha Lloyd was made ordained & appointed Sole Ex^{tx} thereof And this Deponent further Saith That he this Depon^t together with John Bodicoate & Geo: Short did at ye same time Subscribe their names as Witnesses thereto in ye p'sence of ye said Testator.

BENJ^n MANNING.

Jurat' 14° Octobris, 1713.
coram TH^o: ABNEY.

Above: a copy of a deed by Edward Lloyd, assigning an annuity of £10.00 a year from his wife Elizabeth over to Richard Elford, whom Lloyd described as his 'very good friend' and later appointed overseer of his will. The document was drawn up in January 1712, indicating that Elizabeth must have died before the commonly accepted date of October 1712. This is confirmed by the deposition of Benj. Manning (below) affirming that Martha, Lloyd's third wife, had been made beneficiary of his will at the same time.

Numb. 20.

LLOYD's NEWS.

London, *October* 15. 1696.

Ghent, October 17. The French Troops under the Mareſchal Villeroy have plundered all the Churches near Bruges, carried away the Bells, broke all the Windows, and cut down all the Hedges and Trees in the open Countrey; and the Damage they have done to the Churches as alſo to the Cloiſters in the Abby of Oudenburgh, is computed at 10000 Gilders. On Sunday and Monday laſt 9 Regiments of Horſe came into Garriſon here. The Elector of Bavaria hath refuſed to grant Paſſports to divers Ships bound to this Conntrey with Wine and other French Commodities.

Amſterdam, October 19. Letters of the 11th inſtant from Arch-Angel Advise, That 7 Engliſh Ships arrived there, who upon Notice that ſeveral French Men of War were Cruiſing about Shotland, changed their Courſe and ſteered between Shotland and the Orchades. Letters of the 6th inſtant from St. Maloe adviſe, That the main reaſon of the haſty return of Monſieur Renault with his Squadron from the Weſt-Indies was becauſe he had loſt about half his Men by a Sickneſs which raged among them, and moſt of the reſt were ſick; ſo that if he had tarried longer he muſt have left his Ships behind him for want of Men to bring them home; beſides, which Squadron, there are 3 Men of War come to an Anchor in the Road of Rochell, which are believed to be the Ships of Monſieur de Genes from the South Sea.

Rome, September 29. The Pope hath privately ordered Troops and Arms to be ſent to the Frontiers of the Eccleſiaſtick State, that he may be provided againſt all that may happen in caſe a Neutrality ſhould not be accepted of or finiſhed in Italy. The Reſident of Savoy had this Week another Audience of the Pope, who received him with all the marks of an extraordinary Affection; and declared himſelf extreamly pleaſed with the Conduct of the Duke his Maſter, who had already obliged Italy with the dawnings of a Peace.

Falmouth, October 10. On the 28th paſt put into this Port the Duke of Bavaria, of and for Oſtend, and ſailed again this Morning for Cork. Yeſterday His Majeſties Ship Trident arrived here with 2 Coaſters under her Convoy from Plimouth; as alſo His Majeſties Ship Dunwich in 5 days from Milford, where ſhe left the 10 ſail of Ships that arrived there from Berbadoes, with the Childs-Play their Convoy. Laſt Night ſailed hence His Majeſties Ship Jolly, with 3 or 4 Coaſters for Mounts-Bay. The Groin Pacquet-Boat is juſt now going to ſail for Corunna.

Plimouth, October 11. Yeſterday the Mercury Advice-Boat ſailed hence to Cruiſe on the French Coaſt, and the Intelligence-Brigantine to the Weſtward. On the 9th arrived here the Cheſter-Frigate with 2 Maſt-Ships for our Docks.

Cowes, October 12. Yeſterday and this Morning ſeveral of the outward-bound Ships which lay in this Road ſailed for Spithead to join their Convoys, being adviſed they will ſail ſuddenly. This Morning came into this Road His Majeſties Ship Pendennis, Capt. Arden Commander, from Norway; whence he came

Above: *issue number 20 of* Lloyd's News. *76 issues in all were produced, all but seven of them still extant at the Bodleian Library in Oxford.*

knitter") but it is generally believed that he did not serve his apprenticeship in this craft; indeed, at a guess, he may very well have gone to sea as a youth, which would account for his lifelong interest in ships and sea-faring folk.

Yet from the research undertaken by Warren Dawson in the Guildhall and City Church records, it emerges that by 1680 Edward Lloyd was a married man with at least two children, living in the parish of All Hallows Barking. (A son of his, Edward, was buried that year in All Hallows church, and two other children were baptised there – Mary in November 1680 and Hugh in December 1681.) He was "the owner as well as the tenant of a house in Red Cross Alley, afterwards called Red Cross Court . . . a little turning off Tower Street, between Mark Lane and Seething Lane, immediately opposite the porch of All Hallows church".

Evidently it was a cramped little place, because the yearly tax was only a few pence, and sometime in 1682 he moved with his family down Tower Street to a better and more centrally located house in the parish of St Dunstan's-in-the-East where, that October, the infant Hugh was buried. Here the Lloyds lived for the next ten years and had four other children who were baptised in the parish church. In all probability, before setting up on his own, Edward Lloyd worked for some other coffeeman. "He would be unlikely to embark upon the enterprise of proprietorship without previous knowledge or experience of the trade" surmises Warren Dawson. "It is well known that the proprietors of many famous coffee-houses had been, before setting up on their own account, head waiters of other houses."

Then, sometime in 1686 or 1687, he either took over an existing coffee-house, or started up a new establishment of his own. The choice of Salutation Precinct was deliberate: he set out to cater for skippers and their crews.

Many of the ships' captains at this period had gone into the service of the East India Company as ships' "husbands", and after making their fortune abroad had come back home and put their specialised knowledge to good use by dabbling in marine insurance. No one knew the hazards better than they did, and their experience on the trade routes enabled them to gauge the rates for a ship and the voyage it was making. They knew the risks involved because they had done the journeys themselves.

Edward Lloyd's gimmick was a good one. He kept a special corner for the captains and concentrated on the provision of shipping information. Within a short time he was well enough known for newspaper advertisements to refer to him simply as "Mr Lloyd". And by 1691 he had done well enough to be able to move into newly built premises in the midst of the old established coffee-houses grouped around the Royal Exchange, in the very heart of the business world. Obviously a better coffee-man than a journalist, he succeeded in becoming a figure of some importance in the City, as coffee-house owners often were (like the Badrutts in Berlin and the Sachers in Vienna) and as such may have had a finger in quite a few pies. He married three times, had at least seven children, and was buried at St Mary Woolnoth's, where for many years he was a church-warden. (Though his remains are generally assumed to have been dug up in 1892 and reburied in a common grave at Ilford Cemetery, in fact his remains must have been turned out when the old church was rebuilt by Hawksmoor in 1716–27, for the building had a great vault beneath it which necessitated the removal of many feet of earth below the old floor level. The statement that "his remains, with those of other persons buried in the Church, were transferred in 1892 to Ilford Cemetery, where they lie under a common monument" is therefore suspect.)

The coffee-house in Lombard Street was his creation; the stage on which he built his reputation. But of his personality, of the flesh and blood man, there are only hints. He is known to have adopted a foundling child left on his doorstep, which suggests a kindly heart. Against this, a touch of independent spirit and ruffled pride can be detected in his Answer to Their Lordships under somewhat daunting circumstances at the Bar of the House: rather than print a correction in his paper, he preferred to kill off *Lloyd's News* on the spot. To have been placed in such a false position was obviously not to his taste, and even after nearly three centuries the proud but plebeian figure of the coffee-man at the Bar of the Lords gives an impression of a no-nonsense individualist with more time for commoners who paid their bills than portentious peers (who probably didn't).

From issue No 58 of *Lloyd's News* dated Tuesday 12 January 1696, there is a rather less endearing insight. In it the whole front page is given up to an ordinance from Barbados announcing that anyone importing a Christian servant of British nationality aged between sixteen and forty in good physical condition would receive a cash payment of £18 (as against the "Christian servant" who was to be given his board and twenty-five shillings a year). This trade, known as "indentured labour" (or white servitude), flourished with the West Indies and Virginia in the latter half of the 17th century and was, in substance, a process of kidnapping – or "spiriting" as it was called – by well organised agents who made their living by shanghaiing victims and handing them over to the ships. The master mariners were the key figures in the game, and it seems probable that the Coffee-man and Church-warden from Lombard Street who gave publicity to the ordinance was not entirely unconnected with this profitable practice (which, to

be fair, was no more disreputable than the Press-gang – and, after all, the wealth of the first British Empire was derived largely from the slave trade).

In the archives at Lloyd's is an invoice made out by Edward Lloyd to a shipowner called Captain Bowrey in 1703. It was for the "protection" from the Press-gang of the crew of his ship, the *Riseing Sun*, when she was due to sail for the East Indies, and for organising a letter of Mart, or passport. So, in addition to his other activities, Edward Lloyd seems to have run the 18th century equivalent of a tourist office, and, it must be admitted, something suspiciously like a protection racket.

Be this as it may, the short specimen of his handwriting on the invoice is one of the few direct personal contacts which remain today with Edward Lloyd, and while too brief for a proper graphological study it has enabled Heidi-Marie Wolff of Berlin to draw a few conclusions about his character.

She sees him as a stocky, muscular, medium-sized man with a strong personality, whose surprisingly modern handwriting discloses that he was far better educated than might be expected; that he had a quick brain and a good head for business; was straightforward in his dealings and knew exactly what he was doing; that he was rather vain, very ambitious, quite imaginative and probably a bit ruthless; a self-confident man who would let nothing stand in his way and did not suffer fools gladly; and that while neither particularly generous nor impulsive, he had a well balanced, engaging personality which inspired confidence in others. She adds that he was obviously a good mixer who enjoyed being the hub of his own busy world.

Here for what it is worth is the portrait of an average, active Englishman: at once materialist and moral, aggressive and religious, self-satisfied and self-critical, affable and strict, who spent his days behind the counter in his smoky, noisy, cheerful rooms with their wooden pews and the "auction pulpit", and handed round the plate at St Mary Woolnoth's on Sundays. An average Englishman who achieved unexpected immortality.

The last few months of his life were dogged by illness and filled with incident. Late in 1711 he lost his second wife, Elizabeth. The following year he married his third, Martha. On 30 January 1713 he saw the wedding of his daughter, Handy, to his head-waiter, William Newton. A fortnight later, on 15 February 1713, he died, leaving a substantial estate to his family and the coffee-house to his newly married son-in-law.

Edward Lloyd: A man born at the time of the second Civil War, who grew up in Cromwellian England, lived through the Plague, the Fire, the Dutch at Medway, the persecution of Dissenters and the "flaunting of Papists at Court", a Protestant who started his business during the eventful days of the "Glorious Revolution" (when Church benefices were filled with Roman Catholics and Magdalen College, Oxford, was turned into a Papist seminary while the Orange colours flew in High Street), who prospered during the War of the Spanish Succession and died a year before Queen Anne. Edward Lloyd was undoubtedly a Londoner of his time, yet in many ways he was ageless. He would have been equally at home in the 20th century as an entrepreneur, a Mine Host, a betting-shopowner or the chairman of Christies. Who knows, he might even have become a Name at Lloyd's.

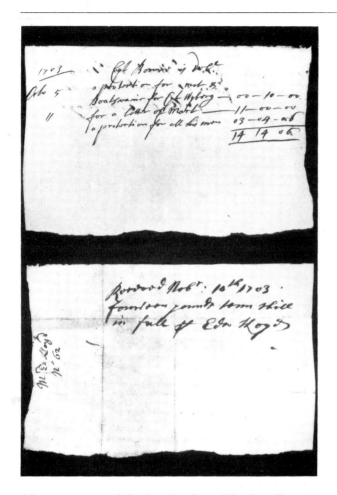

Above: *a copy of the invoice from Lloyd to Captain Bowrey, October 5 1703, for 'protection for a mate and boatswaine . . . and for a letter of mart (marque)', and beneath it Lloyd's receipt for the money.*

Below: *an enlargement from a photograph of Edward Lloyd's signature.*

Lloyd's in the Eighteenth Century and Afterwards

On previous page: *a mail-coach about to leave the General Post Office in Lombard Street. By its proximity to the GPO Lloyd's was enabled to reach a lucrative agreement with the authorities, whereby underwriters received news quicker—and cheaper— than anyone else in the City.*

THE EXPANDING WORLD: 1700–1770

IN OCTOBER 1702 Edward Lloyd posted, at the Lombard Street Coffee-house, a list of ships bound for the Far East but presumed or known to be missing. This lugubrious document has survived, even if the ships did not. Taking into account all the other cargoes that assuredly did reach their destination, it testifies to an already flourishing East Indian and Chinese trade. For nearly a century the East India Company's ships had plied the Chinese waters in the hope that Cathay "would aforth a most liberall vent of English clothes and kersies". What use the Chinamen made of English kersies must remain a matter of speculation, but by the end of the 17th century the company's trading-posts were doing a heavy reciprocal trade in tea and spices. Japan too had at one time appeared a promising outlet, after William Adam (one of the company's captains) had settled there and married a Japanese wife. But in 1641 Japan embarked on its great period of isolation and its ports, however tempting, were barred to English vessels.

The routes, then, to India and beyond to the Spice Islands, were well known in the 17th century and premiums on voyages to the East Indies, though high (15 to 20 percent according to Malynes, who was the first English writer on insurance) were commonplace. The navigators' maps – if still prone to cover up any hiatus with a statutory dolphin or two – were by 1700 the product more of observation than imagination. William Dampier had returned from his epic voyage in the *Roebuck* in 1699 with intriguing news of land ("New Holland") to the south of Java and Guinea. He concluded he had stumbled on a mass of islands, and Jonathan Swift, entranced, took him at his word and christened one of them Lilliput. There were others, however, who were convinced of the existence of a great southern continent, if only in the apparently reasonable belief that one was required "south of the Equator to counterpoize the land on the north, and to maintain the equilibrium necessary for the earth's motion". Doubtless the argument raged long and passionate among the fraternity at Lloyd's, as it did elsewhere in the City which was eagerly promoting speculative South Sea projects – more eager in fact to float a company than a ship. For in spite of the semi-piratical circumnavigations of Anson in 1740, of "Foul-weather" Jack Byron (with his unique knack of never missing a gale if there was one about) in 1764, and of Carteret and Wallis in 1767, no English ship entered the Southern Pacific from the west until Cook sailed in the *Endeavour*.

Yet the 18th century was an intensely curious not to say credulous age. Defoe's apocryphal voyages – of Robinson Crusoe, Cpt George Roberts et al – were no less incredible than the stories brought back (and widely believed) by even the more reputable explorers. The age-old myth of a race of Patagonian giants "who run swifter than horses and are exceedingly jealous of their wives" gained new and convincing currency after the return of Byron's expedition in the *Dolphin*. "We are informed" announced the *London Chronicle* on 12 July 1766, "that the giants found by Commodore Byron measured from $8\frac{1}{2}$ feet to 10 feet in height, and every way stout in proportion. The men's feet measured 18 inches." Equally notorious was the invention by a London magazine in 1708 of a totally fictitious piece of geography attributed to the no less spurious Spanish "Admiral de Fonte". This intrepid officer was supposed to have discovered a North-West Passage at 53°N, sailing north-east along rivers and lakes until he encountered a ship from Boston. "De Fonte" was resurrected during the renewed enthusiasm in the 1740s to discover a short-cut to India, and his findings were taken quite seriously by expeditions seeking to earn the Government's £20,000 reward for the discovery of a passage from Hudson's Bay to the Pacific. Even in 1768 a learned, but happily anonymous, analysis of his "voyage" found its way into print.

Fortunately, perhaps, for the underwriters there was no lack of genuine and more trustworthy discoverers either: James Cook, George Vancouver, George Bass and Captain Phipps (with whom Nelson served as a midshipman). Cook in particular brought an unprecedented measure of scientific accuracy to his surveys in the Pacific, and set new standards in hydrography. His mapping of the east coast of Australia and also of New Zealand in 1769–70 and of the north-west coast of America in 1778 stood up well to the tests of time. The mathematical exactitude of his observations was matched by the care with which he prepared for his expeditions, despising the relative comforts of frigates or East Indiamen for his voyages and opting for shallow-draught north-country colliers (which must have given them food for thought at the coffee-house).

Slowly the maps of the world began to take on a less putative aspect, as Britain, Spain, France and Holland continued their inexorable expansion of their trading empires. Throughout the century virtually all Britain's military adventures were directed towards this end – indeed Pitt's War (from 1756–62) had the sole objective of destroying French commercial power beyond all hope of recovery, and if the gouty old premier had had his way he would have extended it to Spain as well. To a lesser degree Marlborough's wars, the struggle over the unfortunate Jenkin's ear, and even the war of American Independence were partially motivated by trade rivalries. For the underwriters at Lloyd's, men like William Braund, this succession of wars could thrust them as easily to the brink of bankruptcy as they could make their fortunes: Braund himself came perilously close to disaster in

A LIST of what SHIPS are Sail'd from England, for East-India and China, and are not Return'd, nor known in England to Miscarry, and to whom they belong.

Note, O, stands for Old; E, for English Company; and P, for Private-Trade.

	Ships Names.	Commanders Names.	Tons.	Guns.	Men.	Where Bound.	When Sail'd.	
P	Buckhurst	—— Penluce	380	40	60	Muscat	August 16.	1698.
E	Mountague-Gally	John Collier	460	30	80	Surrat	April 8.	1699.
E	Julian	Charles Coatfworth	260	18	50	Borneo	Ditto	
E	Rook-Gally	George Simons	250	20	50	Surrat	August 16.	
E	Trumball-Gally	Henry Duffield	340	30	56	Borneo & China	October 10.	
P	Gosfright	—— Harrifon	330	30	50	Borneo	November 9.	
O	King William	John Braddyll	600	36	120	Fort St. George	30.	
O	Maderas	John Aprife	250	24	50	Bencola	30.	
E	Eaton-Frigate	George Phillips	340	27	68	China	December 15.	
E	Summers-Frigate	John Douglass	400	32	97	Coast & Bay	January 27.	
E	Limpoy	Thomas Monke	160	16	130	Stays in India	February 22.	
P	Mansell-Frigate	John Clarke	400	26	70	Borneo	March 23.	
E	Albermarle	William Beawes	350	28	65	Surrat	April 24.	1700.
O	Martha	Thomas Raines	600	40	80	Bombay	May 14.	
P	Rebecca	Thomas Maftin	120	10	20	Malegafcar	June 25.	
E	Borneo	Henry Berry	300	24	56	Borneo	July 4.	
O	New Advice	—— Redhead	160	16	36	Fort & Bay	6.	
E	Rifing-Eagle	Benjamin Boucher	160	16	40	Bay	September 17.	
E	Difcovery	John Evans	208	16	42	Mocoe	November 1.	
E	Rifing-Sun	Arthur Holford	140	12	27	China	Ditto	
O	Northumberland	Charles Richards	250	24	50	Ditto	13.	
E	Seaford	Martin Gardner	240	24	46	Ditto	19.	
O	China-Merchant	Francis Hofier	170	14	35	Ditto	Ditto	
E	Sarah-Gally	John Roberts	275	22	55	Ditto	Ditto	
E	Sretham	Roger Myors	350	30	70	Coast & Bay	December 4.	
O	Hampshire	Zachary Tovey	375	26	75	Fort St. George	27.	
O	Bedford	John Hudson	750	46	150	Ditto	Ditto	
O	Sidney	Lewis Whitwell	475	36	95	Bengall	Ditto	
O	Dafhwood	Marmaduke Raden	320	26	64	China	Ditto	
E	Neptune	Stephen Lafhley	270	22	55	Ditto	Ditto	
E	Bengall	Henry Trenwith	390	30	78	Coast & Bay	January 5.	
P	Eakins-Frigate	—— Stettell					Ditto	
O	Josiah	Randolph Pye	500	36	100	Bengall	22.	
O	Phoenix	Thomas Lambert	400	28	80	Ditto	Ditto	
O	Dutchefs	Hugh Raymond	450	28	91	Ditto	Ditto	
E	Degraves	William Young	520	36	104	Coast & Bay	February 19.	
P	Sophia	George Luke Burwifh	400	26	70	Coast of India	20.	
P	Anne	Adam Spencer					Ditto	
O	Loyal Cooke	Richard Boulton	330	30	66	Maderas & China	March 3.	
O	Sufannah	William Ingledew	350	24	70	Surrat	April 1.	1701.
E	Catharine	William Holeman	208	20	51	Bay	16.	
O	Nathanael	Charles Hill	250	26	50	Surrat	20.	
E	Rebow	Thomas Dennett	150	14	50	Ditto	Ditto	
O	Loyal Blifs	Robert Hudson	350	28	70	Bombay	May 30.	
O	Herne-Frigate	John Lane	150	20	30	Ditto	June 29.	
O	John & Mary	Bayly Kent	200	16	40	Bencola	July 15.	
E	Upton Gally	John Cammell	180	16	40	Surrat	August 3.	
E	Macclesfield Frigate	Thomas Robert	312	30	60	Borneo	September 15.	
O	Orenzebe	John Blewitt	425	32	87	China	October 1.	
O	Chambers-Frigate	Thomas South	350	30	71	Ditto	Ditto	
P	Conftant Friend	John Lackey	220	22	44	Coast of India	November 2.	
P	Profperous	—— Hilliard	220	20	40	Ditto	22.	
E	Canterbury	Enock Kingsford	340	28	66	China	December 7.	
E	Hallifax	Henry Hudson	340	20	70	Ditto	Ditto	
E	Arabia-Factor	Abram Jackson	140	16	28	Moco	Ditto	
E	Union	John Palmer	208	20	40	China	} Now in the Downes.	
E	Robert & Nathanael	John Smith	230	20	46	Ditto		
E	Macclesfield-Gally	John Hurle	250	20	46	Ditto		

Preparing to SAIL.

	Ships Names.	Commanders Names.	Tons.	Guns.	Men.	Where Bound.
E	Tankervill	Charles Newnam	425	34	85	
O	Wentworth	Thomas Sax	350	34	70	
O	Colchefter	Benjamin Roufe	500	36	90	
O	Howland	Thomas Hayes	400	30	80	
O	Fleet-Frigate	Thomas Burges	280	22	56	
E	Norris	James Allifon	500	—	100	Bay of Bengall
E	Panther	Robert Robinfon	400	24	70	
E	Legorn-Frigate	Jacob Wright	130	20	36	Borneo
P	London	George Matthews	400	34	90	Ditto

SHIPS Arriv'd in the River of Thames.

	Ships Names.	Commanders Names.	Tons.	Guns.	Men.		When Arriv'd.
O	Howland-Frigate	William Prower	400	30	80	———	May 15.
O	Chambers-Frigate	Thomas South	350	30	70	———	Ditto
E	Antelope	Henry Hammond	460	34	90	———	16.
P	Tufcan-Gally	Mark Duell	250	16	40	———	June 18.
E	Canterbury	Enoch Kingsford	370	30	66	———	July 2.
E	Macclesfield-Gally	Jonathan Hurle	280	18	50	———	8.
E	London	George Matthews	400	34	80	———	August 3.
O	Colchefter	Benjamin Roufe	500	36	90	———	14.
O	Wentworth	Thomas Sax	350	34	70	———	Ditto
O	Fame	William Browne	440	30	81	———	Ditto
O	Loyal Merchant	Matthew Lowth	400	30	80	———	18.
O	Dorrell	Samuel Hide	250	20	50	———	September 2.
E	Tankervill	Charles Newnam	400	34	80	———	Ditto
E	Panther	Robert Robinfon	400	24	70	———	Ditto
O	Taviftock	Matthew Martin	700	50	150	———	October 12.
P	Herne	—— Peacock	—	—	—	———	13.
O	Anna	Francis Nalle	350	30	70	———	December 1.
P	John-Gally	Thomas Warren				Plunder'd by Pirats.	August 14.

Above: *Captain Cook raising the British flag on the Sandwich Islands, and below it, a detail from Dampier's chart of his discoveries in the Spice Islands and New Holland 1699–1700.*

Left: *Frontispiece from an account of Admiral Byron's circumnavigation in 1766, depicting the legendary race of Patagonian giants.*

Opposite: *the list of missing ships published by Edward Lloyd in October 1702.*

1741 during the war with Spain, only to emerge from the Seven Year War, twenty years later, a considerably richer and more substantial underwriter.

William Braund's one claim to fame – overlooking the disreputable episode in 1754 when, as a Director of the East India Company, his part in a dubious transaction over a quantity of substandard cloth was revealed – is that the majority of his risk books have survived. He was, by all accounts, conscientious and (by the standards of the age) eminently respectable. Winter and summer, he attended regularly at the same box, even when some of his colleagues preferred to absent themselves rather than take on difficult business; he seems to have dealt loyally and honestly with his brokers. And towards the end of his life – when younger bloods like Angerstein began stirring things up – he remained one of the devoted Old Guard at Old Lloyd's Coffee-house. In short, an exemplary Lloyd's man. His account books, which date from 1747–74, and his risk books (1759–74) have been expertly analysed by Lucy Sutherland of Lady Margaret Hall, Oxford. Their meticulous entries show what was, in all probability, a typical pattern of underwriting during those convulsive years. Because of his own long-standing connection with the Portugal trade, his dealings in 1759 (a year selected by Miss Sutherland) show a bias towards the Peninsula: 141 risks written in all. All the other European and Baltic ports account for only another 275 that year. In comparison Braund underwrote 335 voyages across the Atlantic – either to the North American colonies or to the West Indies – as well as 149 Atlantic cross risks (i.e. for journeys to and from ports other than British ones). This was a form of risk which a 17th century writer on insurance had advised against altogether. But perhaps underwriters had acquired a new – if not always well-placed – confidence in the omnipresence of the Royal Navy (though not beyond an average limit of £145 on each risk!).

Braund died before the outbreak of the American War and Britain's subsequent humiliation. But his career, unexceptional though it was, mirrors the general trends of trade in the first three-quarters of the 18th century. The large preponderance of risks accepted on outgoing voyages over incoming voyages (approximately 2:1) underlines that between 1700–1770 Britain's imports fell by more than half. The complete absence of French trade is to be expected, of course, in the middle of a war, as is the high percentage of Portuguese risks after the lucrative Methuen Treaty of 1703. But the scarcity of business in other European ports emphasises the urgency with which Britain was having to seek out new markets in the 18th century – how she was being forced to expand as the world's horizons were expanding.

Wool, which had long been an essential staple of English prosperity, was no longer so badly needed in Europe. The new markets (for wool and increasingly for Britain's embryonic manufacturing industries), as Braund's books vividly illustrate, were in Britain's colonies especially in America. To foster and protect this trade the Navigation Acts, forbidding colonists to trade direct with other countries, were rigidly enforced. Colonial goods could only be re-exported through British ports and ships. These acts, at once a protection and restraint on colonial trade, followed a pattern of commerce which survived well into the next century, and assured a continuing growth of prosperity for merchants and underwriters alike. But it was also these acts which were instrumental in crystallising the American revolt. Had he lived to see that, William Braund's books would have looked very different after 1781. However, Braund has taken us rather ahead of our story.

BUBBLE-MANIA, AND THE FIRST MARINE INSURANCE COMPANIES

IN THE *Spectator*, Addison had spoken of Lloyd's as the place where "auctions are usually kept", and, although by 1710 Edward Lloyd's coffee-house was already the chief commercial sale-room in London, there is no evidence that any significant amount of marine underwriting was transacted there during his lifetime.

Such underwriting was still carried on, as it had been throughout the 17th century, in a haphazard fashion by merchants, bankers and others who subscribed policies as a side-line to their main business, and Hatton (in *A New View of London*, published in 1708) describing insurance in the same breath as bagnios (hot and cold) says: "Offices that insure ships or their cargo are many about the Royal Exchange, as Mr Hall's, Mr Bevis, etc, who for a Premium paid down procure those that will subscribe Policies for insuring ships (with their cargo) bound to or fro any part of the World, the Premium being proportioned to the Distance, Danger of Seas, Enemies etc".

Then, as now, the market was made up of brokers and underwriters, and insurance cover was obtained by going to a broker (known as an office-keeper) who discussed the details of the policy, drew it up, and then hawked the risk around the Royal Exchange and neighbouring coffee-houses until he had managed to get it underwritten. Like betting on the Turf or the Dogs today, marine underwriting was open to anyone who fancied to have a flutter (Pepys, the Admiralty clerk, occasionally wrote a risk, and Daniel Defoe, the author, ruined himself by doing so); and the dangers inherent to marine

Above: *Satire on the South Sea Bubble, one of William Hogarth's earliest engravings, 1721. In the centre of the picture stands the Wheel of Fortune on which gullible investors are being taken for a ride.*

On pp. 42 and 43: *companion broadsheet prints (1720) on the South Sea Bubble, listing some of the worthy and worthless projects floated during that orgy of speculation.*

41

The BUBBLERS MIRROUR: or ENGLANDS FOLLY.

insurance were dramatically brought into the lime-light by the Smyrna Disaster in 1693. During the war with France which followed the accession of William III, a huge convoy of some 400 merchant vessels was pounced on by Tourville and d'Estrées in the Bay of Lagos, and about 100 merchantmen, valued with their cargoes at a million pounds (a stupendous sum in those days) were captured or destroyed by the French.

Although the loss fell most heavily on the Dutch, the London market was hit so badly that in the words of Defoe, "an incredible number of the best merchants in the Kingdom sank under the load". A Bill to force composition upon creditors was rushed through the House of Commons, but subsequently rejected by the Lords, and many of the unlucky underwriters, including Defoe himself, were hard put to meet their obligations.

In the wake of this catastrophe the idea of a chartered, joint-stock insurance corporation to supplant the individual underwriters gained currency, especially during the lunatic wave of speculation that attended the South Sea Bubble.

Methods of state finance might have made great strides since the days of Elizabeth's somewhat penny-pinching warfare against the Spaniards, and the country might have gained in financial soundness, but England was also faced with the bill for the Grand Alliance in Europe. Thus by 1711 government finances had become so chaotic that the Chancellor of the Exchequer sought to re-establish public credit by means of a chartered commercial company, the shares of which were offered in substitution for government stock – tempting investors with a switch, as it were, from gilts to equities. After the Peace of Utrecht, Spain had conceded rights in South America, and the new South Sea Company was to enjoy a monopoly of trading with the Spanish possessions.

Wild-cat scheme though it was, the notion of South America struck a chord in the mind of the average Englishman, who remembered the stories of how Drake and Hawkins and Grenville had sailed into Plymouth with their ships full of gold and treasure, and how more recently the share-holders in the East India Company had been making money hand over fist. Launched with as much ballyhoo as any 20th century promotion, the prospects of unlimited profits sent the shares soaring. Men and women of fashion crowded down to the Royal Exchange to buy stock which was soon worth ten times its nominal value. "The King" Lady Ormond told Swift, "adopts the South Sea and calls it his beloved child". In this heady climate the stock-jobbers of 'Change Alley and Threadneedle Street were soon falling over each other in their haste to promote companies of every description. (One concern was formed to extract gold from sea-water, and another was blandly launched without any object at all.) In a few short years some two thousand enterprises with a total capital of around six hundred million pounds – over five times the cash resources of all Europe – were successfully floated, nearly all of them as joint-stock companies.

"The hurry of stock-jobbing bubbles" reported the *London Journal*, "has become so great . . . as to exceed all ever known. Nothing but running about from coffee-house to coffee-house, and subscribing without knowing what the proposals were. The constant cry was 'For God's sake let us subscribe to something; we don't care what it is' ".

Not surprisingly, insurance came in for its fair share of speculative activity, and projects included schemes for insurance against house-breaking and highway robbery; death by gin-drinking; against the event of horses "dying natural deaths, or being disabled"; for "assurance for lying", and even an "assurance of female chastity" (the rates for which are, sadly, unknown). But most significant of all was the campaign, started in 1717, to supplant individual marine underwriters by two chartered companies.

It was waged with manifestos, petitions and memoranda, and the case for reform is summed up in a letter – now filed in the British Museum (ref: BM 357B 3/62) – from a merchant to his M.P.:

"Put yourself in my position as a merchant" he wrote "and think what my situation is when I insure under the present system. I must go to the office where an office-keeper only attends who can't certainly inform me who shall subscribe my policy but I must leave directions with him to procure me one for such a sum. If it be a large one perhaps it may be some time before I can have it completed and when my policy is completed I find persons' names to it I have no acquaintance with or knowledge of. It is impossible I can be thought to have what satisfaction is necessary in an affair upon which my whole fortune depends."

Even if the petitioners had, to some extent, a good case, their motives were above all speculative; they were less interested in improving the facilities of British insurance than in the prospects of a successful promotion. For a good three years the controversy raged; yet oddly enough, in all the long-winded polemics which were bandied about, there was never any mention of Lloyd's. The name did not even crop up. London's chief mercantile sale-room was obviously not yet the main underwriting centre; in fact it was probably only one of various places – such as Garroway's, the Marine, and others – where insurers could be found. In the second decade of the 18th century, Lloyd's was still in no way synonymous with marine insurance.

The lobbying came to a head when a group of petitioners, led by Lord Onslow and Lord Chetwynd, approached the King with a direct bribe of £300,000. On 4 May 1720 George I sent a Royal Message to

Parliament that the establishment of two corporations for marine insurance "exclusive only of all other corporations and societies" would be of great advantage to trade.

The Monarch's intervention was decisive. On 10 June 1720 Henry Pelham secured formal royal consent for what was known as "The Bubble Act". Twelve days later the charters establishing the Royal Exchange Assurance Corporation and the London Assurance Corporation were formally granted.

But what appeared at first sight to be a disaster for private underwriters in fact placed them in a stronger position than ever before – and led to the emergence of Lloyd's coffee-house as the great centre and stronghold of marine insurance. For the significance of the Bubble Act – which was intended to suppress all undertakings that might prejudice trade – was not so much in the granting of charters to the two new insurance corporations, but in the clause that prohibited the insurance of ships and goods at sea by any partnership or firm.

"Private and particular persons" were free to continue writing policies "so long as the same be not upon . . . the account or Risque of Persons acting in a Society or Partnership for that purpose". Which meant that apart from the two insurance corporations no firm could now write a marine policy without incurring heavy penalties. But private individuals could – and did.

All the same, to compete against the Royal Exchange and the London Assurance they had to become more professional. They had to offer better facilities and at least equal security. They had, above all, to centralise their activities. And so, because of its mercantile and shipping connections, they chose Lloyd's coffee-house as their headquarters.

As it turned out, the competition of the two corporations was less formidable than had been feared. Both companies experienced financial troubles at the outset, and had difficulty in finding experienced underwriters as managers. They tended to concentrate on Fire and Life insurance, and whereas their share of the marine market soon dwindled to a mere ten percent, the influence of the men who foregathered at Lloyd's increased proportionately. Within a generation no one could doubt that they dominated the world of marine insurance.

LLOYD'S LIST

WILLIAM NEWTON, WHO had inherited the coffee-house from Edward Lloyd in 1713, was buried himself at St Mary Woolnoth's only eighteen months later. His death was probably unexpected, because he left no will, and his 21-year-old widow transferred both here affections and her business to the next-door neighbour, Samuel Sheppard. Within eight months, on 16 April 1715, they were married.

Five years afterwards, Handy died, to be survived by her second husband for a further seven years, and when Samuel Sheppard followed her to the grave in February 1727 the business passed to his sister Elizabeth, the wife of Thomas Jemson.

Although a member of the Shipwrights' Company, Jemson must have found his wife's business more rewarding than building ships, for it is as Master of Lloyd's Coffee-house that he is described in Church documents of 1728. Before long he was involved in a quarrel between the coffee-house owners and the press, which is recorded in a pamphlet of 1728 entitled "The Case of the Coffee-men of London and Westminster; or an account of the Impositions and Abuses put upon them and the whole Town by the present Set of News-Writers". Their complaint was that whereas they were obliged, at great expense, to take in every newspaper published, the material contained in the papers was almost all picked up at the coffee-houses themselves (and quite often distorted). Moreover, since the advertisements – which yielded the *Daily Post*, for instance, as much as £3.15.0 a day – derived their value from the coffee-house circulation, the proprietors were "Paid by the *Advertisers* for taking in *Advertisements* and paid by the Coffee-men for delivering them out: which . . . is to have a good Dinner every Day and be paid for Eating it. Here's luck, My Lads!"

Some of the malcontents even thought of starting up an opposition newspaper, and a committee of eleven "managers" – one of whom was Thomas Jemson of Lloyd's – was set up under the leadership of William Fielden of John's to organise the project.

The news-writers countered cheerfully that "These plodding Fellows" proposed to print only ascertained facts – and who wants to read just the truth? In any case, the scheme came to nothing at the time. But indirectly it gave Jemson the idea of publishing a newspaper of his own, and led to the appearance of *Lloyd's List* in April 1734.

At first this was published once a week (then subsequently on Tuesdays and Fridays) but Jemson himself did not live to see the publication launched, which was superintended by his successor, Richard Baker. Unfortunately the first volumes have all been lost; the earliest surviving issue is No 560 dated Friday 2 January 1740. From that date onwards all but two volumes are safely filed in the Library at Lloyd's.

In many ways *Lloyd's List* was a revival, in a more successful form, of Edward Lloyd's old paper. It was similar in size and appearance, a single sheet 12 inches in length by $7\frac{1}{2}$ inches wide (printed matter $10\frac{1}{2}$ inches by $5\frac{1}{4}$ inches); and while the front page

LLOYD's LIST. Nº 560.

FRIDAY, January 2. 1740.

THIS Liſt, which was formerly publiſh'd once a Week, will now continue to be publiſh'd every *Tueſday* and *Friday*, with the Addition of the Stocks Courſe of Exchange, &c.——Subſcriptions are taken in at Three Shillings per Quarter, at the Bar of *Lloyd*'s Coffee-Houſe in *Lombard-Street*.

Such Gentlemen as are willing to encourage this Undertaking, ſhall have them carefully deliver'd according to their Directions.

London *Exchanges* on	
Amſt.	34 11 a 10
Ditto Sight	34 7½a8
Rott.	35 a 1
Antw.	35 11 a 36
Hamb:	33 10 2U a 11 2½
Paris —	32⅝
Ditto at 2U	32⅜
Bourdeaux Uſance	32⅝
Cadiz —	42⅝
Madrid	42⅝
Bilboa	41⅝
Leghorn	51¼
Genoa	55
Venice	51¾
Liſbon	5 4⅞a5
Oporto	5 4½
Dublin	8

Aids in the Exchequer		*Given for*	*Paid off*
18th 2 Shilling	1739	1000000	926800
18th 4 Ditto	1740	2000000	482600
Malt——	1739	750000	501014
Salt——	1734	1000000	910500

Gold in Coin - - - -		3	18	1
Ditto in Barrs - - -		3	18	
Ps of Eight Pillar large - - -	per Oz	0	5	7½
Ditto Small - -		0	5	6½
Mexico large - -		0	5	7½
Ditto Small - -		0	5	6⅝
Silver in Barrs - - -		0	5	7⅝

Annuities

14*l.* per Cent at 22½ Years Purchaſe
1704 to 1708 Incluſive 24½ ditto
3½ per Cent. 1 per Cent. præm.
3 per Cent. 5¾ Diſc.

Cochineal 20s od per. lb. *Diſcount* 00s per Cent.

Lottery 1710.

Prizes for 3 Years from *Michaelmas* laſt are in courſe of Payment
Blanks for 3 Years from *Michaelmas* laſt 1l. 10s *per* Set.

Price of **Stocks.**	*Wedneſday*	*Thurſday*	*Friday*
Bank Stock - - - - -	138½a¾		138½
Eaſt India - - - - - - - -		156	156a56¼
South Sea - - - - -	98¾		98¾
Ditto Anuity Old	110¼a110	110⅝	110⅝
Ditto——New	110⅜a¾	110¼	110¼
3 *per* Cent. Annuity 1726 / 1731			99¾
Million Bank - - -	113	113	113
Equivalent - - - - - -	112	112	112
R. Aſſ. 100l paid in			
L: Aſſ. 13l paid in	10¾	10¼	10¾
7 per Cent Em. Loan	98	98	98
5 per Cent. Ditto	74¾	74¾	75
Bank Circulation	2l 10s od	2l 10s od	2l 10s od
Lottery Tickets	5l 16s od	5l 17s od	6l 00s od

India Transfer Books open the 19th of January
Royal Aſſurance the 20th of January
South Sea New Annuity the 22d of January, 3 per Cent Annuities the 21ſt and 22d of January
South Sea Stock the 4th of February
The 5 per Cent Emperor's Loan, ſells as above without the ſix Months Intereſt of 2 and a quarter per Cent, and 5 per Cent. part of the Principal to be paid of both, are now paying at the Bank
The India Dividend will be paid the 29th of January, South Sea New Annuities the 29th ditto, and the S. Sea Stock the 6th and 7th of February,
Navy and Victualling Bills to the 30th June laſt are in courſe of Payment.

Intereſt per Cent	*Wedneſday*	*Thurſday*	*Friday*	
3 India Bonds new	79	80	80	Shill: Præm:
4 Salt Tallies	¾ a ⅝	¾ a ⅝	¾ a ⅝	

Opposite: *the earliest surviving issue (no. 520) of* Lloyd's List.

Above: *contemporary print of the General Post Office in Lombard Street towards the end of the 18th century. Lloyd's coffee-house was in the same block (rebuilt after the Great Fire), to the east of the buildings shown here.*

contained the rates of the London Exchange on a number of foreign markets, prices of principal stocks, government annuities and so forth, the back page was given over to shipping intelligence.

The issue of 2 January 1740 gives the prevailing prices of gold and silver in coin and bars, and the modern investor may be interested to learn that the quotation for gold then fluctuated between £3.18.1d and £3.18.4d per ounce, and silver between 5.7d and 5.9d per ounce. The price of cochineal (the dye which frequently featured in the sales at Lloyd's) was 15.5d to 15.10d per pound, while the quotations for stocks were: Bank Stock 136–140; East India Company 155–160; South Sea Company 102–108.

The shares of the two chartered insurance companies were also quoted in every issue, but showed very little improvement during 1740–41; in fact after twenty years of activity both were selling at under par (Royal Exchange £100 at 89–90; London Assurance Nominal £12.10.0 at £10.10.0 to £11).

The front page of *Lloyd's List* also contained legal and company notices, and the times of the high water at London Bridge. The back page was entirely filled with short news items concerning the arrivals and departures of ships at various ports as well as reports of accidents to vessels.

On the whole, the news transmission from English ports to Lloyd's was fairly good: Cowes, Southampton and Gravesend took a day or two; Bristol and Falmouth two to three days, but ten days to a fortnight were required from Scottish ports against only a week from Lisbon. The mail from Livorno took twelve days (which is about the same as it takes today!). New York, however, required two months at the very best.

Postal rates were expensive to be sure. It cost 1.4d to send an ounce for any distance over eighty miles, while letters from Scotland and Ireland bore a 50 percent surcharge. Since underwriters needed to have up-to-date news continuously from at least two dozen English and foreign ports, the expense would have been prohibitive, either for an individual or a newspaper, had someone at Lloyd's – probably Jemson – not hit on a brilliant solution. An agreement was negotiated with the postal authorities that, against an annual payment of £200, port correspondents would send their reports free of charge direct to the Post Office, simply marked "Lloyd's". Since the coffee-house was just down the street, this meant that Lloyd's not only received the news cheaper, but also much quicker than by normal mail delivery.

This postal privilege was the backbone of the paper's success, and in its turn the publication became a landmark in the history of Lloyd's itself, now growing in strength and repute. It heralded the beginning of a fruitful exchange of shipping news with the government, who in turn obligingly sent word to the coffee-house of any great victory at sea.

Though sometimes as in March 1739 it was *Lloyd's List* who got the scoop: "Mr Baker, Master of Lloyd's Coffee-House in Lombard Street, waited on Sir Robert Walpole with the news of Admiral Vernon's taking Porto Bello. This was the first account thereof, and, proving true, Sir Robert was pleased to order him a handsome present". The source of these sensational tidings was also given, and shows how far afield the coffee-house had already cast its net: "Mr Baker had his Letter of Advice by the *Tichfield*, Captain Gardner from Jamaica, who sailed from thence with the *Triumph*, Captain Renton, and got to Dover a Day before him".

JENKINS' EAR

THANKS TO Sir Robert Walpole's enlightened policy of peace abroad and freer trade for all, the country soon recovered from the depression caused by the bursting of the South Sea Bubble in 1720, and the following two decades were a time of great prosperity for England. Manufacturing cities like Birmingham and Manchester doubled in size; Bristol and Liverpool became wealthy ports; exports boomed, and the demand for insurance cover increased proportionately.

But free trade, unbridled competition and an out-and-out rush to establish new colonies and open fresh markets in Asia and South America inexorably brought British shipping into a collision course with that of Spain and France. For nineteen years, Walpole's common sense kept Britain out of war with Europe, despite the often vociferous pressure of his colleagues to revive the old Whig feud against the Bourbons. "Madam" he proudly told Queen Caroline in 1734, "there are 50,000 men slain this year in Europe, and not one Englishman". But in the end the hostilities which he tried so consistently to avoid broke out in 1739 over the Spanish right of search. Inflamed by the knowledge that English vessels trading in the Spanish Main were being boarded by Spanish coastguards and English sailors dragged off to jail in chains, the country was spoiling for a fight; and when Captain Jenkins appeared before the House of Commons with one of his ears in a cardboard box, saying that it had been cut off by Spanish customs officials in Havana, he was readily believed. A few spoilsports protested that they knew Robert Jenkins, and that he had lost his ear in a pillory, but nobody paid any attention to them. (Equally, Oxford Common Room talk would have it that it was not his ear but a more private part of his body.) Popular fury boiled over, and Walpole was obliged to take action. When at last he declared war, the bells of the City rang out and bonfires blazed.

The war provoked by Jenkins' ear soon escalated from a localised campaign off the South American

SLAVERY.

Above: *Slavery, a satire of 1738 'dedicated to the worthy and most injured Merchants of Great Britain' on the so-called crisis of Jenkin's ear. It is an attack on Walpole's peaceful policy, which supposedly allowed the Spanish to treat English merchants (left foreground) like common plough-oxen. The British lion is rampant in anger (right foreground), as English ships are fired on and the hapless Jenkins (top left) has his ear lopped off.*

coast into the long drawn-out struggle of the Austrian Succession, and then the Seven Year War. As H.A.L. Fisher has said, "It was a struggle not of courts and cabinets, but of men on the spot, of sailors and merchants, smugglers and privateers, of lumbermen, settlers and free-traders, of rival mercantile companies, brawling and quarelling either along the Spanish Main or in Acadia and Newfoundland, or along the banks of the Ohio or the St Lawrence, or under a burning Indian sky, among the rice-fields of the Carnatic, or the canes and mango trees of Bengal".

As such, it was an underwriters' war: the first taste of wartime marine insurance since they had adopted Lloyd's coffee-house as their headquarters, and in the early days there were some traumatic moments. Enemy cruisers and privateers swarmed into the Channel and the Soundings, seizing British craft within sight of the coast; trade with America and the West Indies was almost brought to a standstill, and the long list of captured ships and cargoes made sorry reading for the inmates of Lloyd's, by whom 90 percent of the lost tonnage was covered. Many paragraphs in *Lloyd's List* during the years 1740–48 are taken up with casualty reports: No 589 of 24 April 1741 announced a whole batch of English ships captured by the enemy, and as the war proceeded the losses grew: 307 in 1714; 457 in 1745; and 297 in 1748. "They are ringing the bells now" Walpole had the doubtful satisfaction of saying when his peace policy collapsed, "soon they will be wringing their hands." For the underwriters at Lloyd's, this was nearer the bone than most. Practically every policy they wrote covered the risk of capture, seizure and detention, and if the Navy failed they were ruined. "The angle from which most of us were taught our English history makes it difficult to think of the Navy as having been at any time other than admirable," remarks D.E.W. Gibb, "but there were periods in the 18th century when (usually through the folly of White-hall) it was a very insecure shield." Yet, if the hostilities continued with only a short break (co-inciding with the Pelham Ministries) for some twenty-four years, both England as a whole and the underwriters as a group did well out of the war, as William Braund's risk books show. The remarkable coalition of pride, folly and incompetence shown by George III, Lord North and the "King's Friends" resulted, ultimately, in the loss of the American colonies; but at least Canada and India were gained, and as Horace Walpole was one of the first to notice, Great Britain became an Empire. At the outset underwriters managed to keep in the black by insuring Spanish and French ships – apparently a profitable business – until insurance of enemy property was prohibited in 1748; and as time wore on the high premium income from wartime rates turned marine insurance into a golden gamble.

GAMBLING FEVER AT LLOYD'S

AT THE ACCESSION of George III there were only 174 British peers (of whom twelve, being Catholics, could not sit in the House of Lords). These men, their friends and dependents, governed the land. They had been brought up to do so. But for all this, many of them lived empty, frivolous lives. "It is a gaudy, thoughtless age" wrote Richard Cumberland, "and they who live up to the fashion of it, live in a continual display of scenery, their pleasures are all pantomines, their dinners steam along the columns of every Daily paper, and their suppers and assembleys dazzle the guests with tawdry lights and suffocate them with suspicious odours." The great families tended to live in the country and to come to London for the Season; they had their Town houses in Mayfair and indulged in a hectic social schedule, if Horace Walpole is anything to go by. "I had been" he wrote to a friend, "at the Duke of Cumberland's levy, then at the Princess Amelia's drawing-room, from thence, to a crowded House of Commons, to dine at your brother's, to the Opera, to Madam Ceilian's, to Arthur's and to supper at Mrs George Pitt's."

A man of fashion would begin his day at eleven, assisted by his valet and his barber and attended by minor relatives and friends (who had surfaced at a less elegant hour). "We rise by nine" said John Macky in his *Journey through England*, "and those that frequent great men's levées find entertainment at ten till eleven. About twelve, the *beau monde* assembles in several coffee or chocolate houses. We are carried to these places in chairs or sedans. If it is fine weather, we take a turn in the Park till two, when we go to dinner. The general way is to make a party at the coffee house to go and dine at the Tavern, where we sit till six, when we go to the play, unless you are invited to the table of some great man. After the play, the best company generally go to Tom's or Will's Coffee house ad-joining, where there is playing picket and the best of conversation until midnight."

The conversation might well be that of Johnson or Burke, and the gambling more than just picket. Indeed so widespread was the craze for gaming that people of all stations indulged in it. They played whist and picket, hazard and pharaoh (or faro), ombre, loo, quadrille, pope-joan, bassett, passage, commerce, costly colours, Queen Nazarean, post and pair. "The boys and girls" complained Lady Hertford to her friend Lady Pomfret, "sit down as gravely to whist tables as the Fellows of Colleges used to do formerly. It is actually a ridiculous, though I think mortifying sight, that playing should become the business of the nation, from the age of fifteen to four-score." The high play which characterised Whites from its chocolate house days spread to Almacks and Crockfords in the middle of

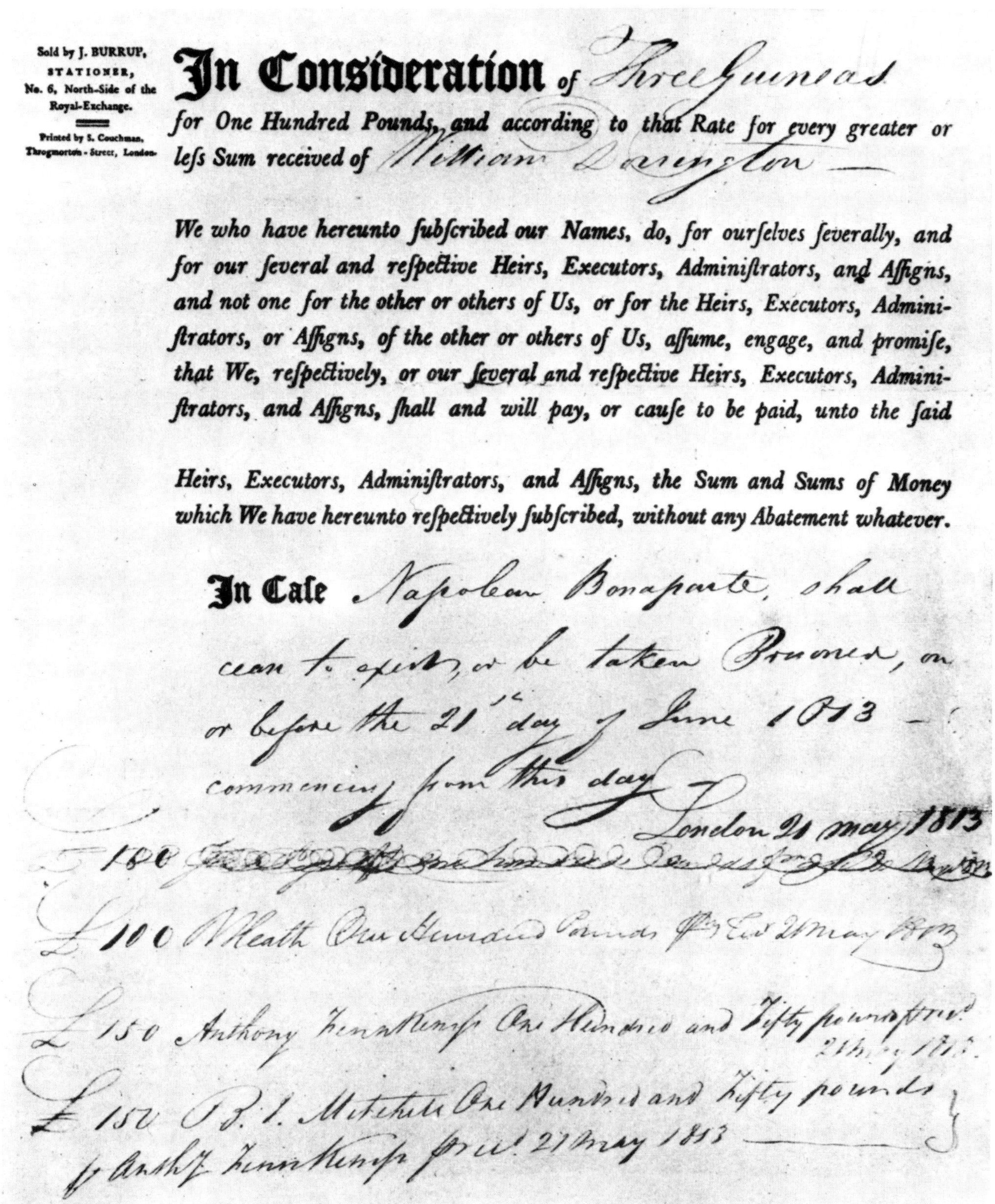

Sold by J. BURRUP,
STATIONER,
No. 6, North-Side of the
Royal-Exchange.
———
Printed by S. Couchman,
Throgmorton-Street, London.

In Consideration of *Three Guineas*

for One Hundred Pounds, and according to that Rate for every greater or less Sum received of *William Darington* —

We who have hereunto fubfcribed our Names, do, for ourfelves feverally, and for our feveral and refpective Heirs, Executors, Adminiftrators, and Affigns, and not one for the other or others of Us, or for the Heirs, Executors, Adminiftrators, or Affigns, of the other or others of Us, affume, engage, and promife, that We, refpectively, or our feveral and refpective Heirs, Executors, Adminiftrators, and Affigns, fhall and will pay, or caufe to be paid, unto the faid

Heirs, Executors, Adminiftrators, and Affigns, the Sum and Sums of Money which We have hereunto refpectively fubfcribed, without any Abatement whatever.

In Cafe *Napolean Bonaparte, shall cease to exist, or be taken Prisoner, on or before the 21st day of June 1813 — commencing from this day*

London 21 may 1813

£ 100 ...

£ 100 H Heath One Hundred Pounds P° Ew 21 May 1813

£ 150 Anthony Tenntkins One Hundred and Fifty pounds rec'd 21 May 1813.

£ 150 P B I Mitchell One Hundred and Fifty pounds by Anth Tenntkins pr ... 21 May 1813 —

Above: *a gambling policy on the life or arrest of Napoleon 'on or before the 21st day of June 1813', at a premium of three guineas percent.*

the 18th century, and betting books were formed in every club and coffee-house and even in University Common Rooms. A Scotsman at Blackheath bet that a friend would drive his feather bale 150 yards once in three times; the wagers in the Combination Rooms at Cambridge dealt with the position of the wranglers; whereas the members of Whites were chiefly concerned with the longevity of their male friends and the fertility of their female ones, or such sporting bets as "Mr Cavendish bets Mr H. Brownrigg 2/1 that he does not kill the bluebottle fly before he goes to bed" (which apparently he succeeded in doing!).

If the theatres, the pleasure-gardens, the masquerades and the ridottos, the cock-fights and dog-fights and prize-fights offered plenty of diversion for a man in Society, his daily routine always included a vist to the club and the coffee-house for a game of cards. And as the century wore on and the middle classes grew more prosperous, so they too began to get showy. "When I see young shop-keepers keep horses, ride hunting, learn dog-language and keep the sportsman's brogue upon their tongues I am always afraid for them," grumbled Defoe, as he noticed that such people were beginning to wear swords and long perukes, and to be seen increasingly at balls and masquerades, as well as on the race-course and at gaming houses. Under the circumstances it was hardly surprising that profligate habits should find their way even into the solid precincts of Lloyd's which until 1769 remained a coffee-house to which all the world had access – and would write any risk on any voyage for any amount. The fat underwriting profits during the Seven Year War were a magnet for speculators hoping to make a quick fortune who were inevitably disillusioned when peace brought a collapse of the high wartime premiums and a levelling-off of underwriting profits.

The result was an outbreak of gambling that had nothing to do with regular marine insurance. Money was free and opportunities for investment limited. To gamble on insurance risks was an obvious temptation. And so people went in for a "flutter". Horace Walpole, himself a gambler, considered that insurance was "nothing more than a particular game, a more solemn species of hazard . . .".

Gambling policies on ships had been prohibited by an Act in 1746, but wager policies on the lives of prominent people became so popular that Thomas Mortimer was moved to publish a scathing attack on the jobbers of Jonathan's and the merchants at Lloyd's who made bets ". . . insuring on the lives of such unfortunate gentlemen as may stand accountable to their country for misconduct". There was even less justification for making a book on the lives of well known personalities who happened to be ill. It hardly improved an invalid's morale to

Above: *contemporary caricature of John Wilkes by Sayers. Wilkes, pamphleteer, radical politician and Lord Mayor of London, was a favourite subject of gambling policies in the mid-18th century.*

Oxf. Mag. Sep. 1774.

BOREAS.

Rohis

I Promise to reduce the Americans.

Above: *George III (another target for the betting men) as he appeared in a contemporary satire of the War of American Independence.*

read in the paper that 90 percent odds were being offered against his recovery.

Henry Gray notes that the life of Sir Robert Walpole was for a long time a standing dish, the premium varying according to the circumstances of the day. Charles Edward, the Young Pretender of 1745, was another popular risk. Large stakes were placed on the Duke of Newcastle when he was prime minister, on Admiral Byng, and on Lord Nithsdale when imprisoned in the Tower.

Nithsdale's escape by disguising himself as his wife was little to the taste of the underwriters who had made their book on the basis that he already had one foot on the scaffold. When George II fought with his troops at Dettingen, 25 guineas percent was paid against his return.

The fact that news travelled slowly offered plenty of opportunities for exploiting inside knowledge. "It is a well known fact" said the *London Chronicle*, "that a certain ambassador insured £30,000 on Minorca in the war of 1755 with advices at the same time in his pocket that it was taken."

According to Mortimer, the merchants of Lloyd's had put up a notice in the coffee-house banning such wager-policies. But in 1768 the *London Chronicle* carried a leader criticising:

> "The introduction and amazing progress of illicit gambling at Lloyd's Coffee House . . ."

and going on to say:

> "Though gaming in any degree . . . is perverting the original and useful design of that Coffee House, it may in some measure be excusable to speculate on the following subjects:

> Mr Wilkes being elected member for London, which was done from five to 50 guineas percent,

> Ditto for Middlesex, from 20 to 70 guineas percent

> Alderman B--d's life for one year, now doing at 7 percent,

> On John Wilkes' life for one year, now doing 5 percent (warranted to remain in prison during that period),

> On a declaration of war with France or Spain: 8 guineas percent . . . But when policies come to be opened on two of the first Peers in Britain losing their heads at 10/6d percent and on the dissolution of the present Parliament within one year at 5 guineas percent . . . it is surely time for Authority to interfere, and . . . put a stop to it."

Such a betting-shop atmosphere brought discredit on the place and upset some of the more reputable merchants and underwriters who did their business at Lloyd's. Insofar as this group can be identified at all, the evidence from Braund's papers would indicate that it was the younger (and perhaps more earnest) broking element, such as

Angerstein and Brook Watson, who took the matter most to heart. So seriously did they object to the way things were going that a number of them felt that the time for a radical change had come. And so they decided to break adrift from the old coffee-house and set up a rival Lloyd's of their own.

POPE'S HEAD ALLEY AND THE ROYAL EXCHANGE

THE ADVERTISEMENT IN the *Public Advertiser* on Monday 20 March 1769 was decorous enough:

"To the Merchants in general, Owners and Freighters of Ships, Insurance Brokers etc, etc. Thomas Fielding, Waiter from Lloyd's Coffee-House begs acquaint them that his House in Pope's Head Alley, Lombard Street is now genteely fitted up and will open for the reception of Gentlemen, Merchants, etc Tomorrow the 21st instant by the name of New Lloyd's Coffee-House, where he hopes to receive their favours which shall be gratefully acknowledged by
Their most obliged servant,
Tho. Fielding."

But its meaning was plain. By arrangement with the chief waiter, an appreciable slice of the underwriting community was deserting the old headquarters and transferring its allegiance to a New Lloyd's Coffee-house.

Suddenly now there were two establishments called Lloyd's. Fielding carried to Pope's Head Alley many of the new generation of merchants, brokers and underwriters, while the old rooms retained the stalwarts along with the flashier clientele whose activities had provoked the secession. The original *Lloyd's List* – as well as the coffee-house of course – remained the property of Thomas Lawrence, who had inherited it six years before from his brother-in-law Samuel Saunders. He therefore still supplied shipping intelligence to the government (in fact, it was probably some time before the authorities realised the significance of the schism). But his rivals meant business. They speedily reached a similar agreement with the Post Office, and before long a *New Lloyd's List* appeared in print.

For some years, the rivalry between the old and the new was acute. But, looking back, it is clear that Lawrence had very little chance. His establishment was run purely in his own interests on ordinary coffee-house lines, whereas New Lloyd's represented a determined attempt by leading city men to put their business on a better regulated footing. Above all, they were determined to be an exclusive professional group, limited by membership.

Whereas today Pope's Head Alley is just a narrow slit between Lombard Street and Cornhill, in the

Above: *the interior of the second Royal Exchange, before it was destroyed by the fire of 1838.*

Above: *the label of Loss and Arrival Book of the New Lloyd's begun in 1774.*

18th century it was a distinctly smart address. Yet, "genteely fitted up" though Fielding's new rooms may have been, the building itself was old and (according to a description in *Public Characters of 1803–4*) the accommodation was "extremely inauspicious to health and inconvenient in respect of business, on account of its size and situation". No sooner had the move been made than it became clear that the premises were far too cramped and uncomfortable, while at a grass-roots level the feeling crystallised among underwriters that they needed something more than just a convenient public place in which to meet. Some sort of an organisation with premises of its own, a code of regulations and a self-governing body had become necessary. And so on 13 December 1771 seventy-nine merchants, underwriters and brokers met in the coffee-house and drew up the most important document in the history of Lloyd's.

> "We, the underwriters" ran the text, "do agree to pay our several subscriptions into the Bank of England in the Names of a Committee to be chosen by ballot for the building of a New Lloyd's Coffee-House."

Each of the seventy-nine subscribers pledged £100, and by this action the Society of Lloyd's was officially born. Henceforth Lloyd's would no longer be the property of the coffee-house Master, but of the subscribers; and from now on its frequenters were to be bound together in a loose but formal association, controlled by an elected committee.

The subsequently published "List of the Subscribers to Lloyd's, from the Foundation in 1771 to the 1 June 1800" names a miscellaneous collection of merchants, bankers, shipowners, underwriters and insurance brokers, brought together by a common interest in marine insurance, and from the minutes it is known that the first committee comprised Martin K. van Mierop, John Wilkinson, John Townson, Joshua Readshaw, James Black, John Ewer, James Bourdieu, John Whitmore and Brook Watson. Van Mierop, who is supposed to have led the secession in 1769, presided over the first general meetings, and so it was a Dutchman (although never officially elected) who was historically the first Chairman of Lloyd's.

According to the minute book, these early meetings were held for the subscribers "to plan for the Building or removing another House for the more commodious Reception of the Gentleman Underwriters etc". But house hunting proved trickier than expected, and a subsequent minute records ruefully that "there have been several meetings of the commitee, but as nothing was determined at any of them, no Notice was taken of them". One scheme was to buy the lease of the house adjoining New Lloyd's; another to take over Will's Coffee-house in Cornhill. A lengthy correspondence with Magdalen College, Oxford, centred around the draft lease for two houses in Freeman's Court owned by the College, but negotiations eventually fell through, and after two years of humming and hawing the committee were still no nearer to a solution than when it started.

At this point a young underwriter who was not even a member of the committee took matters into his own hands. The minute book of the Gresham Committee of the Mercers' Company records that "Mr Angurstine (sic) from the Gentlemen who attend New Lloyd's Coffee-house Attended to be informed if there was any large room to be lett over the Exchange. The Committee ordered the Clerk with the Surveyor to let Mr Angurstine view the two Rooms late in lease to the British Fishery".

An article in *Public Characters in 1803–4* goes on to relate that John Julius Angerstein proceeded to negotiate the lease of the Rooms in the Royal Exchange on his own initiative, personally guaranteed the rent of £160 a year, and then "called a meeting of the subscribers, and having obtained their consent to be invested with temporary authority he, in his own name, procured for *their* accommodation the large and lofty apartments occupied by the British Herring Fishery".

At all events, on Saturday 5 March 1774 the shutters were put up for the last time at New Lloyd's Coffee-house in Pope's Head Alley, and the following Monday morning the premises over the north-west corner of the Royal Exchange were opened for business.

CONTEMPORARY SELF-ANALYSIS

COMPARED TO POPE'S Head Alley, Lloyd's new quarters in the Royal Exchange were at once spacious and comfortable. The Outer Room, to which the public was admitted, was fifty feet long; and the inner "subscribers'" sanctum was even wider and loftier, with three great chandeliers, a series of carved oak coffee-house-style "boxes" ranged down the side walls, and a specially designed pulpit for "The Book" – a large green vellum volume which recorded arrivals, losses, and the latest shipping news. Over the years, indeed, as the walls became covered with placards of ships about to sail, humorous advertisements and lists of the City's sworn brokers, the Rooms acquired a sort of clubhouse cosiness.

Hitherto, of course, the premises had been owned by the Masters, and Subscribers had simply been customers at the coffee-house. Now the Subscribers themselves owned the establishment, and the Masters became not only their tenants but contractors as well to the committee.

Admittedly, the Masters were not yet employees, or Head Waiters, as they later became. They were

Above: *portrait of Thomas Tayler, Master of Lloyds from 1774 to 1796.*

still responsible for rent, rates and taxes. They engaged and paid the staff. They provided coal, candles, newspapers, and stationery; they had to butter up Post Office officials and remit the fees to Lloyd's correspondents at the ports. They drew their income from the annual subscription of £2 due by each person frequenting the Rooms, from catering profits and from the sale of Lloyd's List. On top of which they kept the loss and arrival records, dealt with intelligence reports, and signed official correspondence.

Pleasantly informal though their relations with the committee and the Subscribers appear to have been, the job of Master was certainly no sinecure, and the minute books show that Thomas Tayler (who was appointed Master in 1774 on the death of Fielding) was constantly complaining of the non-payment of dues – at one point 109 Subscribers were in arrears – and the perennial difficulty of keeping the general public out of the Subscribers' Room.

To this inner sanctum admission was dependent not on a subscription but on a lump-sum payment. On the original 179 Subscribers who had pledged £100 each, a call of £20 per head had been made, but after meeting all expenses the committee was able to return £5 to each of them, and henceforth the admission fee was fixed at £15 for life-member-ship of Lloyd's. (Today it is £2,000 plus, of course, the deposit!)

As it turned out, quite a number of City men were prepared to pay their £15 for the privilege of membership, and in practice anyone who put down – or even promised to pay – his £15 could become a Subscriber. There was no formal election or even a check-up on the applicant's financial position, and as a result the Rooms were crowded with people who had but little knowledge or experience of marine insurance.

A cantankerous old Subscriber called John Weskett, who published a massive book called the *Complete Digest of the Theory, Laws and Practice of Insurance*, gives an intimate, nit-picking, but probably quite accurate picture of Lloyd's in its early days at the Royal Exchange. "The most distinguished Features of our present times" he wrote in 1780, "are Frivolousness, Ostentation, and Rapacity." Miffed by what he considered to be the folly of underwriters, the chicanery of brokers, and the sheer dishonesty of so many insurers, he com-plained that "Ligitation is become so rife, there is a necessity, however strange it may appear, for the almost daily attendance, which may be ob-served, especially in Term-Time, of no less than four or five attorneys at Lloyd's Coffee-house! What a Degradation is this of mercantile Character and Abilities, even in a single Branch of Com-merce!" If underwriters were imbeciles who fol-lowed their leaders like a pack of sheep (Weskett seems to have overlooked the fact that if every underwriter were to negotiate the details of each risk again from scratch it would have been virtually impossible to complete a policy) there was no question in his mind that brokers were worse: "Although they may be deficient in a gentleman-like address" he rasped, "at least they should try and develop a civil and candid personal behaviour." These, in fact, were the real villains, and the underwriters simply their foolish victims; and he went on to take a swipe at "The loose, hasty, and often crafty Manner in which Insurances are effected in Lloyd's Coffee-house . . . the frequent want of Penetration, Judgement or Attention on the Parts of the Insurers; and of Explicitness or right information on the Part of Assureds and Brokers, and especially the affected Ignorance, Silence and Indifference . . . as to material Facts and Circumstances".

Fruity stuff. Yet there must have been a good deal of truth in what the old windbag had to say. For undoubtedly all attempts to organise the business of marine insurance and to codify insurance laws had so far fallen by the wayside. Beyond being subscribers to the New Lloyd's, neither brokers nor underwriters were in the smallest degree organised; and, although by law brokers were supposed to be registered with the Lord Mayor and Aldermen and pay a yearly fee of forty shillings, in actual fact no insurance broker took the slightest notice of this statute.

"The history of Lloyd's is a history of continuous growth and change; but no step forward was ever made until its necessity had been proved by some crisis in the affairs of the House" remark Wright & Fayle, "Lloyd's, as a body, has seldom looked ahead. It has confined itself to reorganising and dealing with the pressing needs of the moment. Hence its progress has been slow, but it has never had to retrace its steps."

A significant step forward was made at the general meeting of subscribers on 12 January 1779 (called, as it happens, to discuss new "decorations" for the coffee-house) when it was decided to adopt a standard form of policy.

The earliest English policies, derived from the Italian, had been written by hand. The first printed policies appeared in the middle of the 17th century and in the archives of Lloyd's there is one dated 20 January 1680 on the *Golden Fleece* and a cargo from Lisbon to Venice. But the habit had grown up of improvising clauses and conditions in such a way that, legally, many policies were void from the start. The minutes of this meeting held just under a century after that of the *Golden Fleece* record the two resolutions that were passed:

"That no policy be subscribed from this time *knowingly* that may be printed in words different from a Form now produced."

"That we will not underwrite to any person or persons who may hereafter tender any policy otherwise printed."

Even the testy Weskett was jubilant about this development which, he said, achieved more "at only one meeting of the Insurers . . . than could have been done by *Fifty* Law Suits", although in truth Lloyd's policies continued to raise legal eyebrows.

In 1791 Mr Justice Buller grumbled that "A policy of Assurance has at all times been considered in a court of law as an absurd and incoherent instrument", and Sir Douglas Owen wrote in 1914 that "If such a contract were drawn up for the first time today, it would be put down as the work of a lunatic endowed with a private sense of humour".

Yet even in this nuclear age, every marine policy subscribed at Lloyd's incorporates, practically without alteration, and with only three important additions, the form in use 300 years ago. For, clumsy though its wording may be, the meaning is clear – as Sir Douglas Owen went on to point out (*Ocean Trade & Shipping*, Cambridge 1914, page 155) – and even if overriding clauses have had to be added to provide for contingencies undreamt of in 1779, the merit of a Lloyd's policy, consecrated as it has been by three centuries of usage, is that all the parties concerned know precisely to what it commits them.

With it the reforming zeal of the 18th century exhausted itself. No other development of any consequence took place during the next two busy decades, and in fact affairs were conducted in such an informal fashion that during the fourteen years from 1780–93 only seven general meetings were held, of which four were in 1786, and those to discuss an extension of the premises. (At the last of these all business was postponed until the next meeting – which was not held until 1791!) Clearly all that subscribers asked of their committee was that it should provide them with satisfactory accommodation.

By now there were several hundred subscribers as against the original 179, and once again under the guiding hand of Angerstein the premises were extended – and lavishly too, according to the *Public Advertiser* of 21 July 1791, which reported lyrically: "Lloyd's: The new room just opened at this coffee-house, for the use of underwriters, is in stile of finishing, and point of elegance, the first in the kingdom; connected as it is with the other three, the *tout ensemble* forms the most perfect suite of any in Europe appropriated to commercial purposes . . . in this room the daring hand of the underwriter, with pen and paper, is to brave the united force of Neptune and Boreas."

To say nothing (forsooth) of Mars. For if the routine of underwriting continued to remain substantially as it had been in 1774, Lloyd's itself was nevertheless maturing fast. And the reason for this growth was undoubtedly war.

THE WAR OF AMERICAN INDEPENDENCE

BARELY ELEVEN WEEKS before the move to the Royal Exchange, Samuel Adams with a party of men disguised as Mohawk Indians had boarded three ships in Boston Harbour, and thrown their cargoes into the water; and George III's punitive measures in retaliation for the "Tea-Party" of 16 December 1773 led to war with the American colonies. In the long run a rift between the high-handed, aristocratic legislators in London and the raw democracy of the English colonisers in the New World would probably have been inevitable. But the underlying causes of the American War of Independence were economic – and confronted the subscribers of Lloyd's with the most searching test they had yet experienced. From the outset they were deeply involved, and after Benjamin Franklin had triumphantly persuaded a reactionary French Monarchy to support the American republicans the war risks escalated.

There must have been long faces in the Royal Exchange on 23 September 1779 when it was "up at Lloyd's" that the French and Spanish fleets (combining a total naval strength of ninety ships-of-the-line against the Royal Navy's seventy-two) were off Portsmouth, and it was touch and go whether Hardy, with the Grand Fleet, could escape being blockaded, leaving the whole trade of the country at the enemy's mercy. Yet, although sailors were reported to have wrapped their clothes round the bust of King George II so that "he should not see the English fleet chased up their own channel", the immediate danger was somehow staved off.

But not for long. Disaster struck eleven months later when the Spanish fleet under Cordova – with French reinforcement – fell on an outward-bound East and West Indian convoy three hundred miles off Cape St Vincent and captured fifty-five out of sixty-three ships.

Commercially speaking, it was the biggest blow since the assault on the Smyrna Fleet. The loss was estimated at a million and a half pounds, and coming on top of a number of minor disasters, it shook Lloyd's to the core. Many of the most respected underwriters failed, and even thirty years later, at the height of the Napoleonic Wars, August 1780 was still remembered as the blackest month in the history of Lloyd's. Among those who stopped payment was John Walter, the founder of *The Times*. Sadly he recorded: "I was twelve years an underwriter at Lloyd's coffee-house, and subscribed my name to six millions of property; but

Opposite: *an early example of New Lloyd's 'revised and confirmed' policy of 1779. This example gives cover for a voyage from Plymouth to Guernsey in 1780—a more perilous journey than it sounds, for French privateers were active in the Channel and an abortive invasion had recently been made on the Channel islands.*

S. G.

Printed according to the Form
revised and confirmed at New
Lloyd's, on the 12th Jan, 1779.

Sold by W. Mudge, Royal-Exchange.

IN the Name of God, Amen. Mess.ᵣ Langston & Dixon as well in *their own* Names, as for and in the Name and Names of all and every other Person or Persons to whom the same doth, may, or shall appertain, in Part or in All, doth make Assurance, and cause *themselves* and them, and every of them to be Insured, lost or not lost at and from

Plymouth to Guernsey

Upon any Kind of Goods and Merchandizes, and also upon the Body, Tackle, Apparel, Ordnance, Munition, Artillery, Boat, and other Furniture, of and in the good Ship or Vessel called the *Richard*

whereof is Master, under God, for this present Voyage, *James Bennett* or whosoever else shall go for Master in the said Ship, or by whatsoever other Name or Names the same Ship, or the Master thereof, is or shall be named or called; beginning the Adventure upon the said Goods and Merchandizes from the Loading thereof aboard the said Ship, *Richard*

upon the said Ship, &c. *Commencing the Risk at Spon the 14 Nov. 1780.* and so shall continue and endure, during her Abode there, upon the said Ship, &c. And further, until the said Ship, with all her Ordnance, Tackle, Apparel, &c. and Goods and Merchandizes whatsoever shall be arrived at *Guernsey*

upon the said Ship, &c. until she hath moor'd at Anchor Twenty-four Hours in good Safety; and upon the Goods and Merchandizes, until the same be there discharged and safely landed. And it shall be lawful for the said Ship, &c. in this Voyage, to proceed and sail to and touch and stay at any Ports or Places whatsoever *without being deemed any deviation*

without Prejudice to this Insurance. The said Ship, &c. Goods and Merchandizes, &c. for so much as concerns the Assureds, by Agreement between the Assureds and Assurers in this Policy are and shall be valued at *Four Hundred Pound upon the Ship*

Touching the Adventures and Perils which we the Assurers are contented to bear, and do take upon us in this Voyage, they are of the Seas, Men of War, Fire, Enemies, Pirates, Rovers, Thieves, Jettizons, Letters of Mart and Counter Mart, Surprizals, Takings at Sea, Arrests, Restraints and Detainments of all Kings, Princes and People, of what Nation, Condition or Quality soever; Barretry of the Master and Mariners, and of all other Perils, Losses and Misfortunes, that have or shall come to the Hurt, Detriment or Damage of the said Goods and Merchandizes and Ship, &c. or any Part thereof. And in case of any Loss or Misfortune, it shall be lawful to the Assureds, their Factors, Servants and Assigns, to sue, labour and travel for, in and about the Defence, Safeguard and Recovery of the said Goods and Merchandizes and Ship, &c. or any Part thereof, without Prejudice to this Insurance; to the Charges whereof we the Assurers will contribute each one according to the Rate and Quantity of his Sum herein Assured. And it is agreed by us the Insurers, that this Writing or Policy of Assurance shall be of as much Force and Effect as the surest Writing or Policy of Assurance heretofore made in *Lombard-street*, or in the *Royal-Exchange*, or elsewhere in *London*. And so we the Assurers are contented, and do hereby promise and bind ourselves, each one for his own Part, our Heirs, Executors, and Goods, to the Assureds, their Executors, Administrators, and Assigns, for the true Performance of the Premises, confessing ourselves paid the Consideration due unto us for this Assurance by the Assured at and after the Rate of *Two Guineas & a half to Return 25 P Ct if departs with Convoy for the Voyage & arrives*

In Witness whereof we the Assurers have subscribed our Names and Sums Assured in London.

N. B. Corn, Fish, Salt, Fruit, Flour and Seed, are warranted free from Average, unless General, or the Ship be Stranded, Sugar, Tobacco, Hemp, Flax, Hides and Skins, are warranted free from Average, under Five Pounds *per Cent.* and all other Goods, also the Ship and Freight are warranted free of Average under Three Pounds *per Cent.* unless General, or the Ship be Stranded.

The following Insurance is upon the Brig Richard Valued at £500
£100 R Nicholson for Edm.d Higginson One hundred Pound G..d 17 Nov.r 1780
£100 W.m Days one hundred pound paid 17 Nov 1780
£100 J. Pickersgill one hundred pound G.. rec.d 17 Nov 1780
£100 James Crabb f. R. Thornton One hundred Pound G.. Rec.d 17 Nov 1780

Above: *18th cent. mezzotint of John Paul Jones shooting a Sailor who attempted to lower the colour.*

was weighed down, in common with above half those who were engaged in the protection of property, by the host of foes this nation had to combat in the American war."

As if the damage inflicted by enemy fleets was not sufficient, there was the additional hazard of privateers. John Paul Jones's exploits in the Irish Sea and off Scarborough – where, coming on a rich convoy of forty-one sail from the Baltic, he treated spectators on the clifftops to one of the fiercest combats ever witnessed off the English coast – earned him a far grander tomb in the naval academy in Annapolis than Nelson's in St Paul's. Yet he was only one of the many corsairs who played havoc with British commerce. From every free port in New England fast, well armed vessels put out to prey on traders in the Atlantic, and in all between 1776 and 1783 a total of 3386 British ships were taken. Of these 485 were recaptured, 507 ransomed; and 2384 remained in enemy hands. Wright and Fayle calculate in their history of Lloyd's that if the yearly average of British shipping were put at 6200 units, the annual ratio of loss was over 9 percent – or, allowing for recaptures, about 8 percent.

On top of these alarming figures, underwriters were also concerned with enemy casualties. By the standards of the times, trading with the foe was considered as fair game, if a profit was involved; but this could be costly too. When in 1781 Rodney seized the Dutch island of St Eustatius – a tiny blob in the Atlantic which had been built up into an important entrepôt for the supply of the American States and the French West Indies – and appropriated over three million of accumulated stores, this British success was greeted by an enraged howl of fury from those unfortunate underwriters who were suddenly faced with steep claims to settle with enemy claimants.

Privateering was a business in itself, and a profitable one too. Often by accepting a ransom bond, the privateer could avoid the necessity of tying up a prize crew to look after the captured vessel, and could go on with its cruise. The captain of a privateer, and the syndicate which sponsored it, were only too glad to let their victim free if it was made worth their while; to them the only question was whether it was more profitable to accept a bond, or to carry in the prize and sell her.

This practice was even more convenient for the captured ship. It saved the crew from a French or a Spanish prison and saved the ship for her owners. And even if the underwriters found the practice objectionable, decreasing as it did the incentive to avoid capture and the chance of wiping out the loss by the recapture of the prize, nevertheless the payment of a ransom bond usually cost less than if a ship and its cargo were taken into an enemy port.

The threefold war risks that the underwriters ran – capture by the enemy, capture by privateers, and seizure in port – on top, of course, of the natural hazards, meant that premiums were high. Yet, although in 1782 the basic rate on a voyage from London to Jamaica was 12 percent with convoy or 20 percent without, no sensible businessman could now dare to neglect taking adequate cover.

THE EFFECTS OF THE WAR ON LLOYD'S

UP TO THIS point, it must be said, the regular insurance of ships and cargoes had never been regarded as a mandatory precaution. Merchants and shipowners who had rushed to get cover during previous periods of conflict tended to jib at the expense no sooner than peace was proclaimed. But now for a period of forty years – practically the life expectancy of the average citizen – Britain was to be at war. The American struggle for independence and the Napoleonic wars, which pitted this country against the principal maritime nations of the world from 1775 to 1815, brought vividly home to traders the absolute necessity of covering all risks and thus spreading the losses, which would have been ruinous to a single individual, over the whole market.

For those who knew their business, there were undoubtedly big profits to be made, and the boom in premiums tempted many of London's richest merchants to become insurers of maritime property. Where formerly the normal amount staked by an underwriter seldom exceeded more than a few hundred pounds, henceforth tens of thousands figured in the "line" of a single name.

Statistically, Britain's trade had trebled since the days of Edward Lloyd. The value of imports (for re-export) and exports themselves had risen from ten million pounds in the first decade of the 18th century to thirty-two million pounds in 1774 On top of which the progressive swing of ocean transport from Amsterdam to London meant that the transit trade also increased. All of which brought more grist to the mill for the underwriters. Not only was the whole of British commerce now insured, but the figures were swollen by the insurance of men-of-war carrying prizes and bullion, as well as the cover given to foreign shipping.

Moreover, an immediate effect of the warfare, was to canalise foreign business from all parts of the globe on London, and the mass of this insurance was placed at Lloyd's. The two chartered companies did very little. Evidence given before the parliamentary commission on marine insurance in 1810 brought out, for instance, that the policies placed on the *Diana* frigate for a journey from Vera Cruz homewards in 1807 amounted to £656,000, of which £631,800 was underwritten at Lloyd's and the

Right: *an anonymous caricature of Lloyd's Coffee House in 1798. The news in the morning papers— perhaps of some engagement against the French— appears to have come as a shock to some of the members.*

remaining £25,000 by one of the companies. One underwriter alone, Thomas King, had £10,000 on this policy and several others wrote lines of between £3,000 and £5,000. By the beginning of the 19th century, the annual premium income of a prosperous underwriter at Lloyd's was likely to be in the region of £40,000 gross, and the total premiums taken in the Room was certainly not less than five million pounds.

Large insurances could be effected with astonishing ease. Where seventy years previously a £10,000 policy was something out of the ordinary, in 1810 Angerstein was able to place £40,000 on a ship from Tonningen, £60,000 on a West Indiaman and cargo, and £200,000 on a regular ship from Quebec. From a risk book of 1807, Gibb quotes the figures given by an underwriter whose firm still exists, which show that in a single year, and for his account alone, he took in premiums of £54,452 and paid out claims of £22,802, leaving a gross balance of £31,650 – a figure which, if achieved by an underwriting member today (even discounting the incidence of income tax, surtax and a tenfold inflation factor) would still be considered outstanding.

Of course, as Gibb goes on to stress, there was no such thing as an underwriting member of Lloyd's at that period. Anyone who had access to the Room could write what he liked, and as much as he liked, irrespective of his means. Some men made a fortune; others, with inadequate backing and no previous experience in insurance, came seriously to grief. As John Weskett commented in his *Complete Digest*: "We see not a few Instances even of Tradesmen, Shopkeepers, etc, lured by the golden, but delusive Bait of Premiums, especially in time of War, drawn like Gudgeons, into the Vortex of this perilous abyss, Insurance."

THE NAPOLEONIC WARS

THE WAR WITH revolutionary France was quite different from the struggle against the revolting American colonies. Formidable though the coalitions facing England may at times have been – and there were periods when the odds against her must have seemed quite overwhelming – the balance was shifting fundamentally since the days when a Franco-Spanish armada could chase Hardy up the Channel. The First of June, St Vincent, Camperdown, Aboukir, Copenhagen and finally Trafalgar, all contributed to the clear supremacy of the Royal Navy.

For all this, there were plenty of sleepless nights for those who staked their money at Lloyd's. Even after Trafalgar, the enemy's lighter craft could still terrorise the Trade routes. Not only was every French Channel port a nest of privateers, but strong squadrons of frigates were still able to make sorties against British commerce in home waters and in the Mediterranean; Mauritius remained a running sore to East India shipping; Sourcouf took his toll in the Bay of Bengal, and the French islands in the West Indies were a constant source of anxiety.

On top of which, the renewed outbreak of war with the United States brought fresh dangers to British shipping. The *Essex*, cruising against the southern whale fishery, cost underwriters £600,000. A single Salem privateer, the *America*, took in twenty-six prizes which sold for more than a million dollars.

Napoleon's Berlin and Milan Decrees (aimed at preventing the import of British goods into Europe) and the measures taken by the British government to counteract them, caused a whole series of embargoes, seizures and reprisals. Country after country was compelled to close its ports to British shipping, and English goods were confiscated throughout the greater part of Europe. Yet, oddly enough, trading with the enemy continued to be allowed in England, even if it was subject to many restrictions. The "Traitorous Correspondence Act" of 1793 prohibited the insurance of vessels or goods belonging to any person resident in France, or her colonies or any shipments to a French port. For all Charles James Fox's opposition on the grounds that "as the premium was always more than equal to the risk" the advantage in fact lay with the insurers, it nevertheless passed into law. As time wore on the economic pressures intensified. Both sides were prompted by mercantilist theories: Napoleon did his utmost to exclude British products from the continent and thus cripple Britain's financial lever in Europe, while the British government was equally determined to force British products into central Europe.

To achieve this, plenty of dodges were employed. The goods were carried in neutral ships to Tonningen and the Baltic ports, and given neutral bills of lading to prevent their confiscation under the Berlin and Milan Decrees. Certain firms specialised in these forged shipping documents, and a policy dated 1808 (now in the Library at Lloyd's) covering a shipment of indigo on the *Johanna*, from London to Holland, unashamedly states "with liberty to carry simulated papers". The premium was a hefty 40 percent. And despite all the hazards, a certain amount of direct trade was kept up with France itself. In 1808 John Janson wrote a line, at 50 guineas percent, on a voyage "London to France", and shipments of claret from Bordeaux to London were regularly taken at 8 to 12 guineas percent.

From 1797 until 1806 both Britain and France were at peace with the United States. But even this state of non-belligerence had its attendant risks, for American ships were just as liable to capture by British cruisers if they were carrying cargoes for

Above: *The Death of Nelson, from a painting by Samuel Drummond. Admiral Nelson's friendly connections with Lloyd's are commemorated today by the Nelson Room in the present building, which houses a priceless collection of plate, trophies and documents.*

AM at 8 Observed the British Fleet forming their Lines the head most Ships
from the Enemys center 8 or 9 miles the Enemys force consist of thirty
three Sail the Line five Frigates and two Brigs light Winds & hazy with
a great Swell from the West. English Fleet all Sail set Standing towards
the Enemy them on the Starboard Tack at 8 ½ answd Lord Nelsens Sigl
for Captain Blackwood and went immediatly on Board the Victory, took
our Station on the Victorys Larboard Quarter and repeated the Admirals
Sigls at 10 observed the Enemy varing and comming to the Wind on
the Larboard Tack at 11 – 40 repeated Lord Nelsens Telegraph Message
I intend to push or go through the end of the Enemys line to
prevent their getting in to Cadiz Saw the Land bearing ENE 5 or 6 Leagues
At 11 – 56 repeated Lord Nelsens Telegraph Message, England
expects that every Man will do his Duty at Noon light Winds and
a great Swell from the West. Observed the Royal Sovereign (Admiral
Collingwood) leading the Lee Line bearing Down on the Enemys Rear line
being then nearly within Gun Shot of them Lord Nelsen leading the Weather
Line bore Down upon the Enemys center Captain Blackwood
from the Victory Cape Trafalgar SEBE about 5 Leagues Lat 12w

Signals made &c on the 21st October 1805 –

P m		a m		By Whom	To Whom	No	P m		a m		By Whom	To Whom	No
H	M	H	M				H	M	H	M			
1	50	"	"	Euryalus	Sirius	A & B Gun			7	"	Euryalus	Repeated from the Victory	13
1	55	"	"	Sirius	Euryalus	55 / 52 Num			7	40	Do	Do	76 End
2	"	"	"	Euryalus	Sirius	26			0	"	Victory	Euryalus	Captn
2	10	"	"	Do	Do	58 / 39½ Num 36½			Noon		Do	Repeated from the Victory	63 Prepare
4	10	"	"	Do	Victory	413 N / with 2 Guns							
4	20	"	"	Do	Naiad & Phoebe	100							
5	10	"	"	Do	Do	154 N / 2 Guns							
5	25	"	"	Do	Do	10 N with 1 Gun							
5	45	"	"	Do	Victory	55 / 362 2 Guns							

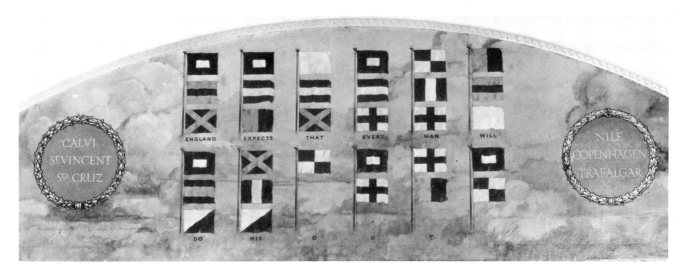

Left: *a page from the log-book of H.M.S.* Euryalus, *containing Nelson's famous signal 'England expects...' before the battle of Trafalgar. The signal is also commemorated at Lloyd's (above) by this modern mural.*

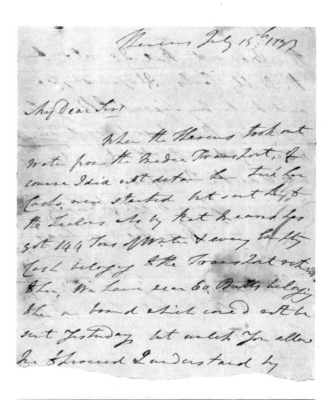

> AUTOGRAPH LETTER FROM CAPTAIN HORATIO NELSON
> TO SIR JOHN JERVIS
>
> Theseus July 15th 1797
>
> My dear Sir,
>   When the Theseus took out water from the Medea transport, of course I did not detain her till her Casks were started but sent her to the Zealous who by that means has got 144 Tons of Water & every Empty Cask belonging to the Transport returned to her. We have near 60 Butts belonging to her on board which could not be sent yesterday but unless you allow me to proceed I understand by (verso) this Moment that I must send the Empty Casks. If you say so and make my Signal to Bring too or Anchor they shall be sent directly. We will go to Work & hoist our launch out & do the needful,
>
>   Yours most faithfully,
>   HORATIO NELSON.
>
> If you make no Signal I shall go on, with the Casks we have not 140 Tons of Casks on board.
>
>   Presented to Lloyd's in 1931 by E. S. Lamplough, Esq.
> L.96.

Right: *among other precious exhibits in the Nelson Room is an autographed letter from Nelson to Captain John Jervis, dated 1797.*

Above: *the Battle of Trafalgar, 1805.*

France as to seizure by the French if they were trading with England. In January 1794 *Lloyd's List* enumerated some eighty American vessels that were awaiting prize court proceedings at Guadaloupe.

Obviously, against such odds, the writing of war risks was a complicated and adventurous form of livelihood. And while, as Fox had pointed out, the premiums were calculated in accordance with the risks, there were nevertheless times when the stability of Lloyd's was tested to the utmost. In 1794, for instance, the unexpected outbreak of war with the Netherlands led to the seizure of all Dutch ships and their cargoes in British ports. Most of them were covered to the hilt on the London market, and the consequent claims were so serious that the committee of Lloyd's took the matter up with Pitt himself, but to little effect: every shilling of the amounts insured had to be considered as a total loss. The following year Rodney captured thirty out of sixty-three ships in a convoy from the Levant and one Lloyd's man alone, Robert Sheddon, was faced with claims for £190,000. In 1797 came the French and Spanish condemnations of American vessels, and in 1799 the Emperor Paul suddenly laid hands on all British shipping in Russian ports. Finally there were the great Baltic seizures of 1810. On the ships impounded in Swedish ports alone, Lloyd's had policies to the tune of nearly a million pounds.

"And a very trying time it was" Angerstein told a parliamentary committee. But, although there were failures, the evidence suggests that in proportion to the volume of business transacted they were neither numerous nor significant. Despite all the hard knocks and the daily wear and tear on the nerves (voiced by Thomas Reid in an outburst to the Select Committee: "The labour, the agitation, the perpetual vexation is not to be described; I would rather begin the world again and pursue any other line") the four decades of war were a period of great prosperity for both brokers and underwriters – most of whom ended up a great deal richer than before – and brought Lloyd's as a whole to a new level of wealth and prestige.

A SPECIAL RELATIONSHIP WITH THE ADMIRALTY

FROM THE MOMENT that war broke out, Lloyd's had been in close and continuous touch with the Admiralty. Lists of ships in convoy – or licensed to sail without convoy – were routinely sent by the Admiralty to the Masters, who for their part reciprocated (in copperplate script) with a flow of intelligence from their agents abroad. It was an amiable arrangement that suited both sides. On 30 June, 1774, for instance, at Angerstein's personal request, a warship was stationed off Ostend to give warning if the port should fall into French hands. And four years later, under pressure from Lloyd's, an Act was passed compelling all vessels engaged in foreign trade to sail in convoy unless specifically authorised by the Admiralty, and severe penalties were imposed on captains who disobeyed the orders of the escort commander.

Over this vital matter of convoy discipline there was very close liaison. Some of the faster sailing ships were all to inclined to break convoy in the hope of reaching their markets ahead of the others, and as this naturally added to the underwriters' risks, the committee was continuously pressing to have the offending skippers brought to task. On the other hand the captain's complaints against the escort commanders – and sometimes their tributes for the protection they had received – were punctiliously passed on to the Admiralty.

Lloyd's, in fact, became the acknowledged link between the merchant navy and the government authorities. But perhaps what gave the most warmth to this special relationship was the open-handed activity of subscribers in promoting funds for seamen and their families. The fighting man might momentarily become a hero; but once his usefulness was over, he was forgotten or ignored; and in the absence of any sort of official aid his dependants were forced to rely on private charity or go begging in the streets. By taking the lead in raising funds for them, the members of Lloyd's won the lasting friendship of the British Navy.

These impromptu whip-arounds were started at the bar of Lloyd's. Within an hour of the news of the "Glorious First of June" reaching the coffee-house, a thousand guineas had been subscribed. Similar collections were held after the battles of St Vincent, Camperdown, Aboukir and Copenhagen, and by such spontaneous gestures a total of over £130,000 was raised (of which £52,609 after Camperdown in 1797, and £38,436 at the news of Aboukir the following year).

The funds were administered by volunteer committees whose bounty was so wide-ranging that the first recorded grant, oddly enough, was a small donation for "distressed haymakers", and shortly afterwards, during a food shortage, a soup kitchen (the first on record) was set up in Spitalfields. But most of the money was ear-marked for seamen. Acknowledging the Copenhagen Fund, Nelson wrote on 15 June 1801 from aboard the *St George* in Kioge Bay: "I feel – and I am certain every Officer and man in the Fleet does the same – much indebted to the gentlemen of the committee for the attention they pay, and the trouble they experience on this occasion. I hope in a few days to have it in my power to pay my respects personally to them."

On another occasion he wrote: "We are all obliged by your humane attention to us seamen,"

and was prepared to do a good turn for Lloyd's when he could. When a brig called the *Unity* was found in circumstances suggesting negligence and probably fraud, he made a point of reporting it.

Seafarers had another good reason for feeling grateful to the men at the Royal Exchange, since it was Lloyd's above all who helped to develop the lifeboat.

As a young ship's carpenter, Henry Greathead had once tipped underwriters off about a blatant case of stranding (endemic, it would seem, among a certain type of captain at this period) and as a result of this connection a group of subscribers headed by Angerstein's partner, Peter Warren, financed his experiments in building an "insubmergible" boat. His first "safety-boat" (it was only later called a lifeboat) was launched in 1785, and in 1802 a grant of £2,000 was made from the corporate funds at Lloyd's for the construction of a number of lifeboats on the British and Irish coasts. By 1825, with the assistance of Lloyd's, lifeboat stations had been established at twenty-six different coastal points.

Up until the Peace of Amiens, these various funds had been raised unofficially to celebrate a particular victory. But on 20 July 1803 thirty-three of the subscribers called a general meeting to inaugurate a Patriotic Fund, as it was called,

"For the Encouragement and Relief of those who may be engaged in the Defence of the Country and who may suffer in the Common Cause . . . so that the Mite of the Labourer combining with the Munificent Donation of the Noble and the Wealthy . . . shall inspire our Seamen, our Soldiers and our Countrymen at large . . . and shall impress on the minds of our Enemies the appalling conviction *that the Energies of this* great Empire are irresistible as its resources are incalculable."

The meeting resolved to raise the Fund by public subscription,

"To animate the efforts of our Defenders by Sea and Land . . . for the purpose of assuaging the anguish of their Wounds, palliating in some degree the more weighty misfortune of the Loss of Limbs – of alleviating the Distresses of the Widow and Orphan – of Soothing the Brow of Sorrow for the fall of their dearest Relatives, the props of unhappy Indigence or helpless Age – and of granting Pecuniary Rewards or honourable Badges of Distinction, for successful exertions of Valor or Merit."

This stirring appeal touched people's hearts. War had flared up afresh with Napoleonic France a couple of months previously, and in a burst of patriotic fervour Londoners of all classes, once again faced with an invasion alarm, dug deep into their pockets. Within a fortnight the impressive sum of £70,312 had been collected at the coffee-house. Six years later the Patriotic Fund stood at

Above: *a Soup Kitchen at Spitalfields. Funds raised at Lloyd's, in particular from collections after notable naval victories, were frequently channelled into such charitable enterprises.*

Left and Above: *Henry Greathead and his first 'safety-boat' (lifeboat). Many such boats were built with funds donated by the members of Lloyds, and lifeboat stations founded up and down the country.*

Above: *Grace Darling was one of those presented with an award from Lloyd's, for her daring rescue of the crew of a stricken trawler off the Northumberland coast.*

Below: *as well as gold medals and silver plate, engraved ceremonial swords were awarded from the Patriotic Fund to officers who had distinguished themselves in the war. These are still to be seen in the Nelson Room at Lloyd's.*

£400,000, of which over £300,000 had been distributed, and the "badges of distinction", in the shape of gold medals and silver plate, were highly prized by their recipients. When the war ended and the accounts were finally closed, a total of £629,823 had been donated.

These humanistic activities, together with its escalating wealth, gave the coffee-house more than just mercantile prestige. Lloyd's, as a quote from *Public Characters of 1803–04* indicates, was now a significant power in the state, "... an Empire within itself; an empire which in point of commercial sway, variety of powers, and almost incalculable resources gives laws to the trading part of the universe".

LLOYD'S ON TRIAL

INEVITABLY, SUCH A crescendo of success was not to everybody's taste. Along with the kudos came mutterings too. Cobbett, inevitably, objected to "a set of traders at Lloyd's" usurping the functions of the Crown by bestowing honours on naval and military officers, and even the First Lord of the Admiralty condemned what he called "that mischievous system of rewards ... which is held out to the navy as giving greater encouragement than the government of the country". Around this power-house prosperity there grew a climate of envy which culminated during 1810 in what was to all intents and purposes the trial of Lloyd's by Parliament. Ostensibly it was an attack on the monopoly enjoyed by the two chartered corporations since 1720. But everyone knew that if a monopoly existed, it was at Lloyd's.

In granting these two companies their charters, the intention of Parliament had been that they should replace, or at least compete with, the private underwriter. But, as it turned out, their marine business was negligible compared to Lloyd's. They concentrated on fire and life insurance, and turned down all but the most cast-iron marine risks. On the evidence of the stamp duties, for instance, their joint marine premium income in 1809 was £6,150,000 – a mere 4.5 percent of the total. And, although some private underwriting was carried on in a bookseller's shop at Glasgow and in the Exchange Coffee-Room at Liverpool (under the guidance of W.E. Gladstone's father) as well as at Bristol, Hull and Newcastle, fully three-quarters of the marine insurance of Britain was transacted in London, nearly all of it at Lloyd's.

In 1810 this state of affairs was challenged. A group of influential merchants presented a petition to repeal the existing monopolies and secure an act of incorporation for themselves. Lloyd's speedily organised a counter-attack. Joseph Marryat, MP for Sandwich (and father of Captain Frederick Marryat, the novelist) was their soft-spoken but articulate advocate.

On 14 February, William Manning, a West India merchant who sat for the City of London (and was the father of Cardinal Manning) opened the promoter's case – which was concentrated mainly on what he called the "instability" of private underwriters. Marryat, in a vigorous reply, stressed the importance of the underwriters' specialised knowledge, and reminded Parliament of the public services rendered by Lloyd's. The House was thinly attended (only twenty-seven members voted) but by a narrow majority the motion was passed and a Select Committee was appointed to study the whole question of marine insurance. Both Manning and Marryat were appointed as members; but Manning was named as chairman, and very soon turned the enquiry into a full-scale indictment of Lloyd's.

For a month the Select Committee took evidence, much of which turned out to be little more than hearsay opinions and vague complaints. A somewhat suspect procession of witnesses were trotted forward to testify that underwriters charged such over-high premiums that business had increasingly to be written abroad; that they wriggled out of settling claims whenever they could and were not always financially stable; and that (to add insult to injury) they were frequently unavailable in the autumn, not on holiday as they suggested, but because they wanted to avoid writing winter risks.

Angerstein it was who put the record straight. At seventy-five, with the authority of more than half a century of insurance experience behind him, he spoke quietly and unboastfully about the pre-eminent position which Lloyd's had built up for itself. He made it clear that Lloyd's had moved with the times and that the sheer variety of risks which could be placed at the coffee-house would be unthinkable elsewhere. But, of his highly convincing evidence, what must surely be of major interest today to the specialist (and perhaps even the layman) is his description of broking techniques a century and three-quarters ago:

"If I have a cross risk to make, if it is from America, I go to a box where there are Americans to give me information; and so it is from the Baltic or any other part; I generally go to the box or the people whom I think best conversant, for they are the people who can begin the policy for me better than the others, and I can by that means get it done. It is of no use applying to a Baltic merchant on an American risk; he does not do it, simply because he knows nothing about it ...

"There are so many people frequenting the coffee-house that, even if an underwriter does not himself understand a question, he soon procures information, and makes me master of the subject at the same time."

That underwriters were quick to side-step claims he denied. "There are a great many claims which

Above: *Extraordinary News, a caricature by Ansell in 1808, satirising the dismay of City men when the terms of the Convention of Cintra were published (following the French evacuation of Portugal). The rotund gentleman has misread 'sixty rounds per gun' to be carried by the French as 'sixty pounds per man'. Behind the doorway of Lloyd's is just visible.*

are now allowed; but the underwriters cannot cheat the merchant, except in one way, that is by being a bankrupt.

On the other hand, he added, "There are so many frauds about insurances, and, I am sorry to say I have made many through my own office, so I do not wonder where proofs are called for. The demands from foreigners particularly are past all belief." Far from being evasive, underwriters often went out of their way to settle a claim. "I have known them pay a loss where the merchant has made a mistake, and called it ship instead of goods, or goods instead of ship, and the underwriter, knowing it, took no advantage and paid the loss. . . . I have known a ship insured from some place in Europe, when she came from another, and that has been paid." Private underwriters would always settle the loss for a "man of character", but naturally not so readily for anyone they had any reason to suspect.

Angerstein went on to express doubts whether the new company would be of benefit to British trade. From enquiries at the stamp office he had checked that the tax on private underwriting policies during the previous year had been £312,000, on a premium income of nearly £125,000,000. If nine-tenths of this business were to be offered to the company (which seemed likely, since "nine-tenths of the greatest merchants and people of consequence are connected with the promoters") it would accept about £80 million, "selecting the best risks at the best seasons" but turn up its nose at the balance, the "bad ships, cross-voyages, and other bad risks".

There, he pointed out, was the rock upon which the speculation must split. "You will no longer have men of property attending the coffee-house to write policies . . . for every part of those £40 million (balance) will be supposed to have been shown to the companies, whether it has been or not, and these insurances will only be done at a very exorbitant premium, if at all."

Other merchants, underwriters and brokers amplified the picture given by Angerstein, and John Fisher Throckmorton invoked the many instances of hanky-panky with which insurers were faced (such as the *Eagle*, insured by its American owner after it had sunk; the *Adventure*, deliberately sunk off Brighton in 1802, and for which the captain had been hanged; the *Hannah & Mary* from Boston, likewise fraudulently sunk after being heavily insured; and dozens of other cases such as the ship from Livorno, insured for a cargo of silk while actually carrying brimstone).

But after the Committee had solemnly moved to its conclusion, the report submitted to Parliament was so biased that it presumably must have been drafted by Manning himself. Ignoring the evidence of the thirty-six witnesses – except when favourable to the

Above: *Lloyd's Subscription Rooms in the second Royal Exchange drawn by Pugin and Rowlandson in 1800, and published in 1809.*

petitioner's case – it blandly recommended that the exclusive privileges of the two chartered companies should be repealed, and that the petitioners should be allowed to proceed with their own incorporation.

Scarcely was it out than Marryat published a counterblast of his own. "The writer of this report" he declared, without mincing his words, "has treated the evidence, which should have formed the basis of his observations, much in the same manner as the Edinburgh Reviewers frequently treat those productions which they profess to review. After giving the title-page of the work, and the name of the author, they present their readers with a very clever Essay upon the same subject as that to which the author in question undertakes to discuss; but take no more notice of him, or of his work, than if neither the one nor the other had ever existed". He went on to prove that the Report was outrageously unfair, and it was only normal that petitions against the Bill should be submitted by both the corporations as well as Lloyd's before the debate on 30 May.

But, as it happened, the Bill was not proceeded with. Just as the real fisticuffs were about to begin, the petitioners unexpectedly backed down, possibly to rally their forces. They returned to the attack the following year, and on 28 February 1811 the Bill was debated in Parliament. Marryat drove home the monopoly argument: to him the ultimate object of the Bill was "the establishment of a great combination to do away with every other form of insurance. At present there was a monopoly *de jure* but not *de facto*; if this measure succeeded there would be a monopoly *de facto*, though not *de jure*". In the place of some 1,500 individuals there might be twenty companies, who would rig the premium rates between themselves.

To the last moment, the issue was in doubt. But, whether it was the legal argument or an instinctive mistrust of monopolies, when it came to the division the votes cast were twenty-five for the Bill and twenty-six against. "So" in official language, "it passed into the negative", to the satisfaction not only of the coffee-house, but also of the correspondent whose letter appeared in *The Times* on the morning of the vote. "Shall that 'cloud cap't tower' Lloyd's" he asked, "prodigal in loyalty and extensively munificent in charity, be shaken to its very base; the subscribers and their families ruined; and the community at large deprived of its extending and necessary influence, to gratify a few interested and ambitious men? God forbid."

THE GRANDEES: LLOYD'S CELEBRITIES DURING THE NAPOLEONIC WARS

OF THE TWO thousand-odd habitués who thronged the Subscribers' Room during the Napoleonic Wars, there were plenty of romantics, eccentrics, and plain solid merchants of impeccable dullness. But there were also some others who bestrode the cosy confines of the coffee-house like giants, and any "who's who" of Lloyd's at that period would include, without doubt, the following names:

John Julius Angerstein (1735–1823). Probably the most celebrated of them all, who organised the move to the Royal Exchange, and so largely moulded both broking and underwriting in his image that he is traditionally known as the "Father of Lloyd's".

Sometime in the 18th century a branch of the Hanoverian family (which took its name, in the Jewish fashion, from the village of Angerstein, near Göttingen) extended its activities to St Petersburg. There Julius was born, though already at the age of fifteen he was sent off to London to work in the office of Andrew Thompson, a well known Baltic merchant. He did well enough to be taken on as a junior partner by Alexander Dick, and in 1757 the firm of Dick & Angerstein appears in the registers as an insurance office in Cowper's Court, Cornhill. Eleven years later the firm of Dick & Perrot was in the old office, and Angerstein was in a new one on his own at the same address. In 1778 his firm appears as Angerstein & Lewis, Throgmorton Street, and in 1783 Angerstein, Crokatt & Lewis, over the Exchange. He played a leading role in the 1769 secession, and apart from his activities as an underwriter became a broker of such distinction that (to quote the Dictionary of National Biography) "Policies sanctioned by his subscription acquired so great an authority that for some years they were called 'Julians'". Indeed when his name appeared on a policy it was sufficient recommendation for the rest to follow without further ado.

During the course of his long career he acquired the sort of patrician *grandeur* that is now associated with a Rothschild or a Rockefeller, and Farrington, who often mentioned him in his Diary, records that "He told me his habit now is to ride every morning before breakfast from half past seven for an hour and a half to two hours – breakfast at 10 – go to London to City business abt 11 and return a little after 5 – in October He annually goes for two months or so to Mr Bouchere's in Lincolnshire . . . and there He hunts almost daily, beginning with 2 or 3 hours and increasing to 4 or 5 hours; but his hunting is for air and exercise and not to perform feats".

In one way or another, he was a friend of most of the great figures of his time – such as Dr Johnson, Garrick, Jonas Hanway the philanthropist, Sir Joshua Reynolds and Sir Thomas Lawrence – which belies the suspicion that he was probably a dull dog outside the office. Nelson once told him that he hoped "he should die in battle", and William

Above: *portrait of John Julius Angerstein, Chairman of Lloyd's, by Sir Thomas Lawrence.*

Below: *a gallery of notable Lloyd's men at the beginning of the 19th century from a series of etchings by R. Dighton.* From left to right: *James Dewar, Pulsford, and Richard Thornton.*

A View at Lloyd after a Stormy Night.

Write 'em or let 'em alone.

Pitt took his advice on financial matters, including a scheme for state lotteries. Thanks to his efforts, moreover, an act was passed through Parliament which prevented the owner of a ship from changing its name – a common and often fraudulent practice with unseaworthy vessels.

In 1806 he was Chairman of Lloyd's. Yet, great though his influence in the City may have been, to the world at large he was best known as an art collector, and after his death in 1823 his collection was acquired for the nation and formed the nucleus of the National Gallery – which was, in fact, at first located in his town house at 100 Pall Mall (now the site of the Reform Club). Here and at his Blackheath home, he entertained society's heavy cream in a stately but offhand manner, to judge from Farrington's description: "Mr J.J. Angerstein's I dined out. We dined at 6 o'clock. The dinner consisted of 2 courses, viz: a fine Turbot at the top, a sirloin of beef at the bottom and Vermicelli soup in the middle, with small dishes making a figure of dishes. – The remove roast ducks at the top and a very fine roast Poulet at the bottom, macaroni – tartlets, etc, etc, afterwards Parmesan and other cheese and Caviare with toast. – Champagne and madeira were served round during dinner . . . I observed that Mr Angerstein drank very little wine *after dinner*. – While the conversation went on He for some time slept – after He awoke He eat an orange with sugar. He appears to consider His Health, but looks very full and well. His dress was a Blue coat, striped pointed waistcoat – drab cloth breeches – mixed coloured worsted stockings – buckles in His shoes, very plain, but respectable". And to complete the portrait "The Princess of Wales dined at Mr Angerstein's yesterday, and in the evening there was a rout. . . . The Princess supped there with a small party and remained till half past 3 o'clock, but Mr Angerstein went to bed before Supper".

Sir Francis Baring (1740–1810). He founded the famous banking house of Baring Brothers, also came over from the continent. He was the grandson of a Lutheran pastor, and, although deaf from a boy, he built up a multi-million business which in 1830 was estimated to be worth seven million pounds. A Member of Parliament and in 1792–3 Chairman of the East India Company (which rated him a baronetcy) he wrote a number of treatises on banking, and at the time of his death was described by Lord Erskine as "unquestionably the first merchant in Europe, first in knowledge and talents, and first in character and opulence".

Zachary Macauley (1768–1838). An astringent but admirable do-gooder who, went out to Jamaica at the age of sixteen, was so appalled at the miseries of the slave population that (after a stint as Governor of Sierra Leone) he returned to England

A GREAT MAN on CHANGE.

Two views of Sir Brook Watson, Chairman of Lloyd's from 1797–1806.

Above: *in his robes of Lord Mayor of London by John Singleton Copley.*

Right: *as seen, with his wooden leg, by Dighton.*

and virtually ruined the prosperous West African business of Macauley and Babington by devoting his life to the abolition of the slave trade. A fellow of the Royal Society, he was friendly with such people as Chateaubriand, Sisismondi and Madame de Stael, and on his death a memorial was erected for him in Westminster Abbey. He was also, of course, the father of Thomas Babington Macauley, the historian.

Sir Brook Watson (1735–1807). Orphaned at the age of six, he went to sea and had his leg bitten off by a shark at Havana when he was fourteen – which did not prevent him from becoming commissary general to the army in Canada, and subsequently Member of Parliament for the City of London; a director of the Bank of England and Lord Mayor of London in 1796. He was indeed at the height of his reputation when elected Chairman of Lloyd's (in 1796) which he remained until his death. A controversial figure whose support of the war brought him into collision with the Whigs, his pugnacious manner and stumping wooden leg made him the target of the *Rolliad*:

"One moment's time might I presume to beg?
Cries modest *Watson* on his wooden leg
That leg in which such wondrous art is shown,
It almost seems to serve him like his own;
Oh! had the monster who for breakfast ate
That luckless limb, his nobler noddle met
The best of workmen, nor the best of wood
Had scarce supply'd him with a head so good."

Richard Thornton (1776–1865). An irrepressible self-made tycoon, "Dicky" sailed his own ship to Memel during the Napoleonic blockade, and had to fight off a Danish gunboat; but he brought back thousands of tons of hemp for the Admiralty. Two years later (in 1812) his brother, who was still in Memel, sent him an express message that Napoleon was retreating from Moscow – and, since the news reached "Dicky" three days before the government or anyone else, he was able to net £200,000 on the Exchange, subsequently dazzled the City by his speculation in tallow and foreign loans. He insured the risk of Queen Victoria having twins, and would stand with his back to the fire in the Subscribers' Room offering all newly married members 100 to one against a similar occurrence. Once, when offered first sight of a risk on a shipment to Russia of £250,000 worth of bullion by Baring Brothers, he is reported to have taken the "slip", very slowly put down the figures twenty-five, and added nought after nought until he had completed the whole sum. Upon which, seeing the look of consternation on the broker's face, he rapped out: "Young man, you can show this slip to Mr Thomas Baring, and if he thinks I have taken too much you can tell him that I will deposit exchequer Bills to that amount until the risk is run off."

"Good for three millions" he used to boast of himself – and when he died at nearly ninety he in fact left something like four million pounds.

THE IMPACT OF PEACE

AROUND THE TIME of the Peace of Amiens, Wordsworth looked down the Thames and rhapsodised that "earth has not anything to show more fair" than the sight of the City of London from Westminster Bridge. Thirteen years later, when Napoleon sailed to St Helena as a prisoner on a British man-of-war, the scene was even more gratifying to English eyes. The forest of masts (there were often over two thousand ships lying in the river between London Bridge and Deptford) testified to Britain's wealth and power. Thanks to her naval victories she possessed eleven-twelfths of the world's shipping and the carrying trade of the globe was in her hands. The rich markets of North and South America, the West Indies and India lay wide open to her manufactured goods, and her commercial tentacles spread into every corner of the yet undeveloped world. Though the twenty-two years' struggle with revolutionary France had cost over £700 million, Great Britain's export trade had more than doubled and her revenue trebled, while the population of her empire had exploded from twenty to seventy million – no bad achievement for an island of thirteen million itself. Thus it was that the survivors of the 30,000 British soldiers who fought at Waterloo returned to a country that was richer than ever before. The City of London had become the economic capital of the world.

Yet for the underwriters at Lloyd's there was also another face to all this burgeoning success; the period between 1793 and 1815 had been one of continuous war during which business confidence had often been seriously shaken. While a good number of marine underwriters had done well out of the inflated wartime rates, the heavy losses at sea had meant that other, less experienced, underwriters had been ruined. Now the return of peace had brought a decline in premiums (on voyages which had hitherto carried a rate of five to eight percent underwriters had to make do with one to 1.5 percent) whereas the risks for shipping had not, in fact, vanished. For many privateers the switch to piracy had been an all too tempting and easy step. Unrest in Europe and the internecine struggles of the new states themselves had given the pirates their chance.

Within a few years the activities of Greek corsairs in the Mediterranean had compelled Lloyd's to ask the Admiralty once again to provide convoys for British shipping heading for the Levant; and not long afterwards privateers under the flags of Buenos Aires, Brazil and Columbia

Mr. Rotchchild

London Pubd by Thos McLean. 26, Haymaket. 1824.

were plundering merchantmen and sometimes committing atrocities too. Added to which there were Portuguese squadrons blockading Oporto, Funchal and Terceira, while Spanish cruisers seized British ships for allegedly breaking the blockade of Buenos Aires. While the material prosperity of the country (though occasionally chequered by sudden depressions) may have seemed to many Englishmen to be the most assured thing in the world, it was not necessarily so on the first floor of the Royal Exchange – especially when in 1824 the agitation for a repeal of the insurance monopolies exploded again.

The narrow defeat of the new marine insurance project of 1810 (known sarcastically at Lloyd's as "the five million scheme") had removed the steam from behind such initiatives; or had done until Nathan Meyer Rothschild appeared on the scene. He it was who began the marmoreal saga of the House of Rothschild.

Nathan's father, Meyer Anselm (whose family name was Bauer) had originally been groomed to become a Rabbi, but had opted instead to set up as a money-lender at the sign of the Red Shield (Rothschild) in Frankfurt's Judenstrasse. In due course, he sent Nathan (1773–1855) to Manchester to act as purchaser of manufactured goods. But Nathan did much more than this. With a bare £80 in his pocket, he opened a tiny money-lending business. Five years and £200,000 later, bulwarked by a soaring financial reputation (no one else had multiplied his capital 2,500 times in five years) he transferred his activities to London.

"Nathan unwearily kept to the multiplication table, entering into the hunt for gold with a zest and an eagerness far outdistancing that of any of his competitors, including such veterans in the field as the Goldschmidts, Coutts and Barings" comments Frederick Martin. "Having got into intimate relations with the government of the day, through being always ready for large advances, even at the darkest period of the continental war, Nathan Rothschild commenced speculating in the funds, on a scale never before attempted, and with the most brilliant results."

The secret of his immensely varied activity lay in the knack of getting advance information about events abroad. He employed carrier pigeons and fast sailing boats to transmit news from carefully chosen agents on the continent. Not only was his private intelligence vastly more efficient than most of the government or indeed of Lloyd's, but he knew precisely how to exploit the knowledge when he had it, and no one could match his brand of financial judo when it came to promoting a bull or bear climate on the stock market.

He was at Brussels on the eve of Waterloo, not as a guest at a fashionable ball, but as a beady-eyed witness of the battle itself. As soon as the outcome was clear, he rushed back home (crossing the Channel in foul weather in an open boat) and for twenty-four hours was the only man in England who knew whether Napoleon or Wellington had been victorious. He immediately bought stock which had plummeted on the news of Blucher's defeat two days previously, and in those twenty-four hours (in the view of the pundits) a clear million pounds sterling was added to the fortune of Nathan Meyer Rothschild.

This was the man who, by an amiable City tradition, was leaning one spring morning in 1824 against his favourite pillar in the Royal Exchange (the Rothschild pillar, of course) with his hands in his pockets when his cousin ran up to him in a state of great excitement.

"Vat ish de matter?" queried Nathan. Whereupon the other (to quote Martin's account) recounted, in gasps, how he had been applying for the vacant actuaryship of a large insurance company, and had been turned down, though admittedly the most qualified candidate, on account of his religion, the directors saying that they would have no Jew. "Vat!" he cried, disengaging his hands from his pockets and grabbing his cousin by the shoulders. "Not take you because of your religion. Mein Gott! Den I will make a bigger office for you dan any of dem."

Suspect though the tale may be, there was nothing apocryphal about the way Rothschild armed such top money men as Alexander Baring, Samuel Gurney and Sir Moses Montefiore to launch the "Alliance British and Foreign Fire and Life Assurance Company" (with a capital of five million pounds divided into 50,000 shares of £100 each) and sent shock waves reverberating through the Room at Lloyd's with a fresh petition to Parliament for repeal of the 1720 Act.

Thomas Fowell Buxton (the member for Weymouth married to a Gurney, who was chosen to pilot through this new Bill) knew little or nothing about marine insurance, and his statements about Lloyd's would have been laughable had it not been for the high reputation he enjoyed as leader of the anti-slavery party. He painted a harrowing picture of the fate of a shipowner or merchant who placed an insurance at Lloyd's. There would be a number of underwriters on the policy, and when it came to settling a loss after a lapse of two or three years some of them might be dead and others bankrupt. "A company does not die" he asserted, with stunning disregard for the facts, "its insolvency is in the highest degree improbable."

Lloyd's counterattacked with the well worn argument of a *de facto* monopoly, and regretted that "Unhappily, His Majesty's ministers were disposed to lend too fond an ear to any suggestion coming from that mass of wealth which has been put into motion on this occasion."

Above: *even in peace, merchant shipping was still
prey to wandering corsairs and privateers, as shown
in this wood-engraving from a magazine of 1825.*

The trouble was that the government was known to be in favour of removing the restrictions on marine insurance. After an interview with Huskisson (then President of the Board of Trade) James Barnes of Lloyd's reported that the minister was "obstinately biased in favour of Free Trade".

Also, of course, that Buxton knew how to rouse the House. The second reading of the Bill was carried on 28 May 1824 by 51 votes to 33.

Lloyd's made an appeal *ad misericordiam* to the Lords. The Bill, they pleaded, meant that underwriters would be ruined and the great agency and intelligence system created by Lloyd's would wither away. "It would be trifling with the misfortunes of your petitioners to assert that the private underwriters would still exist," they concluded sadly.

But Their Lordships were unmoved, and on 24 June the Bill received Royal Assent.

There was an immediate stampede to form new marine insurance companies – some of them floated by Lloyd's subscribers themselves who fancied that the days of the coffee-house were numbered. John Stanniforth (who had been a member of the 1811 house committee) floated the Indemnity Mutual Assurance Company with no fewer than twenty-two Lloyd's men among its twenty-six directors. Yet, as it turned out, the impact on Lloyd's was hardly perverse enough to set any teeth chattering after all.

The newly formed companies were starting business on a falling market, and a spate of commercial speculation in 1825 definitely rumpled their prospects. Many of the newcomers collapsed and the two major concerns, the Alliance and the Indemnity, were far too prudently managed to indulge in the sort of free-for-all rate-cutting that underwriters had feared. Other new ventures were barefaced swindles which soon swallowed up the savings of their unsuspecting investors or survived until exposed by the Select Committee of 1841. In contrast, some famous companies were founded during this period, such as the Guardian Assurance (1821); the Yorkshire Insurance (1824); the Scottish Union and National Insurance (1824); the Standard Life (1825); and the Scottish Amicable (1826).

Towards all of them the private underwriters remained implacably hostile, partly through pique and partly through a persistent feeling that too many birds were now chasing too few worms. By now much of the bounce and excitement had gone out of the Room, and the decade that followed the Act of Repeal was probably the gloomiest in the history of Lloyd's. Many subscribers hedged their bets by joining the companies, and in 1841 a solicitor named Duncan voiced privately held fears when he told another parliamentary select committee that "from the extent and character of the business and the enormous amount of the risks being undertaken" he thought it better "if gradually private underwriting were extinguished and marine insurance confined to responsible joint-stock companies".

As the legal adviser to one of the marine insurance companies, it may be suspected that Duncan had an axe to grind. Yet the fact was that what with depressed rates, aggravated by a heavy stamp duty which drove a good deal of business abroad where it could be placed much cheaper, many underwriters had fallen on evil days. In 1814 there had been 2,150 subscribers of which nearly all had qualified by signing the Trust Deed. By 1825 the number had fallen to 1,504, by 1830 to 1,264, and a decade later this figure sank to under a thousand. In 1828 a sharp-tongued (and unpopular) underwriter called Francis Fortune castigated the committee for mismanagement of affairs and spoke of "distressed proprietors, many of whom we see daily begging on the stairs of the House" – a clear overstatement, although two sons of subscribers were glad to be given jobs in the Room as waiters, and in 1832 a benevolent fund was established to give relief to "worthy unfortunate members of Lloyd's, their widows, or children".

Undoubtedly, nerves were on edge. The quarrel with the committee (mainly about the remuneration they received) escalated into a violent attack on the chairman, Alderman Thompson, who had (perhaps tactlessly) accepted the more sonorous than rewarding position of honorary President of the Sunderland Joint Stock Marine Premium Insurance Company. Such violation of the ground rules meant that he had to go. But he was succeeded by G.R. Robinson, a capable and well liked underwriter who was also MP for Poole, who was destined to preside over the Room for the next critical decade and a half – during which Lloyd's regained a good deal of its old prosperity and prestige.

For coinciding with his election came some slight but significant changes for the better. A new Stamp Act was introduced which reduced the duties of insurance policies; *Lloyd's List* (which unlike *Lloyd's Register* belonged to Lloyd's itself) was put on a new footing and became a daily newspaper with an immediate increase in circulation; and the Agency system was extended giving greater lustre to Lloyd's image abroad. But even as a hint of optimism once again crept into the Room, disaster suddenly struck. The Royal Exchange was burnt to the ground, and Lloyd's found itself homeless.

VICTORIAN LLOYD'S

Above: *the second Royal Exchange as it appeared
just before the fire.*

On previous page: *The Telegraph Room at Lloyd's
in the second half of the 19th century.*

THE FIRE

A FIRE, AS Bernard Darwin once remarked apropos clubs, amounted almost to a patent of respectability. In 1825 there had been a disastrous conflagration at Lord's; the Royal Blackheath (which claimed an unbroken descent from the Scottish courtiers of James I) had all its records reduced to ashes in the latter part of the 18th century; while the blaze at White's in 1733 was so spectacular that both George II and Frederick Prince of Wales jumped out of their beds to watch it.

For Thomas Bolton, as he went about his routine duties as Master of the Captains' Room at Lloyd's, the talking point that evening on Wednesday 10 January 1838 was almost certainly the prolonged and shivering cold snap which had frozen the Thames clean across. At five o'clock the Subscribers' Room was closed as usual, and three hours later, with the help of a porter, he checked that the grates were raked over in the Captains' Room, and that all the lamps were extinguished before locking up and leaving. Then, soon after ten, passers-by spotted that flames were coming out of an upper room in the north-west corner of the Royal Exchange. An alarm was given, and within twenty minutes the first fire-engine was dragged up to the north gates – only to find that they were securely locked and that nobody knew where the keys were kept. When (grumbling that he had no orders to do so) the watchman refused to let them be broken down, someone rushed off to the Mansion House to alert the Lord Mayor, and returned to find that a detachment of the Grenadier Guards, stationed at the Bank of England, had arrived on the scene and were frantically trying to force their way in, with the help of the firemen and a gathering crowd of spectators. As the minutes slipped by, the flames spread, and by the time they finally broke down the gates the building was burning from end to end. And, to make matters worse, the fire-engine's hose had frozen stiff.

By midnight, when the Mayor and other officials arrived, Lloyd's premises upstairs was "all one body of flame" which (according to a newspaper report) could be seen as far away as Windsor in the west and Theydon in the east. Reinforcements of Guards were summoned from the Tower to clear the crowds and make way for further fire-engines, but there was little the firemen could do, since the water froze as soon as it came out of the nozzles, covering them with ice and turning the ground into a skating rink. However, as another newspaper reported, "amidst the tumult of the population, the shouts of the firemen and the crash of falling masonry" the bells in the campanile began to play tunes – including, incongruously enough, "There's nae luck aboot the hoose", until they too came crashing down.

Left: *the fire at the Royal Exchange on the evening of January 10 1838.*

Above: *the ruins of the building afterwards.*

1802			1803		
July	Wilson Sestock		July	Wheelwright C A Junr	
	Waring James			transferred to a subt for C.A.W.	
	Wathen Josh		Augst	Woodhouse Math	
August	Weguelin I.C.			Wylde E.A.	
Septr	Wathen Josh		October	Wilson Willm	
	a substitute for				
Novembr	Wright Henry		1804		
	a substitute for		January	Ward John	
1803				Wolfe Lewis	
Jany	Waymouth C B			Ward Willm	
	Wilkinson C 2		Feby	Ward Samuel	
Feby	Walter John 2			Woolcombe Wm	
April	Wylde Thos Junr		March	Wivel P.L.	
	Wallis Willm		May	Wray Amos	
	Willcox F.D.			Webb Josh	
May	Wall John				
	Westinghausen JW		September	Wyllie Jo	
	a substitute for		May	Wyill Chard	
	Williams T.S.			a substitute for	
	a Substitute for				
	Wollaston WH				

Left: *one of the few record books saved from the fire at the Royal Exchange by Guthrie, still showing the damage sustained at the edges.*

Yet one stroke of luck there was. An underwriter named Guthrie happened to be in the neighbourhood, and with the aid of a small band of helpers he set about salvaging whatever was possible from the coffee-house. Ripping off "the upper parts of tables and desks" they rushed them out of the building, together with as much of the archives as they could lay hands on, before the flames and the smoke made them give up. Thanks to their efforts, many irreplaceable documents were saved – and even today the firestained pages and crumbling edges recall that but for them the whole of Lloyd's early documentation would have perished.

By dawn, nothing but a blackened shell remained of the "Palladium of English Merchants". A prompt and generous offer of accommodation from the proprietors of the Jerusalem Coffee House (who had dashed an advertisement into print by 1.30 a.m.) averted the danger of a total stoppage. But when subscribers and committee foregathered there at nine in the morning, it was immediately obvious that the premises were far too cramped to be anything but a stopgap. In the borrowed boardroom of the London Assurance Corporation committee members spent two anxious days conferring about what was to be done, and on the Saturday G.R. Robinson was able to tell subscribers that after considering a number of possibilities (such as rooms in the East India House, the Excise Office, the Auction Mart, the Commercial Sales Rooms in Mincing Lane, the Jamaica Coffee House and the City Club House in Broad Street) the choice seemed to lie between moving to the Drapers' Hall in Throgmorton Street or the South Sea House on the corner of Threadneedle Street and Bishopsgate. Forty-eight hours later the matter was settled, and Tuesday's newspapers carried the announcement:

> "*Lloyd's* – the business of Lloyd's will be CARRIED ON in the GREAT HALL of the SOUTH SEA HOUSE, Threadneedle Street, on and after Wednesday next.
> London 15 Jan 1838   W DOBSON, Secretary"

And so, for the next eighty-two months, Charles Lamb's "stately relic" was to be the home of Lloyd's.

LLOYD'S IN EXILE

"Reader, in thy passage from the Bank . . . didst thou never observe a melancholy looking, handsome, brick and stone edifice, to the left, where Threadneedle Street abuts upon Bishopsgate? I dare say thou hast often admired its magnificent portals ever gaping wide, and disclosing to view a grave court, with cloisters, and pillars, with few or no traces of goers-in or comers-out – a desolation something like Balclutha's.

"This was once a house of trade – a centre of busy interests. The throng of merchants was here – the quick pulse of gain – and here some forms of business are still kept up, though the soul be long since fled. Here are still to be seen stately porticos; imposing staircases; offices roomy as the state apartments in palaces – deserted, or thinly populated with a few straggling clerks; . . . with venerable faces of beadles, door-keepers – directors seated in form on solemn days (to proclaim a dead dividend) at long worm-eaten tables, that have been mahogany, with tarnished gilt-leather coverings, supporting massy silver ink-stands long since dry . . . such is the SOUTHSEA HOUSE. At least, such it was forty years ago, when I knew it – a magnificent relic!"

In his first essay printed over the signature of Elia (which appeared in the *London Magazine* of August 1820) Charles Lamb was dreaming back to the days when, as a fifteen-year-old office boy, he had worked in the South Sea House before moving over to the India Company, and from all accounts it had changed little when Lloyd's moved in that Wednesday morning. Nor can the next few years have been very comfortable for the underwriters. The Great Hall was not large enough to accommodate them all, and the Court of Directors of the South Sea Company had haughtily refused to allow any part of the building to be used as a coffee-house, so that the Captains' Room had to be set up in the London Tavern – and later in a house at 80 Bishopsgate. So it is not entirely surprising therefore to find that membership fell from the 1,211 subscribers in December 1837 to a new low of 945 at the end of 1843.

Yet, upsetting though this period of exile may have been for the men of Lloyd's, it was not by any means entirely a wasted time. Due to the ingenuity of James Bischoff, for instance, a useful development called the *Index to Lloyd's List* was put into use. By means of it, underwriters could keep continuous tabs on ships in whatever part of the world they might be sailing. The index showed, against the names of the vessels in alphabetical order, the dates of the issues in which their relevant departures, arrivals, speakings or casualties were recorded. While no computer, it nevertheless improved efficiency and helped Lloyd's to maintain its position as the hub of the marine world; while on a more esoteric level, members' appreciation for the practical help and goodwill shown by other organisations finally scotched their hostility towards the insurance companies, and in March 1840 a proposal by the committee to "furnish information similar to that which is now received by the two chartered corporations to all public establishments" was carried by a large majority.

At the same time, a revision of the byelaws opened the doors as widely as possible to the mercantile world, and while still in exile Lloyd's became divided into two groups: the *Members*, who paid an entrance fee of £25 as well as a £4-a-year

subscription; and *Annual Subscribers*, who could use the facilities against the simple payment of a yearly subscription of £4. Any person "underwriting in his own name, or empowering another to write for him" had, of course, to be a member and was eligible to vote; and thus control was kept in the hands of the underwriters. Meanwhile William Tite's design for the new Exchange was approved in 1840, and on Monday 17 January 1842, almost exactly four years after the fire, Prince Albert laid the cornerstone of the new building. It was a splendid occasion. A canvas pavilion to hold 1,450 guests had been erected on the site; the floor was covered with crimson cloth, and the sun came out as the Prince took up the trowel. The workmanlike way in which he spread the mortar delighted spectators who "gave vent to their feelings with a round of cheers". A medal was struck to commemorate the occasion, but underwriters had to wait for another two and three-quarter years before the architect could conduct Prince Albert through the finished Italian-style building with its Roman portico and the sculptured frieze which had a ten-foot high figure of Commerce in the centre.

On 28 November 1844 it was opened. Multiple bands played "See the conquering hero comes", as the Duke of Wellington (whose statue in front of the Exchange had been unveiled that June) arrived on the scene. Cabinet ministers, politicians and bigwigs were there by the hundred. The bells in the campanile chimed "God save the Queen" (in B flat); addresses were presented, and after heralds had made the proclamation the Queen received a slip of parchment from Sir James Graham and declared ("in an audible voice"): "It is my Royal will and pleasure that this building hereafter be called 'The Royal Exchange'." For the banquet held in what was to be the new underwriting room, there were four long tables, according to the *Illustrated London News*, "Spread with every conceivable delicacy and profusion of the finest wines" and which *John Bull* described in greater detail as "A magnificent baron of beef weighing upwards of 20 stone and surmounted by a figure of St George and the Dragon" served on "massive gold plate of the most exquisite workmanship".

Oddly enough, very few of the Lloyd's underwriters received invitations to this feast in their own premises. But though the press made some waspish comments on this lack of courtesy towards them, they cannot have minded too much. For on Monday 26 December they were back at the Royal Exchange, with accommodation which was regarded as the last word in comfort and magnificence. "The lavatory is on a scale approaching to luxury" commented Chambers' Edinburgh Journal. "The elegant soap dishes, the spotless napkins, the china basins, the ivory-topped cocks for the supply of hot and cold water. . . ."

Above: *the Underwriting Room at Lloyd's in the third Royal Exchange, circa 1875.*

Various Victorian views of Lloyd's published at different times in The Graphic.

Top: *The Underwriting Room in 1886.*

Left: *the Loss Book in 1877.*

Above: *the Reading Room in 1890.*

Even if some of them may have missed the cosiness and restrained comfort of the old building, they were all delighted to be back home.

TOWARDS THE PATTERN OF HIGH VICTORIANISM

INEXORABLY–THOUGH PERHAPS without realising it– the country was moving into an entirely fresh ambience since the day that, as dawn rose through the elms in front of Kensington Palace, the Arch- bishop of Canterbury and Lord Conyngham had woken a young girl with the news that her uncle had died and she was now Queen. For on that June morning of 1837, as the 18-year-old Victoria per- formed the stately minuet which led from school- room to throne, a new period of British history had begun.

Yet in truth, the English were not yet basking in that complacent and corsetted glow which later would be known as "Victorian". It was still a rumbustious age, unashamedly paternal with its well etched pattern of patrician and squire, trades- man and pleb. But on all sides the traditional values were being challenged by science and the industrial revolution, and the muscular energy of horse and man were losing ground to the mechanised power of steam and cog. With astonishing vigour, a new breed of *entrepreneurs* were building up their factories and mills and mines in the Midlands, all too often through heartless exploitation of the poorer classes; and, even as Britain attained a living-style thus far unknown in the history of the world, Karl Marx and his crony Friedrich Engels (who could observe the repulsive conditions of factory workers in his father's cotton-goods mill in Manchester) were gathering material in the British Museum to denounce capitalism and sow the seeds of a world revolution which they believed would be sparked off in this island.

As part of this pulsing activity, England had flung across its countryside some 5,000 miles of shining iron rails in less than a decade – plunging the country into a frenzy of speculation (in 1844 alone, Parliamentary committees approved twenty- six projects totalling 800 miles) and provoking Wordsworth to write his sonnet against the Kendal and Windermere Railway:

"Is then no nook of English ground secure From rash assault? . . ."

Yet, oddly enough, sails were still the staple of the merchant fleet at mid-century. Even in 1858 the ratio of steam to sail was about forty-five to one; and for the most part ships were still built of wood. The first transatlantic crossing by steam had been made in 1819 by the *Savannah*, an American packet of 320 tons using an auxiliary 90-hp engine. By 1838 England had the *British Queen* and the *Great Western* (1,320 tons, 325 feet in length) which with her 400-hp engine travelled at a rate of nine knots, so that her voyages averaged fifteen days on the outward trip from London to New York and thirteen days homeward. That year also saw the first Atlantic crossings of the *Sirius*, the *Fort William* and the *Liverpool* (which carried fifty saloon passengers and 150 tons of cargo) as well as the foundation of a new line by Samuel Cunard – a Halifax Quaker who secured the government steam mail contract and immediately began build- ing four Cunarders.

All of these vessels, like the ill fated *President* and the *Britannia* (in which Charles Dickens travelled to New York in 1842) were paddle steam- ers, charging an average of £30 for the transatlantic trip. While relying on their boilers, they retained their masts for extra speed. But Fulton's torpedoes – the first piercing impact of which was felt at the battle of Sinope in 1840 – showed the need for less penetrable hulls. In 1843 the *Great Britain* was completed to the designs of Isambard Kingdom Brunel, the builder of the Great Western Railway. An iron ship of 2,984 tons, she was driven at a speed of twelve knots by another innovation: the screw propeller, with six arms (each about seven feet long) connected to a shaft geared by chains to low- pressure engines. Three hundred and twenty-two feet long, with six masts and five watertight bulk- heads, she was the grandest thing afloat (300 people could dine at long tables running the whole length of a vast saloon), and yet for underwriters and the marine world the use of an iron hull heralded a spate of unseaworthy vessels that *Punch* later lampooned as "coffin ships".

Punch's unintellectual badinage mirrored the clubhouse swagger of those lofty new Rooms in the Royal Exchange. For, to be sure, Beau Brummel had only just died and the age of the dandies was not quite past. D'Orsay's waistcoats and cravats were still the wonder of the fashionable world, and Disraeli had delivered his maiden speech in the Commons with his hair carefully curled, wearing a bottle-green coat and a waistcoat covered with gold chains. Even in the City men could, and did, wear clothes of every colour: short frock coats with deep velvet collars; shirt cuffs turned back over coat sleeves; low-cut waistcoats of stunning patterns – and few members would dream of going down to the Subscribers' Room without a grey or white top hat. (Hair was usually worn long, and, although most men were clean-shaven, side-whiskers were be- ginning to appear.) Even if Thackeray was moved to write a sad little ecological piece for *Punch* about a man driven almost to suicide by the thought that almost everything he ate, and the air that he breathed, was full of poison ". . . if my Thames is a

Above: *the launching, by Prince Albert, of Brunel's Great Britain at Bristol in 1843—iron-hulled and driven by a screw propellor, she was one of the great achievements of Victorian engineering.*

regular Lethe, in which every eel is a mortal writhing serpent, and every white bait a small dose of death, what is the odds of taking a little more pyroligneous acid in my coffee?''. There is little doubt that members of Lloyd's, notwithstanding ''coffin ships'' and Luddites and volatile premium rates, were managing to keep themselves comfortably above the breadline.

As an example of this, Alexis Soyer, the celebrated chef at the Reform Club, described the sort of dinner party a City man would give when he got home from the Royal Exchange: ''You order your carriage, which lands you within five minutes of the appointed time at your host's door, and after passing through the hall lined with servants in and out of livery, you are ushered into the presence-room. About ten minutes after, dinner is announced, and your hat is taken from you as you descend the stairs to enter the drawing room . . . a delicate soup and turtle are handed round, nothing on the tables except flowers and preserved fruits in old Dresden baskets, a bill of fare placed next to every person, a turbot with lobster and Dutch sauces, and a portion of red mullet with cardinal sauce are offered to each guest; cucumber and the essential cruet-stands bringing up the rear. The ''flying dishes'', as the modern cooks call the oyster or marrow patés, follow the fish. The entrees are carried around, a *suprème de volaille aux truffes*, a sweetbread *au jus*, lamb cutlets, with asparagus, peas, a *fricandeau à l'oseille*; carefully avoid what are called flank dishes, which if placed on the table are usually cold, and are quite unnecessary; either venison, roast saddle of mutton, or stewed beef *à la jardinère*, are then produced, the accessories being salad, beetroot, vegetables, French and English mustard. A turkey poult, duckling, or green goose, commences the second course; plover's eggs in aspic jelly, a mayonnaise of fowl succeed; a *macedoine* of fruit, *merinques à la crème*, a marasquino jelly, and a chocolate cream, form the sweets. Sardines, salad, beetroot, celery, anchovy and plain butter and cheese, for those who are gothic enough to eat it. Two ices, cherry-water, and pine-apple cream, with the fruit of the season, furnish the dessert. Two servants or more, according to the number of the party, must attend exclusively to the wine; sherry Madeira, and champagne, must ever be flowing during dinner. Coffee, hot and strong, ought always to be served in the dining room with liqueurs. . . .''

By the time that subscribers took possession of their fine new quarters in the Royal Exchange, Lloyd's had been in existence for over a century and a half, and was shedding its coffee-house image (although official communications were addressed to ''Lloyd's Coffee House'' until the end of the 1914–18 War). It was, in fact, by gradual steps becoming institutionalised. The haphazard collec-

Above: *a Victorian waiter at Lloyd's.*

103

Above: *the Merchants' Room at Lloyd's. Members read the news of the victory on the Alma during the Crimea War.*

tion of freelancers, linked by a common interest in underwriting, was evolving into a society with an entity of its own, and an international credit rating which was only as strong as the weakest of its members. If only for this, the security of a Lloyd's policy had to be defined, and then sustained. Here, in the *laissez-faire* atmosphere of the mid-19th century, lay the preoccupation of the committee for the next quarter of a century, and it culminated in the Parliamentary Act of Incorporation in 1871.

The return to the Royal Exchange, and a revival of trade following the repeal of the Corn Laws, led to a marked increase in membership. In 1846 this was divided into two classes: active underwriters, who were allowed to write risks; and non-active underwriters, who were not permitted to do so. Surprisingly, there were at that time 185 underwriting against 621 non-underwriting members, though twenty-five years later the balance had changed and the active group formed two-thirds of the total membership. Even more surprising for those who imagine Lloyd's to be restricted to Englishmen (as it later became, and remained until 1969) was the continental flavour of many of the names – such as Mussabini and Shunk; Spartali and Thielke; Zygomalas, Peynado, Segelke, Focca and De Sa, to quote a few of many hardly Anglo-Saxon members.

With this growth of membership came the inevitable need for greater discipline among subscribers. Members could default on their claims and even go bankrupt, but the only offence which rated expulsion from Lloyd's was the non-payment of the annual subscription. As it happens, the standard of commercial honesty was remarkably high, and there were few major scandals (although some instances where members sailed pretty close to the wind). But it should be remembered that insurers themselves still regarded insurance to be a risk in itself. The successive Acts of 1844, 1870, 1872 and 1907 represented gradual attempts by the British Government to control and codify insurance – and it was not, in fact, until 1946 that the Whitehall machine jelled the ground rules on marine insurance. Perhaps (as Gibb has remarked) British insurance was fortunate in not being smothered by cotton-wool in its formative years. But the solvency of members and the back-up to a Lloyd's policy was obviously a matter of topmost importance. In December 1851, it was resolved that: "If any member or annual subscriber become bankrupt . . . or compound his creditors, he shall cease to be a member or annual subscriber."

Yet while this bye-law prevented bankrupts from trading in the Room, it did nothing to ensure the solvency of all the others who were issuing policies. Moreover, new members were still accepted without any particular guarantee. But the committee was beginning quietly to tighten up here too, and one

of the first members to have someone stand security for him (to the tune of £5,000) was H.J.P. Dumas, whose name subsequently became famous in the Room. By the 1860s most new candidates were required to put up either a deposit or a guarantee, and other steps were being taken to ensure that a Lloyd's policy had a cast-iron backing.

Equally, until 1871 there was nothing to prevent part of a risk being placed with Lloyd's underwriters and the balance with outsiders, even though the policy itself appeared to be a Lloyd's one. The Act of Incorporation made it a criminal offence for anyone who was not a recognised underwriting member of Lloyd's to sign his name to a Lloyd's policy. Moreover, to protect it, there had to be an imprint, and the collophon chosen to distinguish a Lloyd's policy was an anchor. For more than a century now, this has been symbolic of Lloyd's.

From 1871 onwards, Lloyd's was a Corporation, established by Act of Parliament. It had a constitution, a set of rules – but no set policies. As in the past, it was a club that provided the premises and the facilities for members to do business "each for his own part and not one for another". Walter Farrant, who for many years was the Caller of the Room, summed the position up best when, asked the question "What is Lloyd's?" he replied, with kindly dignity: "Individually we are underwriters. Collectively we are Lloyd's."

THE DIMINISHING WORLD: 1820–1900

"So GREAT IS the hurry in the spirit of this world, that in aiming to do business quick and to gain wealth, the Creation at this day doth loudly groan" wrote John Woolman in his diaries towards the end of the 18th century. His complaint, it seemed, concerned the headlong rush of the mailstages which were required to keep to schedules of upwards of 100 miles in twenty-four hours. The price of such frenzied abandon, he observed, was the wholesale collapse of exhausted horses in the mud-pitted roads, and mail-boys frozen to death in their seats. Even at this price, try as it might, the Post Office was only as fast as its fastest stage, and even in 1805 the news of Nelson's victory at Trafalgar took seventeen days to reach the London papers (an improvement, nevertheless, on France where it took another nine years to get published). With its special arrangements at the General Post Office and correspondents all over the world, Lloyd's continued to outstrip virtually every newspaper in the speed of its information. While *The Times* was proudly announcing to the world that it had sent a special correspondent to France to witness the execution of Marie Antoinette, Lloyd's already had more than thirty correspondents of its own in several continents. In 1811 it appointed its first official agent abroad (to Madeira), among whose functions was furnishing the committee with "regular advices of the arrival and sailing of vessels and every other information in which the interests of the underwriters are concerned". (Today Lloyd's agents and sub-agents all over the world, reporting day and night to the Intelligence Department, spend well over £50,000 a year in cable bills alone.)

Above: *an operator at work on an early Morse telegraph, circa 1850. Lloyd's had telegraphic communication as early as 1845.*

Left: *a (later) view from* Punch *of the hazards of being a Lloyd's agent.*

LLOYD'S AGENT TOWING HOME THE SHIP OF THE DESERT.

As the 19th century matured, those horizons which had expanded so dramatically over the last 200 years gradually began to contract. True, there were still vast tracts of the earth's surface awaiting their joyful incorporation into the British Empire – the heartlands of Africa or the frozen polar wastes still lured the intrepid and curious – but the seas and coasts which were Lloyd's province were no longer matters of speculation but of scientific investigation. Particularly in means of communication, the years of peace following the end of the Napoleonic Wars saw a remarkable impetus in the technological applications of scientific discovery. Within two decades MacAdam's method of road construction had been adopted and brand-new highways were soon accommodating the ludicrous, belching steam carriages (which were no improvement on the poor exhausted horses at all); the first iron steamships had been launched, and the Stockton to Darlington railway was in business.

But, by the 1830s, the most far-reaching invention of all was incubating in the mind of an American painter. Samuel Morse's electric telegraph was not publicly hatched until 1844, when the election results in Baltimore were magically transmitted to Washington, but within a few years the communications of Britain, not to say Europe and America, had been utterly transformed. Telegraph lines sprang up alongside the blossoming new railroads and were operated by the railway companies themselves. As early as 1845 Lloyd's had made their first telegraphic arrangements with the South Western Railway Company, whose service forwarded lists of shipping casualties from Southampton to London. In 1851 – the same year that Britain

Opposite top: *a characteristic 19th century brig, the* Ituna, *was built in 1834, plied trade to the West Indies and South America for forty years, was dismasted and abandoned in mid-ocean in January 1874.*

Opposite below: *a view in the Whitechapel Road 1831, a nightmarish satire conceived in 1828 of what London would become if the vogue for steam carriages caught on.*

Above: *H.M.S.* Agamemnon *attempting to lay the Atlantic cable in 1857 in the face of many hazards— not least whales getting entangled with the cable. The feat was eventually accomplished by the Great Eastern in 1865.*

Left: *Brunel's* Great Eastern *being at last launched successfully in 1858.*

Below: *the first Cunard steam ship.*

On following two pages: *the Great Gas Illumination of the Royal Exchange in 1856, to celebrate the end of the Crimean War.*

ND THE FULNESS THEREOF

grandly went on show to the world at the Great Exhibition – the first electric instrument was installed in the Royal Exchange itself (in the Merchants' Room).

That year the first submarine cable linking Britain with Europe was completed, though not before a great chunk of it had been dredged up by an innocent French fisherman and offered for sale in Boulogne market, and two years later Lloyd's had hooked itself into the Continent (and ultimately to India) by courtesy of the Submarine and European Telegraph Company. The daunting task of laying a transatlantic cable was begun in 1857 by two Navy ships, the *Niagara* and the *Agamemnon*, but it proved too mighty an undertaking even for ships with such epic names. Barely 500 miles had been laid before the cable snapped. A second attempt succeeded momentarily, barely enabling Queen Victoria to exchange civilities with President Buchanan before the cable frayed and isolated the two continents once more.

Eight years after the first unsuccessful attempt, the greatest liner in the world sailed out of Valencia to try again, armed with stouter cable and more sophisticated tackle. Brunel's *Great Eastern* was an underwriter's nightmare. Its construction took three years, cost one and a half million pounds, and was attended by not a few bankruptcies; its first launching on 3 November 1857 was a disaster leaving a quarter of the monster hanging in mid-air. After three attempts she was finally launched, but the worry of it all killed Brunel who suffered a stroke even as his crowning achievement was undergoing her trials. The jinx followed her to New York in 1860 where a hurricane descended on her and ripped off her paddle wheels like cardboard, swept away all lifeboats and doubled up the rudder-post like a bent nail. She limped back to port miraculously, with a maddened cow running amok in the saloon and the 400 passengers in no better state. (No one was entirely surprised to discover, when she was broken up in 1888, a skeleton incarcerated inside the iron framework.)

The *Great Eastern*'s true vocation, however, emerged with the successful laying of the cable in 1865, justifying Robert Peel's rotund encomium on "... this silver-toned zone to join the United Kingdom and America ... at the very bottom of the mighty Atlantic which beats against your shores with everlasting pulsations". Yet such sentiments, though overblown to our ears, were not totally inappropriate: to the visionary Victorian anything seemed possible now that man had begun to exact obedience from nature. Was he not poised on the brink of the Electric Age? In 1856, to celebrate the glorious if tardy outcome of the Crimean War, the Royal Exchange had been splendidly illuminated with patriotic slogans – in gas. Within two years the first lighthouse, at South Foreland, was lit by

electricity (much to the consternation of shareholders in gas and coal companies), and inside another three Joseph Swan was to demonstrate his embryonic incandescent lamp, and Reis his electromagnetic telephone. Before he was very much older, a Lloyd's man could stroll down to the Mansion House and have his crossing illuminated by giant arc-lamps.

Not every product of this inspired surge of technical creativity, it has to be admitted, was so well omened. Admiral Popov's Circular Battleships were to be seen briefly in the Baltic before being consigned to oblivion; and Bessamer's Hydraulic Saloon (a contrivance whereby the public sections of a ship remained on an even keel irrespective of the rollings of the rest of the vessel) was more notable for its good intentions than its success. But more relevant to Lloyd's underwriters than the fate of these maritime oddities was the quickening improvement in theoretical marine architecture. Since the Royal Navy had sailed into the Crimean War with a magnificent – but totally redundant – all wooden fleet, the gross tonnage of steam ships had increased from 131,000 tons (or 4 percent of all ships) to over two million tons in the 1870s (nearly 30 percent of all ships). That hybrid, the steam clipper, had made its appearance as well as the much mistrusted Ironclad – both of them in their pioneering days subject to the vagaries of master shipwrights who preferred to rely on "experience" than on mathematical study of the new problems involved. Not surprisingly it took a spate of infamous disasters – notably the *Royal Charter* (1859), the *Birkenhead* (1852), the *London* (1865) – to instil a proper sense of responsibility. This came more speedily in fact from the shipbuilders themselves than from the Government (which had abolished the Central School of Mathematics and Naval Construction in 1853 for reactionary reasons of its own) or from the ship-owners.

Some ship-owners indeed were inclined to take advantage of the precarious situation by deliberately overloading their vessels (obviously some disasters were the result of insufficient freeboard, but by no means all). Such "coffin-ships", took a terrible toll on human lives and, of course, insurance. As early as 1865 questions were being asked in Parliament about this malpractice, but not until the strenuous efforts of Samuel Plimsoll made themselves felt in the lobbies of the House did the issue take on any urgency. In 1873 Plimsoll moved for the appointment of a Royal Commission to look into "the practice of certain ship-owners to send to sea vessels that were either not sea-worthy or were so loaded as to be almost certain to sink" and this done "for the sake of the insurance money", according to a contemporary commentator. Out of 2,700 people drowned annually, said Plimsoll, four-fifths were drowned needlessly.

THE COFFIN-SHIPS.

POLLY. "O, dear JACK! I can't help crying, but I'm so happy to think you're not going in one of those DREADFUL SHIPS!"
JACK. "What, Davy Jones's Decoy Ducks! No! no! Lass—never more!—thanks to our friend Master Plimsoll, God bless him!"

Above: *The Coffin Ships, a cartoon from* Punch *by Tenniel, celebrating the tardy passage of Plimsoll's Merchant Shipping Act in 1875 which was designed to prevent unscrupulous shipowners deliberately overloading their vessels to claim the insurance when they sank.*

These tragic statistics appeared to make so small an impression on the House that Plimsoll's long overdue Merchant Shipping Act was postponed twice, in 1874 and in 1875, causing the crusader to defy the rules of the Commons and shout "I will unmask the villains who have sent brave men to death". He was, of course, called on to apologise immediately but was compensated (or silenced) by a makeshift bill requiring a loading-line to be marked on every vessel. Strangely this was to be left to the Master's discretion, and one waggish captain actually painted his on the funnel. Equally strangely there is no plaque to Mr Plimsoll in Lloyd's.

As the century drew to its close yet another important advance was being made in the sphere of communications, which was to affect Lloyd's intimately. In 1896 a young Italian called Guglielmo Marconi patented what he called wireless telegraphy in Britain, claiming he was capable of sending messages through the air for a distance of no less than nine miles. Five years later, flying a crude kite at the end of a length of copper wire on the coast of Newfoundland he succeeded in picking up a faint morse signal from Cornwall more than 1,700 miles away. For some time Marconi's experiments had been exciting the attention of Sir Henry Hozier, then the incumbent Secretary at Lloyd's, whose energy over the past twenty years had established Lloyd's as pre-eminent in marine intelligence (by the end of the century there was scarcely an ocean-going vessel which was not in contact with one or other of Hozier's forty signal stations before reaching its destination). In 1901 Hozier made an arrangement with Marconi for Lloyd's stations to handle ship-to-shore messages on behalf of Marconi's company. It was a short-lived partnership, as it transpired, for as a telegraphic business increased Lloyd's was faced with the prospect either of entering upon a full-scale commercial venture (which would have been irrelevant to its own immediate requirements) or of offering less of a service than Marconi required. Marconi did in fact recover two stations after lodging a legal complaint against Lloyd's, but the issue was decided anyway in 1906 when the Government revoked Lloyd's wireless licence. Once again, as in the days of the mailstages, Lloyd's found itself obliged to enter into an arrangement with the Post Office, which proved not to be the death-knell of Lloyd's pre-eminence in marine intelligence that everyone supposed it would.

THE LUTINE STORY

She sailed out of Yarmouth with the Crown jewels of Holland and over a million pounds of bullion in her hold. The night before her departure the captain and officers entertained the local notables of Lowestoft and Yarmouth at a ball aboard. Within a few hours of leaving she ran into foul weather and, carried off course by strong lee-tides, struck a sandbank between Vlieland and Terschelling. When dawn broke, she had gone to pieces and disappeared without a trace. The news that she had sunk with all hands created a sensation. "In the annals of our naval history" said a London newspaper, "there has scarcely ever happened a loss attended with so much calamity, both of a public as well as a private nature". For more than a century and a half she has been a magnet for treasure-seekers, and a golden prize still awaits anyone who can conquer the shifting sands and bring to light the treasure which went down with the *Lutine*.

As ROMANTIC AND improbable as any tale by R.L. Stevenson, the legend of the *Lutine* has fascinated generations of Lloyd's men, and her bell, salvaged in July 1857, and now hanging in the Room, rings whenever there is news to be given – once for good tidings, twice for news of a disaster. But, to separate fact from fiction, this seems to have been the story of the *Lutine*:

In 1785 the French navy launched a frigate of 950 tons called *La Lutine*. Mounting thirty-six guns and carrying a crew of 240, she was lying at Toulon at the outbreak of war in 1793, and was one of the ships surrendered to Lord Howe to prevent their falling into republican hands. Renamed HMS *Lutine*, she was sent to England after some service in the Mediterranean, and after being fitted with a new deck was used as a convoy ship. In 1799 she was attached to the North Sea fleet with Captain Lancelot Skynner, a Northamptonshire man with a fine record, in command.

Since Europe at this time was in the throes of a financial crisis, the London banking firm of Goldschmidt (forebears *inter alia* of Jimmie Goldsmith the tycoon and his brother Teddy the ecologist) found it necessary to buttress their German operation, and applied for government help in transporting a large quantity of bullion to Hamburg – a necessary precaution, with the North Sea so full of enemy ships and privateers. At that moment it happened that the government likewise had to send cash urgently to the Army in Holland. It was planned, therefore (as a letter from the Treasury to the Admiralty on 27 September reveals) to transport both the Goldschmidt gold and "a sum of money in silver" for the soldiers' pay to Hamburg and the Texel in the same ship. In fact, HMS *Amethyst* was ordered to be ready to sail – which she did on 2 October, but with only the Paymaster's funds on board; the Goldschmidt's bullion was apparently not ready in time.

That same day the Admiralty instructed Admiral Duncan, then at Yarmouth, to send "a brig, or cutter, to Gravesend, for the service of receiving on board some bullion and conveying it to the

Above: *a painting of the frigate* Lutine *by F. R. Mason, which now hangs in the Committee Rooms at Lloyd's.*

Above: *salvage operations in progress on the* Lutine *off the coast of Holland, but nothing of importance has been rescued from the ship since 1861. The bell (left) was brought up in 1857, hangs today in Lloyd's and is rung to signal the arrival of important news once for bad, twice for good.*

Elbe", and accordingly he dispatched an armed cutter, HMS *Nile*, which carried out its mission safely. But a quantity of bullion had been sent by land to Yarmouth, and the bankers asked for another ship. "I complied with their request" reported Duncan to London, "and ordered the *Lutine* to Cuxhaven . . . together with the mails lying here . . . directing Captain Skynner to proceed to Stromness after doing so to take under his protection the Hudson's Bay's ships, and see them safely to the Nore."

These sailing orders reached Captain Skynner just as a ball had started up aboard. It was hastily cancelled, the bullion was loaded, and at dawn on 9 October the *Lutine* set sail from Yarmouth. A last-minute passenger was a certain Captain Cooke who had seen many years of service on the Hamburg run. According to *The Times*, Skynner ran across him in the agent's office and persuaded him to join the trip. Obviously he was far from happy about the weather and felt that his experience would be useful in the already foul conditions. As it happened, a north-west gale blew up. The ship was driven off its course, and it may very well have been Captain Cooke who suggested sheltering in the Vlie. But unhappily the *Lutine* struck a sandbank and sank at once. The only two survivors died within a matter of hours.

The news reached Lloyd's on 15 October (four days before any official report was received by the Admiralty) and underwriters, Angerstein among them, paid out for a total loss – promptly enough, in fact, for another consignment of bullion "equal to that unfortunately lost on the *Lutine*" to be sent only a week later to Hamburg.

The *Lutine* had sunk not far from Terschelling, and when the tides were exceptionally low she was partly visible. Obviously, by law, anything salvaged from the wreck was now the property of the underwriters. But since England was at war with the Netherlands the Dutch government claimed it as a war spoil. In the meantime, the local fishermen had had a field day. The Dutch authorities later admitted that fifty-eight bars of gold, over 40,000 Spanish silver pistoles, and hundreds of gold coins had been recovered, and some reminted, before the shifting sands had once again swallowed up the wrecked vessel and individual treasure hunting had ceased.

It was not until almost the end of the Napoleonic Wars that anything further was done about salvaging the bullion in the *Lutine*. But a certain Pierre Eschauzier, the local "Opper Strand vonder" (a sort of governmental lord of the manor) who lived near the spot where she had sunk, had been doing some private research and had come to the conclusion that what had so far been salvaged was only a tiny part of what still remained. He argued that the markings on the gold bars (which had a G for

Goldschmidt followed by a sequence number) indicated clearly that something like 500 more were still submerged, and he was able to get a Royal Decree (dated 26 July 1814) as well as a government grant for fresh salvage operations. But after seven years of dredging all he managed to bring up was seventeen gold coins.

Even so, he did not give up. In fact, he managed to talk King Willem I into giving him further support, and in 1821 by a second Royal Decree he was awarded exclusive rights to salvage the *Lutine*, on the basis that half of what he recovered would go to the government. He had a large diving-bell made in London, and resumed operations with English divers – but with even less success than before. The changing currents and shifting sands at the entrance to the Zuyder Zee now made it difficult even to pinpoint the location of the wreck, and after a further five frustrating months he finally threw in his hand.

But all this activity had caused a number of underwriters at Lloyd's to prick up their ears. The *Lutine* and its treasure, they felt, belonged to them and not to the Dutch. *The Times* took their side. The Dutch position, it pointed out, was that, as the *Lutine* had been wrecked during a war with Holland, it had become a prize. But (*The Times* went on to argue) "We shall be anxious to learn on what plea the present King of the Netherlands authorises his minister of foreign affairs to treat this ship and cargo as hostile property. In 1799 England was not at war with the House of Orange, but *for* the House of Orange". In any case, the newspaper added, no possession was ever taken of the wreck.

The argument was telling enough for Canning to take the matter up, and the upshot was a compromise. The Dutch government waived its rights but upheld those of Eschauzier. Henceforth (as F. Conyngham, Secretary at the Foreign Office, wrote on 6 May 1823 to William Bell, then Chairman of Lloyd's) Lloyd's would have 50 percent rights and Eschauzier the other 50 percent. "Mr Canning apprehends" the letter concluded, "that it may be advisable for the claimants in this country to agree to the offer now made." Which indeed they did, and in 1828 the King of the Netherlands issued the necessary decree.

But any cross-channel partnership between Lloyd's and Eschauzier was frustrated by the violent anti-British feeling that sprang up in Holland following the separation of Belgium from the Netherlands in 1830, for which England was held to be largely responsible, and for another quarter of a century nothing was done.

Finally salvage operations by Lloyd's and Eschauzier's soon began again in the summer of 1857 when, fortunately enough, a violent gale swept away some of the sands and uncovered the wreck. Mr Ball, Lloyd's sub-agent at the Texal, wrote to the secretary on 1 September 1857 that "Yesterday there was recovered, by means of divers and pincers, $13\frac{1}{4}$ silver coins, being Spanish piasters, 1 gold Louis d'or, 5 brass hoops and casks, and a quantity of cannon and shot". Five days later it was announced that "the vessel is entire", and J.M. Hill, Lloyd's agent in Amsterdam arrived on the scene in an armed gunboat put at his disposal by the Dutch authorities – a wise precaution, as it happened, since by then an armada of private treasure-seekers had turned up to see what could be fished from the wreck.

Operations were held up during the winter months, but with the help of a diving-bell and other equipment lent by the government, bullion and species to the value of £39,203 were salvaged during the following summer. The *Lutine's* bell, which weighed 106 lbs and was $17\frac{1}{2}$ inches in diameter, was brought up on 17 July. Somewhat surprisingly, it bore the name *St Jean* and the date 1779 – as anyone who cares to inspect it in the Room can see. But it is possible, say the historians of Lloyd's "That the *Lutine* may have been laid down as the *St Jean* . . . or that the bell was a secondhand one, returned to stores from a vessel that had been broken up".

In 1860 the ship's rudder was found, and went to Lloyd's where it was made into an ornately carved chair and table for the chairman. But this was about all that was recovered. The sands shifted back again and the operations were suspended. Frederick Martin made out a balance sheet a few years later:

Salvaged	1800–1801	£55,770
	1857–1858	£39,203
	1859–1861	£ 4,920

According to his calculations, the total value of the treasure on the wreck had been £1,175,000. If this were so, over a million pounds remained – rather more than five times that figure in our devalued currency. At 10.18 on the morning of 29 July 1938, two strokes sounded on the *Lutine* bell itself in the Room at Lloyd's and a red-robed "waiter" announced from the rostrum that a gold bar marked FFB 57, weighing about 7 lbs had been brought up by the dredger *Karimata* owned by the Billiton Company which, under licence from Lloyd's, had been systematically dredging around the area of the *Lutine*. But this gold bar, along with a cannon ball and a few coins, was the only booty brought up after 1861, and Warren Dawson may have written the epitaph of the *Lutine* when he said: "Although the wreck lies fairly near the shore, the actions of currents and the constant shifting of sand have rendered salvage operations difficult and costly almost to the pitch of impossibility. A change in the current in a single night will undo the work of months, and it is very doubtful if the greater part of the golden treasure will ever more see the light of day."

All the same, it is there for anyone who cares to have a try.

THE GREAT SECRETARIES

DESPITE THE REFORMS back in 1800, which by shutting the door to non-subscribers had effectively turned Lloyd's into a society, no proper administration had been set up. The collection and distribution of news had remained in the hands of the Masters, and even official correspondence with the Admiralty continued to be conducted by Bennett or White alongside their normal functions of running the coffee-house. But in 1804 the Whitehall *haute-école* turned haughty. When Lord Camden became Secretary of State for War, his first communication was a curt note declining to "enter into epistolary intercourse with the waiters of Lloyd's Coffee-house".

Obviously the snub must have registered, because shortly afterwards a brief note figured in the minutes which "ordered that all letters etc on the business of the Committee be signed by John Bennett Jr as Secretary".

Thus was appointed Lloyd's first great Secretary. While Bennett Senior and White continued with their duties at the bar of the Subscribers' Room, John Bennett Junior (who up to this point had been helping his father with the accounts) stepped into a still unpaid job with enthusiasm. Apart from taking charge of the Loss and Convoy books, he set about widening the system of shipping intelligence. In his eyes, the existing band of correspondents was insufficient; what he wanted was a network of agents throughout the world. Arming in his brother-in-law (a Royal Naval Captain) along with another close friend who was secretary to an admiral, he quickly opened up fresh channels of communication. New correspondents were appointed as far distant as Barbados and the Cape, and a regular stream of information began coming in from India and the United States. In addition, Bennett privately kept up a confidential correspondence with a number of contacts of his own, posting up such extracts as he and the Committee felt would be of interest to the Room. But unfortunately this crusading spirit had unexpected consequences.

In 1811, pressure by France on the Scandinavians led to the seizure of a large number of ships in the Baltic ports – a bad blow for underwriters, who were immediately caught up in a hurricane of claims. When it was revealed that the Committee had not passed on some of Bennett's private information dealing with the escalation of French

Above: *portrait of John Bennett Jnr, first Secretary
of Lloyd's from 1804–34, by Andrew Morton.*

Above: *Lloyd's signal station at Gibraltar, one of many established by Hozier around Britain and in other parts of the world.*

authority in the Baltic (which might conceivably have affected underwriters' judgement of risks) resentment was expressed by a vote of censure against the Committee. The upshot was the nomination of a new Committee under the chairmanship of Marryat. But, more important, it was decided that they should "appoint Agents, to act for the benefit of the underwriters, wherever they may think proper".

Hitherto Agents had acted under power of attorney for individual underwriters; now they were to become representatives for the Society of Lloyd's as a whole. Bennett and the new Committee set energetically about appointing new Agents, and by the end of the year they had already established agencies at many English and Scottish ports, as well as in Spain, South America, the West Indies, Newfoundland, and even on the now hostile coast of America. At the time of Bennett's death in 1834, there were 350 of them, and so vital was their connection with Lloyd's to become that today over 1,500 Agents and sub-Agents now operate throughout the world.

These watchdogs relayed a never-ending stream of information concerning every facet of shipping: the arrivals and departures of vessels, casualties, delays, repairs, recording even the most trivial news items which might concern the marine world. The benefit to underwriters was immediately felt, and the long-term goodwill which the agency system generated was immense. The whole country came to realise that Lloyd's was performing a national service.

John Bennett's life work was one of the most significant contributions made by any single man to Lloyd's. Subsequent Secretaries also made their mark: to Captain Halstead RN, for instance, who was appointed in 1848, went the credit of building up an integrated management. But, after Bennett, the other great Secretary to achieve distinction (not only for becoming Winston Churchill's father-in-law) was Colonel (Sir) Henry Hozier who, loftily dividing mankind into two classes – Officers and Other Ranks – was the virtual ruler of Lloyd's from 1874 until 1906.

The *Windsor Magazine* once described him as "A sturdy, square-built soldier-like figure, he has a cheery face and is of sanguine temperament, full of 'pawky' Scotch humour, loves a joke, and will laugh in his lighter moments with a loud boyish glee that is quite infectious. But he has a sterner side to his character . . .".

This eminently Victorian figure not only ran the place with parade-ground efficiency: he was, perhaps above all, responsible for the establishment of the famous Lloyd's Signal Stations.

Realising that a system of signal stations equipped with telegraphic equipment would be of the greatest value in centralising shipping news,

Above: *drawing of Sir Henry Hozier, Secretary of Lloyd's from 1874–1906.*

Below: *William Farrant, former railway porter, who became Lloyd's most famous Caller. His magnificent voice echoed round the Room for thirty-four years.*

he began to snap up all the stations that were already functioning (starting with the Lizard) and then bought land at strategic sites to erect new ones. At one moment Lloyd's had forty stations in the British Isles under its direct control, and agreements with a hundred others in overseas territories. From Penzance to Flamborough Head, and from Ramsey to Southend, the coastwise watchers hailed and signalled all passing ships, with semaphores by day and light signals by night, and transmitted their messages to Lloyd's.

This was, of course, before Sir Oliver Lodge and Signor Marconi had pioneered the use of wireless telegraphy. But Henry Hozier was not slow to grasp its significance either: in 1901 he became a director of one of Marconi's companies and came to an agreement for Lloyd's stations to handle ship-to-shore messages, until the Postmaster General, Lord Buxton (whose ancestor Fowell Buxton had fought Lloyd's in 1810) withdrew the Corporation's wireless licence and made what Hozier considered to be a derogatory remark about him in the House.

Interpreting it as an attack on his honour, Sir Henry called in his secretary and dictated a letter to the Postmaster General, challenging him to a duel. The venue, he suggested, should be somewhere in France.

Although the challenge was not accepted, it rounded off the story. For if Lloyd's first great Secretary was appointed as the result of a snub from Whitehall, her other great Secretary resigned because of one too.

C.E. HEATH AND THE GROWTH OF NON-MARINE INSURANCE AT LLOYD'S

BY THE EARLY 1880s a noticeable change was coming over London. The earnest gusto of Victorian material success was blossoming into a taste for luxury and indeed ostentation. Apart from such minor annoyances as Irish Home Rule and Socialist agitation, all was well with the state of the nation. Or so at least it seemed. Queen Victoria was Empress of India, the titular head of the greatest and probably the most glamorous empire ever known, and if Dizzie had taken his bow, Mr Gladstone and Lord Salisbury alternately ensured that Britannia continued to rule the waves. To aristocrat and entrepreneur alike, a sunny vista of progress and prosperity stretched endlessly ahead. Perceptibly the corsets began to loosen, the restraints to diminish, and a new, more extravagant atmosphere crept in as chop-houses turned into restaurants and music halls and theatres sprang up like spring flowers. The success of the Lyceum under the princely domination of Henry Irving encouraged first the Savoy opera and then

Above: *drawing of Cuthbert Eden Heath, published in the "Financial Times." Heath was a pioneer of several forms of non-marine insurance at Lloyd's, including fire and theft.*

the Savoy Hotel to come into being, and down in the City – where Mr Punch, after a visit to the Room, had dismissed Lloyd's rather nostalgically as a picturesque survival from the past – underwriters got a much needed shot in the arm.

For to be candid, at this particular juncture, although risk cover was by no means lacking, it was being handled in so stodgy and hidebound a fashion that a great deal of the important business was quietly being siphoned away by the companies. In fact such an inhibiting desire for caution had overtaken the Room that outside the world of shipping little was now to be heard of Lloyd's, and but for the activity of a handful of venturesome underwriters – such as F.W. Marten – there was every indication that Lloyd's was in danger of becoming a past number.

But once again destiny was beckoning. An Admiral's son, who had failed his medical test for the navy, opened a vast new horizon for the coffee-house, and by his experience and achievements in fire and accident insurance blueprinted a pattern of activity which was to revolutionise private underwriting and bring renewed prosperity to the Room. Until 1885 Lloyd's had concentrated on marine insurance. Cuthbert Eden Heath made it the place where (in theory if not always in practice) any risk of any type could be covered. Thanks to his vision, modern Lloyd's emerged as the world centre of risk insurance.

C.E. Heath received his early training in the office of Henry Head and Company, prior to becoming an underwriting member in 1880. When he was elected to the Room, the non-marine market at Lloyd's was hardly more than a sideline for a few underwriters who supplemented their marine business with some fire risks on buildings and equipment. But, as it happened, Admiral Heath was a director of the Hand in Hand (the first purely mutual Fire Company to have been established in England) which, being non-tariff, was having trouble reinsuring its fire business with the companies and their closely banded tariff association. Although the Committee (harking back perhaps to the days of the wager policies) tended to sniff at anything non-marine, there was nothing in the rules that specifically prohibited it. Acting for himself and two others, Heath took his father's business, boosted his premium income beyond all expectations, and, to the dismay of the tariff companies, even began writing policies which covered a loss of profit from fire.

"The business covered at Lloyd's was practically all marine at that time" he later said in an interview. "In 1882 I began to underwrite for myself, and I soon realised the possibilities and the need for extension. Fire claimed my attention, and the first business of any magnitude was a reinsurance contract with the Hand in Hand, which I accepted in 1884. Others were soon induced to come in with me, notwithstanding the marked general disinclination to do this business. Fire insurance began to increase, and I felt that as our expenses were so low we could afford to write this business at tariff rates and make a profit even on second-rate risks."

They were placing bets in the Room, he added, on how long it would take to see him in Carey Street. But far from ruining the fire business, as the pessimists predicted, his innovations caused a revolution which was to regenerate Lloyd's. The diehards might hate it, but he was breaking into fresh ground all the time. And he did not have far to look.

Encouraged by the exploits of Charlie Peace, a new type of criminal was on the prowl, and in the eighties armed break-ins became so frequent that Londoners began speaking of "the burglary season". But while other people discussed plans for arming the police force and forming a corps of *vigilantes*, Heath acted. A broker who was placing a fire insurance on the contents of his house asked him – more as a joke than anything else – whether he would cover him against burglary as well. Heath did, and the first burglary policy was written (the rates came to vary from 2s 6d percent to 5s percent, according to circumstances). Later, when a relative lost her jewellery, which was ensured against theft, but not against loss, he got the idea of covering personal property against deprivation from any cause whatsoever. Thus the "all risks" policy was born, and the rate he quoted of $\frac{1}{2}$ percent remained standard for the next fifty years.

Rather in the same way, when the accountant of a Holborn diamond merchant became worried about the risk his employer was taking as he carried his stock around to show customers, Heath quoted a premium to insure the stock wherever it might be. The accountant was so impressed that he told other diamond merchants and became a broker specialising in jewellers' "block policies" (he ended up as a Name on Heath's syndicate). From that moment onwards, most dealers in precious stones throughout the world have protected themselves by these special "block policies" placed at Lloyd's.

Nor was this by any means the end of his diversification. Always with an eye open for new outlets, Heath soon spotted the growing possibilities of the accident insurance market. In 1880 the first Employer's Liability Act had been passed, but it was really Austin Chamberlain's Workman's Compensation Act of 1897 that turned this into an important growth business. In the meantime, Cuthbert Heath had pioneered the way, and even by 1892 the volume of non-marine insurance being placed at Lloyd's through his initiative had increased to such an extent that the Committee had to issue a warning. Deposits and guarantees lodged with them by underwriting members as security

Above: *Charlie Peace, the notorious Victorian burglar whose activities largely accelerated public demand for Heath's new theft policies.*

We the undersigned underwriting members would agree to hand in to the Committee of Lloyds annually a statement signed by an approved accountant that we were in possession of assets reasonably sufficient to wind up our underwriting accounts.

We suggest that a Committee should be appointed to consider the best method of carrying out the above proposal.

Names	Suggestions
John ? Dawson	
B ? ?	
Geo H. Faber	
? W ?	
Albert ? Read	Provided the suggestion is generally adopted.
? ?	— do —
C. E Heath	
A. ? White	
? ?	do.
Charles ? ?	
B. R. Fleming	
John Fleming	
? ?	
Raymond ?	
Edward Hicks	That statement may be called for any time.
? Poole	
? ?	
H. ?	
Alfred Faber	
George ?	
? ?	

Above: *C. E. Heath's Audit 'manifesto' drawn up by him in 1908 and signed by forty-two leading underwriting agents. An important stage in the campaign for a compulsory audit.*

Opposite: *the end of the Cromdale, one of the last cargo ships under sail, off the Lizard.*

AT LLOYD'S.—WHERE "AN ILL WIND BLOWS NOBODY GOOD."

Above: *a fraught moment at Lloyd's caught by the
famous* Punch *cartoonist Harry Furniss in 1893.*

Above: *cheers greet the announcement in 1890 that the Room will in future close earlier on Saturdays.*

for their individual liabilities could only, they cautioned, be applied to marine and transit claims.

But by now the possibilities of the non-marine market were so clear that not only the marine underwriters, but also newcomers from outside, were anxious to secure a footing in such potentially rewarding profit-centres. And because neither the marine underwriters nor the outsiders could claim any special knowledge of these new markets, a significant change in underwriting took place. The "underwriting agent" made his appearance in the Room, and with him came the "Name".

In its simplest definition, an underwriting agent is an underwriter who writes a line for another member of Lloyd's. Hitherto, it had been each man for himself. But now, with interests widening and bifurcating into new directions, the need for specialised knowledge led a man to approach a successful underwriter like Heath and ask him to accept risks on their behalf and to take a commission for doing so. Thus the underwriting agent came into being. It was a logical development. By spreading the risk, it enabled the underwriter to transact a greater volume of business than he could if writing for himself alone, and for other members to take advantage of his knowledge and success. The risk-writing remained in his hands; the others were merely sleeping partners who put up the money for the business. They were the Names, he their Agent – each individually responsible for his share of the risks.

In this way syndicates were formed. At first they were small; but when traditional marine underwriters, observing the success of these non-marine syndicates, began to offer themselves as Names to the underwriting agents who specialised in non-marine business, the little groups became bigger. Having started with three or four Names (rarely more than six or seven) they expanded progressively to a dozen or twenty and in some cases even thirty Names in a single syndicate, and during the course of the 20th century have continued to escalate, so that today several of the larger syndicates have over 400 Names.

For underwriters, Heath's pioneering efforts represented a clear turning point in their fortunes. But for his resourcefulness (and the deafness which kept him out of the Navy) Lloyd's might very well have remained, as the 1871 Charter intended, purely and simply a corporation for marine insurance. Cuthbert Eden Heath changed all this. And, since a significant proportion of today's £750 million premium income can historically be traced to his vision and initiative, he is rightly toasted, on festive occasions, as "The Father of Modern Lloyd's".

MODERN
LLOYD'S

On previous page: *an early biplane in flight over Southern England. Lloyd's were the first to issue a standard aviation policy—the 'White Wings' policy in 1911.*

RELATIONS WITH THE USA

ONE OF THE enduring testaments to the conspicuous success of Lloyd's in the 20th century has been the progressive stengthening of links between London and the American insurance market. Volume of transatlantic business has expanded so phenomenally over the past seventy years that today American premium income accounts for about half the yearly turnover at Lloyd's – a billion dollars, in fact. If anyone is tempted to put this down solely to affinity of language or culture, let him consider briefly the chequered course of Anglo-American relations since the days when underwriters were cursing the very name of John Paul Jones.

The loss of the American colonies had, as Fox, Burke and the other opponents of the war of 1775–81 had predicted, a profound effect on the pattern of British trade. Gone now were the captive and lucrative markets at Boston and Philadelphia and Charleston (where, for the first time almost in living memory French merchantmen were welcome). In the bitterness of defeat, Britain watched the infant republic – no longer shackled by the exigencies of the old Navigation Acts – search out its own markets, fight its own battles with Barbary pirates, and sell its own cotton and tobacco without dutifully lugging it over to Britain for re-export. Whereas British ships had been re-exporting nearly 300 million lbs of American tobacco in the palmy days before Independence, this trade had shrunk by the end of the 18th century to little more than one million lbs.

Nor were the early years of the 19th century conducive to repairing the damage done by George III and his crony Lord North. Memories, on both sides of the Atlantic, were long. As undisputed lord of the seas, Britain had no intention of allowing American firms to trade with their French enemy: between 1804 and 1807 alone more than 1,000 US merchant ships were confiscated or sunk by the Royal Navy for what was (in the eyes of Whitehall at any rate) illegal trading. Thomas Jefferson's response, the Embargo Act of 1807 forbidding British ships to enter American harbours, did not in fact as expected ruin British trade – if anything it ruined American ports. By 1812 the reaction was inevitable: America declared war on Britain, already at full stretch trying to deal with her Continental foes.

The stirring news that in August 1814 a British force had succeeded in burning both the Capitol and the White House in Washington would have been poor consolation to members at Lloyd's that year, as they scanned the bulletin boards. Hardly a day dawned but reports arrived of yet another British merchantman lost to the accuracy of the American gunners. In thirty months of war American privateers put paid to 1,300 British ships and cargoes valued at forty million dollars. Only the end of the war in Europe, and Castlereagh's enlightened diplomacy, put a stop to the carnage and established a basis for future friendly relations. The spirit of reconciliation survived even President Polk's war-cry in 1844 "Fifty-four forty or fight" (*i.e.* American annexation of all the Pacific coastline as far north as Alaska at the latitude of 54°40′, thus unthinkingly cutting off Canada from the sea). If nothing else the unpleasantness of the war of 1812 had shown that no one was the winner, when the Atlantic was in dispute.

It was all the more unfortunate, therefore, that when the American Civil War broke out in 1861, politicians and merchants alike should have backed the wrong horse. There was no lack of sympathy in Britain, of course, for the North from radicals like John Bright, but precious little in the City (however embarrassing individuals might find the slavery issue). This, and the fact that support for the rebellious South was so uncompromisingly articulated by no less an organ than *The Times*, made it appear that Britain was perhaps more Southern than she was. "The Yankees are cowards" fulminated *The Times*, and wondered why its eminent special correspondent William Russell was cold-shouldered all the way back home by the federal authorities. It might well, indeed, have come to outright war, with Britain smouldering at the unmitigated insult of having two confederate commissioners forcibly removed from a British ship, and the Union deeper and deeper alienated by the depredations of the privateer *Alabama*, which had somehow been allowed to "escape" from custody in Liverpool.

As it was, the legacy of this unhappy partisanship dogged the heels of successive British ministries long after Lee's armies had downed their arms at Appomattox Courthouse in 1865. Claims for compensation over the *Alabama*, amounting to fifteen million dollars, dragged on for ten years until they were paid honourably and in full by Mr Gladstone in 1872. A prompt settlement it may not have been, but it was one well appreciated by American men of business (at a time when businessmen were forging the destiny of a great country). Within a year or two American companies – encouraged wholeheartedly by the steamship lines – were advertising heavily in Britain for emigrants: Northern Pacific Railroad urging the bargain prices of land in Minnesota, Union Pacific offering the blandishments of the sunnier climate of California. Such was the response that a few years later Thomas Cook was supplying special folders for Chicago, St Paul and other rapidly expanding American cities; a century of mutual suspicion, originally engendered by armies of redcoats, was rapidly being broken down by new armies of settlers. By the end of the century, not even a grave diplo-

Above: *The Yankee Torpedo, a satire of the Anglo-US war of 1812, showing the havoc wreaked by the new American torpedo developed by Robert Fulton.*

matic crisis over Venezuela (where both Britain and America claimed influence) in 1895 could seriously dent the growing affinity of the two English-speaking nations.

By the turn of the century the United States was indisputably rich, booming and insurance-minded. The Morgans, the Vanderbilts, the Carnegies and Harrimans had built up their massive empires, and now that Lloyd's had begun to offer non-marine cover, they were glad to look to the London market for those hand-tailored fire risks that were beyond the scope of their domestic concerns – if indeed much confidence remained in American companies after Pulitzer's muck-raking *World* exposed the scandalous deficiencies of the Equitable Life Assurance in 1905.

Lloyd's gave these blossoming American tycoons the type of shelter they wanted, and they took it with both hands and premium-income figures rocketed. Before long Lloyd's became so well known in the States that its name was soon plagiarised by a series of bucket-shop dealers who jumped on the bandwagon and styled themselves "Lloyd's", without having the slightest connection with the London underwriters. This abuse grew to the point that legislation against it had to be introduced; but on the very day before it was passed no less than thirty concerns in New York alone registered themselves under the trademark of Lloyd's. A decade later some of them were still circulating imitation policies, not a few even bearing the anchor.

(In 1936 Neville Dixey, then Chairman of Lloyd's, had to make new arrangements to reconcile the Corporation's position under American law, and to enable the genuine Lloyd's to continue its operations across the Atlantic. Indeed to satisfy American claims, Lloyd's set up the American Trust Fund, financed from local premium income, which now involves something like a billion dollars in cash and US Government securities.)

In due course the actual word Lloyd's came to enter the American vocabulary and became, even in legal pronouncements such as the Illinois Code of 1935, a noun to designate, roughly speaking, the technique of private as opposed to company underwriting. (Even today in the United States it is necessary when referring to the London market to speak of Lloyd's of London*.) That such a formidable reputation grew up in the States was not, of course, entirely fortuitous. But that it happened in such a short space of time was the result of Lloyd's prompt and honourable settlement of claims arising from a disaster which stirred America's heart to the depths.

THE SAN FRANCISCO EARTHQUAKE

THAT NIGHT ENRICO Caruso was appearing as Don José in *Carmen*, and all the nobs of Nob Hill had turned up to hear the vibrant tones of the best voice in the business. Nor were they disappointed. Indeed, when the final curtain fell, the socialites of America's most glamorous and cosmopolitan city raised the roof of their old opera house with cheers.

By midnight they had moved to the Palace Hotel, where some of the supper parties lasted until dawn. It was then that it happened. At precisely 05.12.12 in the morning of 18 April 1906 the earth suddenly writhed and heaved, cracks appeared in the streets, tramlines buckled, water geysered into the air from ruptured mains, and buildings crashed in a shower of dust and splinters. For forty-eight incredible seconds the earthquake went on. It rose (thought William James the philosopher) from crescendo to fortiore to fortissimo, which to the more trained musical ear of Alfred Hertz had "an uncanny mezzo-forte effect – something comparable to the mezzo-forte roll on a cymbal or gong".

An eerie silence followed, and then pandemonium. Guided by columns of smoke, the horse-drawn fire engines rushed to deal with fires which had been started by upturned lamps and stoves. But since the mains had snapped, the hydrants were dry; and by breakfast time the flames were spreading through much of the downtown area. The army was called out, but against a raging inferno there was little to be done without water.

Soon a mass exodus from the city began: wagons, carts, prams – anything on wheels was pressed into service. Among them were some Italians with two carts piled high with oranges. Hidden underneath the fruit was over 80,000 dollars in gold. The manager of the Bank of Italy, at least, was managing to save his cash.

But in truth not much else was saved in San Francisco as the fire swirled through the city and building after building went up in flames. "San Francisco in ruins . . . dynamite used in vain to check the flames" reported the 'World' on 19 April. The following morning its headlines divulged that the flames had swept uptown into the wealthy district, destroying "the magnificent mansions of Nob Hill. . . . First estimates put the loss of lives at over 1,800 and nearly 300 million dollars of damage to property". Over on the East Coast, Wall Street plunged. It was one of the greatest disasters America had ever experienced.

Initial press reports indicated that while there might be millions for fire claims, there was not a cent of cover for earthquake damage; the owners of property destroyed by the earthquake would not be able to collect a dollar under their insurance policies, even though the buildings that fell were later swept by fire.

On the other hand, if "a structure shattered by the seismic disturbance should spread a blaze to an adjoining building, the owner of that building

*The name of Lloyd's has also found its way into the titles of a number of distinguished companies in Europe concerned with shipping and insurance: Lloyd Adriatico, Lloyd Triestino, Hapag-Lloyd, Rotterdamsche Lloyd, Svenska Lloyd, among others.

Weather Forecast: SHOWERS

A Trinity of Triumphs!

4,145	868
World Wants Yesterday!	More Than Same Day Last Year!

967

More Than Any Other New York Newspaper!

The World.

" Circulation Books Open to All."   " Circulation Books Open to All."

12 New Americans a Minute!
The Greatest of all Tidal Waves of Immigration.
Full-Page Photograph in Next Sunday's World.

VOL. XLVI. NO. 16,319.   Copyright, 1906, by the Press Publishing Company, New York World.   **NEW YORK, THURSDAY, APRIL 26, 1906.**   PRICE ONE CENT in Greater New York and Jersey City. TWO CENTS outside of Greater New York and Jersey City and on trains.

PROGRESS OF THE FLAMES ALONG MARKET STREET, IN THE BUSINESS SECTION OF SAN FRANCISCO, WITH THE EFFECT OF THE EARTHQUAKE SHOWN IN MANY BUILDINGS.

VIEW of the CENTRAL PART of SAN FRANCISCO, showing the FIRE BURNING UP MARKET and MISSION Sts. WORK of the EARTHQUAKE is SHOWN by FALLEN CHIMNEYS. EMPORIUM. ST. FRANCIS HOTEL. OLIVER HOTEL. Photo Copyright by Judge Publishing Co. 1906.

BDUCTS HER SON IN AN AUTOMOBILE.

Strange Case of Odd Fellows' Home Boy Made Stranger by Mother's Act.

An automobile going at great speed toward New York a woman in a stunning gown and a hat with flowing plumes might have been seen at 5 P. M. yesterday on the road from Yonkers, the Bronx. She held in her lap a boy of nine years from South Da-...

ASTOR-SHAW WEDDING IS DELAYED BY U. S. COURT.

Arrangements Had All Been Made for Ceremony Last Saturday, When Supreme Bench's Divorce Decision Upset Everything.

(Copyright, 1906, by the Press Publishing Company, New York World.)
(Special Cable Dispatch to The World.)

LONDON, April 25.—Reports that Mrs. Nannie Langhorne Shaw and William Waldorf Astor, Jr., were married last week were unfounded.

The World correspondent is now informed that all preparations had been made for a wedding last Saturday, in the least conspicuous manner possible, but the divorce decision of the United States Supreme Court upset all arrangements. The legality of Mrs. Shaw's divorce may be affected by the decision, so the marriage is indefinitely postponed.

CHILDREN BATTLE WITH ANGRY BOSTON TERRIER.

It Flies at Them in Riverside Drive Park and Bites and Lacerates Two of Them—Beaten Off with Sticks and Stones, It Is Chased to Its Home.

A Boston bull terrier owned by August Hall, a broker, of No. 315 West Ninety-eighth street, attacked some children who were coasting it to join in their games in Riverside Park, at Ninety-eighth street, late yesterday afternoon, and bit two of them before it was put to flight with sticks and stones.

ANOTHER EARTHQUAKE SHOCK RENEWS PANIC IN THE STRICKEN CITY.

Damaged Walls in 'Frisco and Oakland Hurled Down — Frightened People Leave Hotels and Exodus Begins Anew—Relief Work Well in Hand.

By JOHN FAY,
Staff Correspondent of The World.
(Special to The World.)

SAN FRANCISCO, April 25.—An earthquake shock of a few seconds' duration brought down a hundred tottering walls and incited new panic in the camps in the western addition and in Oakland at 3.30 o'clock this afternoon.

The earth's movement was a vigorous one from southwest to northeast.

Many thousands who had made up their minds to remain in the camps are to-night preparing to cross the bay.

In Oakland the people ran out of their homes and many men repairing buildings quit work. In the hotels women screamed and fled downstairs to the street. No apparent damage was done.

Cornices and chimneys shattered a week ago were again set in motion and fell to the street.

The absorbing questions are: "When will the convulsions cease?" "What will be the end?"

Word comes from Lick Observatory and will be well. But this bulletin does that they will soon cease and that the not instil confidence for the people put...

SAVE FIVE DOLLARS TO-DAY

On Your Clothing Purchase.

BASHFUL BOY A SUICIDE.

Young Andrews Couldn't Muster Nerve to Graduate with Girls.

(Special to The World.)

OXFORD, Pa., April 25.—Sixteen-year-old James Andrews, the only boy in a class of seven, committed suicide rather than graduate with girls. His body was found in White Clay creek, where he had drowned himself in about four feet of water. His coat pockets were filled with flatirons and stones.

134

Opposite: *The San Francisco earthquake of 1906, as described in the* New York World. *The promptness with which Lloyd's underwriters met their commitments after the disaster compared very favourably with the procrastination of American insurance companies, and vastly increased the prestige of Lloyd's in the USA.*

could collect his insurance". Yet once a structure had been shaken down by the earthquake, the insurers were not liable. It was a ticklish distinction and six weeks later, on 7 June, the headlines in the San Francisco *Chronicle* insisted that "Insurance Companies must show their hands".

Some of the American Companies, by then, had already accepted the losses. They were following the lead given by Lloyd's underwriters in London who, disregarding the small print on their policies, had begun paying out claims within a week of the catastrophe. By doing so, they established an immense fund of goodwill. The non-marine side of Lloyd's had already made considerable progress in the United States during the previous decade. By its prompt action in meeting claims overnight at San Francisco, Lloyd's laid the foundation of the tremendous prestige that the corporation enjoys in the American market.

EDWARDIAN DEVELOPMENTS

FOR SO LONG the figurehead of the nation had mourned, reclusive. And then, as the new century opened, dustsheets were removed from the furniture in Buckingham Palace and Windsor Castle, and a new, gilt-tinted epoch began. The king of *bonviveurs*, of whom Disraeli as far back as 1881 had said "He has seen everything and known everybody" was on the throne.

A true cosmopolitan, Edward VII set out to dispel the notion that England was insular. Hereditary Princes of the Empire and Russian Grand Dukes formed the shimmering accompaniment to his European travels. Each month had its own well defined destination: Biarritz in March; Paris in April; London in May; Ascot in June; Cowes in August; Marienbad in September; Balmoral in October. It was all delightful and frivolous, if a trifle middle-aged; but Society, patrician and well provided with the world's goods, hastened to follow the monarch's example, and neither Ibsen nor Marx nor Bernard Shaw and the Fabians could do much to dent its amiable but complacent mores.

At Lloyd's, however, the vibrations were different. For one thing, the marine market was once again passing through an unprofitable period. For another, the new trend towards writing in syndicates meant that underwriting agents, unintentionally or otherwise, could misuse their syndicate funds. And on top of all this, some underwriters – following Heath's example but lacking his touch – were branching into risks that ended in red ink.

In 1903 an unpleasant scandal blew up around the failure of the Burnand syndicate. The press were openly critical about the financial back-up to a Lloyd's policy, and the future of Lloyd's as a

THE RACE OF DEATH!

Above: *The Race of Death (1903), a comment from* Punch *on the perils of motoring. In that year a speed limit of 20 m.p.h. for motor cars was introduced.*

whole. Indeed *The Times*, in an article, suggested that Lloyd's had outstripped its underwriting deposits, and that to safeguard its credit, an audit was mandatory.

Not everyone agreed. One influential underwriter called the suggestion "inquisitorial, oppressive, offensive, and disgustingly insulting". But Heath thought otherwise. Picking up a handy sheet of paper, he wrote down a resolution in a few lines and secured a round-robin agreement, signed by forty-two underwriting agents, in favour of a compulsory audit. At the next general meeting, the proposal was unanimously approved. From this point on, all premiums had to be held in trust, and underwriters were required to submit each year to a solvency audit.

But, essential as they were, administrative reforms were not all. Equally significant was the dramatic eclipse of steam in favour of the internal combustion engine, and, although the motor car (and subsequently the flying machine) were whims of the wealthy, they opened new vistas for the insurance market.

Already by 1904 a syndicate at Lloyd's was pioneering a comprehensive policy for cars, on the basis of £1 premium per year for each horse-power; and in due course garages around the country were designated as "official repairers". But while to the general public the marine and non-marine syndicates were virtually anonymous, and certainly nothing more than initials under the magic umbrella of a Lloyd's policy (which could only be negotiated through the filter of a Lloyd's broker) the motor syndicates broke with tradition and adopted eye-catching names, such as Red Star, Kinloch Motor Policies, to be more easily identifiable by the motorist, even if he still placed his business through the Lloyd's broker. All the same, these motor syndicates tended to cater for the local rather than the international market, and they still remain a cosy specialised corner of the Room, covering only a small percentage of the global motor business.

With aviation, however, it was a different story.

EARLY AVIATION

NOTWITHSTANDING ROGER BACON's predictions in the 13th century of "... instruments to fly withall, so that one sitting in the middle of the instrument, and turning an engine, by which the wings being artifically composed may beat the air after the manner of a flying bird. . . ." there were few visionaries on the brink of the 20th century who seriously thought the future of aerial flying lay in the kind of steam-driven monstrosity of steel and silk that Hiram Maxim (better known for his other lethal invention the machine-gun) was championing. As

"THREE CHEERS FOR THE QUEEN!" THE SCENE AT LLOYD'S AFTER THE SINGING OF THE NATIONAL ANTHEM.

Above: *patriotic sentiments in the Room on the occasion of Queen Victoria's birthday in 1900.*

early as 1894 he had launched his edifice along half a mile of special railway track, so constructed as to actually prevent the machine from taking off. As it was, the plane (if such it could be called) tore up the track and plunged riotously through the barrier.

The gentler art of powered ballooning was precarious enough, heaven knew. (Hadn't that crazy Brazilian Santos-Dumont blown up himself and his airship in 1901, trying to fly round the Eiffel Tower, and landed ignominiously on top of the Trocadero?) Yet those pioneering aeronauts were made of sterner stuff than their flimsy machines: Santos-Dumont very soon did succeed in bucketing his way round the Paris landmark, and in so doing inspired a host of other inventors to greater heights. One of these was Samuel Pierpont Langley, a professor at the Smithsonian Institution in Washington. By the autumn of 1903 he was confident enough of the success of his model aeroplanes to invite a crowd of observers and journalists to inspect the first trial of his new, full-size *Aerodrome*. Sadly for his admirable convictions, the Langley flying-machine, catapulted from the roof of a houseboat moored on the Potomac River, did not soar magnificently into the clouds as scheduled – it sank magnificently beneath the waves.

Within months, however, of this all-too-public spectacle, two brothers, bicycle mechanics by trade, had achieved the astonishing feat of staying aloft for no less than fifty-nine seconds, with only a handful of mildly curious locals at hand to watch. So modest in fact had been their meticulous experiments (as they continued to be for several years) that the vast majority of American papers totally ignored the historic flights of Orville and Wilbur Wright along the sands of Kitty Hawk, on the coast of North Carolina. (After their very first historic flight lasting about twelve seconds, a gust of wind caught the plane, turning it over and over; some of the struts were broken and the fabric on one wing had to be renewed – a part of the old fabric somehow found its way to the library at Lloyd's where it is now a prized exhibit.) Scepticism in Europe when the news finally reached there was even more deep-rooted – understandably perhaps, for it was the autumn of 1906 before anyone on that side of the Atlantic (Santos-Dumont once again) contrived to bounce a heavier-than-air machine more than a few feet into the air.

Even then, one London newspaper was rash enough to offer a satirical prize of £10,000,000 to the first man to fly five miles (it is not recorded whether anyone was bold enough to inform them that the Wright Brothers had already done just that). And such were the prevailing public sentiments until the day in January 1907 when Henri Farman triumphantly completed a circular kilometre before the assembled committee of the Aero Club of France. In Britain, in spite of a princely offer of £10,000 for the first London–Manchester flight by the *Daily Mail*, aeronautical progress was, in every sense, pedestrian. Northcliffe's glittering prize hung tantalisingly before the eyes of British pioneers for four years, as they fumed under the futility of trying to urge their ignorant contraptions into flight – indeed until 1910 when it was snatched away by another Frenchman, Louis Paulhan.

By then, aeronautics, even in Britain, had advanced beyond all recognition. Colonel Cody (a naturalised Briton from Texas) had quit his travelling Wild West road-show, unhitched his incredible *Flying Cathedral* from an oak tree at Farnborough one morning in May 1909, and proceeded to make the first official flight in England, of four miles no less. Louis Bleriot had steered his monoplane through the dawn mist on July 25th the same year, from a hangar at Les Baragues to a field outside Dover, then strolled off into town for his *petit déjeuner*. At Rheims the first organised flying meeting had already been held, at which the American ace Glen Curtiss had walked away with the first Gordon Bennett speed prize, at a velocity in excess of forty-six miles an hour!

The success of the Rheims competition not only established aviation as a popular spectator sport, but as an infinitely more dangerous pursuit – as each flying star attempted more and more spectacular exploits to thrill the huge gawking crowds. 1909–10 exacted a particularly high toll of these daring young men performing at often foolhardy public exhibitions, among them many of the most famous: the Frenchmen Lefévre, Delagrange and Le Blon; Americans Johnstone and Moisant, to name only a few. The earliest experimenters, to be sure, had courted death and disaster every time they perched themselves atop (or under) a machine as apt to crumple like matchsticks as to get airborne. But they had performed on secluded airfields, pulled themselves bruised or battered from the wreckage, and dug philosophically into their own pockets (or their sponsors') for yet another try.

The first British meetings, held at Blackpool and Doncaster in the autumn of 1909, vividly demonstrated if nothing else the imminent perils of these public spectacles. At Doncaster in particular only the courage of Hubert Le Blon prevented his machine being sucked by the rising wind straight into the milling mass of people in front of the grandstand: at the risk of his own life, he contrived to crash-land his Bleriot only yards behind the stand and save countless lives. Organisers hastened to provide themselves with some sort of cover against the doings of these madcap birdmen, and before the end of 1910 Lloyd's had accepted their first third-party aviation risk. One of the first (if not the very first) to be taken out was to cover the London–Manchester prize flight in the spring – a wise pre-

NIGHTMARE OF A NEGROPUDLIAN AFTER THE BLACKPOOL FLYING WEEK.

Above: Punch's *report on the aerial antics of Blackpool Flying week in 1909. After several near-disasters at such early meetings, organisers rushed to take out third-party cover at Lloyd's.*

On page 140: *the front page of the* Daily Graphic *after Bleriot's historic flight across the English Channel in July 1909.*

On page 141: New York Herald *report of the Statue of Liberty air race in October 1910. The race was later awarded to the Englishman Claud Graham-White— two years later—after it had been proved that Moisant took off too late to qualify for the race.*

THE DAILY GRAPHIC, JULY 26, 1909.

HOW I FLEW ACROSS THE CHANNEL: BY M. BLERIOT. (See Page 7.)

THE DAILY GRAPHIC
ONE PENNY

LONDON: MONDAY, JULY 26, 1909.

No. 6.22.—Vol. LXXIX.   Registered as a Newspaper.

BRAVO BLERIOT!

M. BLERIOT AND HIS MONOPLANE, IN WHICH HE YESTERDAY ACCOMPLISHED THE FIRST CROSS CHANNEL FLIGHT BY A "HEAVIER-THAN-AIR" MACHINE. THE FLIGHT FROM BARAQUES, NEAR CALAIS, TO DOVER OCCUPIED TWENTY-THREE MINUTES.

THE NEW YORK HERALD.

NEW YORK, MONDAY, OCTOBER 31, 1910.—EIGHTEEN PAGES.— BY THE NEW YORK HERALD COMPANY.]

MR. MOISANT, AMERICAN, WINS STATUE OF LIBERTY FLIGHT BY 43 SECONDS; THREE AERIAL RACERS SOAR OVER BAY

COUNT JACQUES DE LESSEPS JUST AFTER HIS FLIGHT.

CORTLANDT F. BISHOP AND CLAUDE GRAHAME-WHITE.

MISS LOUISE MOISANT, JOHN B. MOISANT AND MISS TILLIE MOISANT.

Triumph Over English Racer in Face of Seeming Defeat

In Blériot Monoplane, Purchased for $10,000 When His Own Is Smashed, Daring Aviator Gains the Prize by Narrow Margin.

PLAUDITS OF 75,000 RESOUND AT BELMONT

Aeroplane Battle for Supremacy Witnessed by a Million Persons, Who See Winged Competitors Fly Over the City and the Harbor.

RESULTS OF CONTESTS AT BELMONT

CLAUDE GRAHAME-WHITE ROUNDING THE STATUE OF LIBERTY.

J B MOISANT PASSING CAPTIVE BALLOON GOING WEST

Speed of Mile a Minute Kept Up for Entire Course

Mr. Grahame-White, Flying Over Coney Island, Covers Longer Route Than Victor in Thrilling Contest.

COMTE DE LESSEPS IN GALLANT STRUGGLE

His Fifty Horse Power Machine Unable to Cope with Rival's —New Record Is Made in Hourly Distance Contest of the Tournament.

PROGRAMME AT BELMONT TO-DAY

THE HERALD'S ANNUAL POLITICAL FORECAST OUT NEXT SUNDAY, NOV. 6

caution as it turned out. At his first attempt in April, Claud Graham-White barely managed to ditch his Bleriot on a railway embankment in Lichfield. His second effort a few days later developed into a race against the sardonic Frenchman, Louis Paulhan, and found him grimly attempting to fly by the light of the moon and the headlamps of his motor cavalcade below. (Once again he was forced down, and discovered hanging onto his wingtips for dear life trying to prevent the machine being blown away.)

Over in Egypt, meanwhile, a prize of £1,000 was being offered to the first person to fly from Heliopolis around the Pyramids and back. Undeterred that a man named Singer had already come to grief in the attempt, Edmund Flower (father of the co-author) ordered a plane from Santos-Dumont, a condition being that the Brazilian aviator first proved its paces by an hour's demonstration flight. Predictably, Santos-Dumont crashed the aircraft; and, on the advice of his engineer, Edmund Flower ordered a Panhard Levassor monoplane instead, which he took out each morning, swinging the propeller himself as the natives, understandably enough, were scared to go near it. By doing first a hop, and then a bigger one – rather like a bird from its nest – he learnt to fly. But just before he was due to try and circle the Pyramids, a violent sandstorm blew the shed housing the Panhard to bits and reduced it to a mass of wreckage – which probably increased his life-expectancy by some 57 years (though depriving him of a small niche in aviation's story) and illustrates the sort of hazard with which underwriters were faced in this pioneering period.

Lloyd's first standardised aviation policy – the "White Wings" policy (still to be seen in the library) – came into existence the following year. Although the planes themselves were uninsurable, a number of owners took out cover at Lloyd's for third-party liability – as well they might, with their machines landing as and where they could, much to the disturbance of irate farmers counting the cost, not only of the plane's damage to their crops but also of that done by the hordes of local sightseers who invariably converged on the plane.

Indeed Lloyd's underwriters, in those infant years, often showed no less daring and enterprise than the aviators. When it was announced by the Belmont Park (New York) authorities that the showpiece of their October 1910 meeting would be a flight round the Statue of Liberty and back, insurance companies in America refused one and all to insure the organisers for any kind of liability. The chosen flight-path was indeed hazardous, crossing as it did large expanses of densely populated Brooklyn. But Lloyd's declared themselves prepared to issue a £100,000 policy – at a premium of no more than £500. As if a reward for the underwriters' initiative, the great event was won by

Graham-White (though only after two drawn-out years of official investigations, which determined that the original winner, John Moisant, had taken off too late to qualify). In 1912, in fact, some underwriters were emboldened to offer cover on a number of aircraft taking part in military trials on Salisbury Plain. But the weather was appalling and crashes were ten-a-penny, and most underwriters having got their fingers burnt were disinclined to accept similar risks before the war broke out and transformed the future of flying.

THE SINKING OF THE TITANIC

LAUNCHED ON 31 May 1911, the 44,000-ton *Titanic* with her four great funnels was the greatest ship afloat. According to the experts, her watertight bulkheads and double-skin hull made her virtually unsinkable. She sailed from Southampton on her maiden voyage with a passenger list of celebrities – narrowly avoiding a collision as she left the docks. Yet, five days later, at 2.20 on the morning of 15 April 1912, in a silent, calm sea in mid-Atlantic, her bow dipped beneath the waves – until the huge liner was nearly vertical in the water. Seconds later, she dived into two miles of water. The unsinkable had sunk.

A few hours before, at 10.25 p.m., one of the liner's wireless operators named Harold Bride had just finished mending the transmitter. It had taken seven hours, and he was dead tired. He lay down on his bunk in the wireless room and dozed off. There was the faintest judder through the gigantic frame of the ship, but he thought nothing of it, until the captain poked his head round the door with the news that the ship had struck an iceberg and a call for assistance might have to be put out.

Even so, it did not seem very serious. The icefloes were abnormally far south this year, but other liners in the past few weeks had had brushes with icebergs and had carried on without assistance. But within a few minutes there were unmistakable sounds of confusion outside the cabin, and the captain reappeared. "Put out the call for help" he ordered. To replace the old call-sign CQD there was now a new one, SOS. "Try that" Bride told his fellow operator, Phillips, "it may be your last chance to send it." Even the captain laughed, though by now he must have known that one side of the bottom of the liner, tearing into the submerged ice at twenty-one knots, had been ripped to pieces. It was not long before the surging water reached the dynamos, snuffing out Bride's calls for help. He had got through to a German steamer, but it was too far away. So really was the *Carpathia*, which had turned about and was heading for the doomed ship at full speed, and the *Olympic* which Phillips just had time to inform that they were

Above: *the Titanic entry in the index to* Lloyd's List *of 1912, showing the date of the report in the* List *of the ship's foundering.*

Left: *the Titanic slip, showing that the insurance on the hull and machinery was valued at £1 million. Below that are the signatures of all the underwriters who subscribed to the policy, and for how much.*

Above: *a painting of the liner as she sank.*

Left: *an artist's impression of the abandoning of the Titanic after it had struck an iceberg in mid-Atlantic.*

Right: *the entry of the disaster in the Casualty Book at Lloyd's.*

Above: *the scene of the distress outside the offices of the White Star Line in New York as news of the catastrophe began to filter through.*

sinking by the head.

By 01.00 a.m. these messages reached New York and the weary newspaper offices. Some papers frankly did not believe the unconfirmed report and ignored it; others hedged their bets by reporting that the liner had struck an iceberg, at the same time assuring their readers the floating monster could not sink (least of all on its maiden voyage). Only the *New York Times* feared – and published – the worst. All the next day it looked as if the *Times* had blundered. Insisting that the boat was unsinkable, the White Star Line offices in New York admitted by lunchtime that there had been a slight mishap; suggested at teatime that all the passengers were safe; confessed at suppertime that there had been a fearful disaster. As it turned out, the news was worse even than anyone had dreamed. Only one ship, the *Carpathia,* had succeeded in picking up any survivors.

Bride himself, his legs broken and semi-conscious, was dragged to safety off an upturned lifeboat – one of the very few to be launched. He remembered a stoker bursting into the radio room and trying to snatch Phillips' lifejacket from his back. Bride had knocked him unconscious and left him to his fate. He remembered being washed off the side as he and some others struggled to release the one remaining lifeboat from its moorings. Then, somehow, he was clinging for his life to a capsized raft. The *Titanic* was about 150 feet away. The ship's orchestra was lined up on deck. They were playing "Autumn", even as the nose dipped beneath the waves. The rails were lined with men – Colonel Jacob Astor among them – waving their tragic farewells to wives and children who had been squeezed into the lifeboats. Here and there were women who had resolutely refused to leave their husband's side. The sea around was alive with swimmers, threshing about to reach one of the already overcrowded boats, until the cold ate into their bones and they gave up the struggle.

The captain was seen, at the end, leaping off the sinking ship, cradling a baby in his arms. He was pulled aboard a lifeboat, but slipped back into the water with the words "I will follow the ship". He was not seen again; nor were W.T. Stead, the famous editor of the *Pall Mall Gazette*; nor Major Butt, President Taft's military aide; nor Millet, the French artist. 1,595 passengers and crew went to their deaths that night. Only 745 were saved, to tell how the ship that couldn't sink sank.

When the tape at Lloyd's printed off the message of this appalling disaster, the Room was staggered, but there were no failures or defaults. Over eighty men had signed the underwriting slip for sums varying from £400 to £75,000 at a premium of fifteen shillings on £200. In all, Lloyd's paid out some £1,400,000 in claims, and such are the intricacies of insurance that even today, over sixty years later, the *Titanic* file has not yet been finally closed.

THE FIRST WORLD WAR

HAD A READER of the *Daily Telegraph* on 28 October 1908 opened his paper at page nine, he would have read a remarkable, brutally frank – not to say ominous – interview with the German Kaiser. The article was liberally peppered with expressions of love and esteem for the British people from the Kaiser himself, but he warned that his subjects "did not like Britain". Readers of the *Daily Mail*, on the other hand, would have found those sentiments reciprocated. Ever since the Kaiser's heavy-handed intervention in South Africa in 1896, Lord Northcliffe had been warning against the German menace: "They will have you yet, those Junkers." The alarming growth of Germany's tough-looking navy, which had shown its teeth at Morocco in 1905 (and was to do so again in 1911), made Britain's lone *Dreadnought* look lonely and vulnerable.

Not since the Napoleonic Wars, nearly a century before, had Britain been involved in a major conflict at sea. There was no knowing what a modern, 20th century war would involve. In 1903, a Government Committee had reached the somewhat surprising verdict that private marine insurance would be equal to any demands such a war might create. If the committee members had known what havoc the Japanese torpedoes were to wreak on the Imperial Russian fleet at Port Arthur the following year (and what losses the underwriters were to sustain) they would doubtless have reached a very different conclusion. Not only had weapons of destruction grown more deadly efficient, but the commercial targets, which only the most romantic doubted they would be used against, had grown a great deal more expensive. Just one liner and her cargo could theoretically now cost an insurer over a million pounds. Wars in the past might have made a few fortunes at Lloyd's, but those wars had been localised and had proved to be no restraint on trade outside a restricted area. No one was rash enough any longer to predict such a happy prospect; indeed since 1898 war risks had not been automatically included on Lloyd's marine policies – though the majority of vessels were separately covered against seizure or capture (in the year before the outbreak of war approximately two-thirds of British tonnage was so insured).

It was, therefore, fortunate for Lloyd's that in 1913 a fresh Committee was assembled to reconsider the matter, and doubly fortunate that the Government should have accepted its recommendations that the State should assume 80 percent of all risks not covered by private enterprise and that the Government's rate should be uniform for all voyages. For under war risk policies forty-eight

hours' notice of cancellation was required from insurer to owner, which in the event of a sudden outbreak of war was useless for ships already laden or on the high seas. And the war, when it came at the beginning of August 1914, was very sudden.

Britain returned home from work on Friday 31 July, troubled no doubt by a little local difficulty in the Balkans and Austria's strange intransigence over an ultimatum to Serbia, but looking forward to a sunny Bank Holiday Monday. When the country returned to work after the holiday on the Tuesday, every major power in Europe was either mobilised, marching or at war. Even if the Stock Exchange took several weeks to recover its nerve, Lloyd's was back at work that Tuesday and ruefully counting up the peacetime policies at 6d or 1/- percent which were now in severe risk. But for the most part the fortuitous arrangements for a State War Insurance Department, which came into force with commendable speed, enabled most underwriters to weather the crisis without disaster.

In practice, the fact that the Government was offering a uniform rate for all voyages meant that for the safer journeys underwriters could quote highly competitive prices (which had been the Committee's object) and often make substantial profits. Indeed over the war as a whole (which of course lasted far longer than those who imagined it "would all be over by Christmas") the Government lost seven and a half million pounds on cargo insurance. Nevertheless on all other forms of insurance it made a gross profit of £32 million – so the taxpayer had little cause to grumble.

For Lloyd's the war was a period of mixed fortunes: the collapse of the German insurance companies – especially when America entered the war in 1917 – brought a great deal of business to London, but the attendant policy of unrestricted U-boat warfare, which precipitated that US entry, hit the underwriters very hard indeed. In the spring of 1917 alone Britain lost nearly one and a half million tons of merchant shipping, when the submarine activity was at its height. This particular menace (though not the scale which it reached in the latter stages of the war) was well appreciated by the early months of 1915 when Allied shipping first began to suffer the depredations of the ubiquitous U-boats. When the war was still young these attacks had the veneer of humanity, with the submarine commanders giving due warning of the assault and allowing passengers and crew time to scramble into the lifeboats.

The sinking of the liner *Lusitania* in May 1915, however, ended these illusions for good. Certain facts have subsequently been marshalled in defence of this barbarity: that warnings not to sail were sent to all passengers in New York and that "official" notices were published in the US press; that the *Lusitania* was stuffed from stem to stern

New York Tribune

First to Last—the Truth: News - Editorials - Advertisements

Vol. LXXV.... No. 25,010.   [Copyright, 1915, By The Tribune Association.]   SATURDAY, MAY 8, 1915.   PRICE ONE CENT In City of New York, Newark, Jersey City and Hoboken. ELSEWHERE TWO CENTS.

WEATHER
FAIR TO-DAY AND TO-MORROW;
SOUTHERLY TO N.W. WINDS.
Yesterday's Temperatures:
High, 64. Low, 50.
Full report on Page 15.

900 Die as Lusitania Goes to Bottom;
400 Americans on Board Torpedoed Ship;
Washington Stirred as When Maine Sank

CAPITAL AROUSED, SITUATION GRAVEST YET FACED IN WAR

Washington Determined That Germany Shall Not Be Allowed to Shirk Responsibility for Deaths.

GREATLY FEARS LOSS OF AMERICANS

President Shows Nervousness as Bulletins of Disaster Come In—Strongest Protest Yet Made Planned Even if No U. S. Citizens Were Lost

[From The Tribune Bureau.]

Washington, May 7.—The news of the heavy loss of life on the Lusitania stirred Washington as it has not been stirred since the sinking of the Maine. The earlier reports that both passengers and crew had been landed safely had quieted apprehensions of an immediate crisis in the relations of the United States and Germany. But when it became clear that when the third of American lives was finally made up few could be found to be missing.

That the situation will be acute when loss of American lives is proved is admitted on all sides. No action will be taken by this government until all the details of the torpedoing of the Lusitania are received. They as one thing certain, however, and that is that Germany will not be allowed to shirk any responsibility for the disaster, should investigation show that the act was performed by a German submarine.

LONDON SEES VITAL QUESTION FOR U. S.

America Is 'Bound to Defend Lives of Its Subjects,' Declares 'Daily News.'

GERMANS TOAST 'VICTORY' AMID 'HOCHS' IN CAFES

Steins Clink as Celebrators Predict Downfall of Britain's Sea Power.

OFFICERS GAY IN CLUBHOUSE

Restaurants Thronged and Entire Families Out to Cheer Kaiser and His Submarines.

U. S. OWES IT TO SELF-RESPECT TO ACT, SAYS ROOSEVELT; 'PIRACY ON VAST SCALE'

[From a Staff Correspondent of The Tribune.]

Syracuse, May 7.—After the appalling details of the Lusitania disaster had been told to Colonel Roosevelt to-night he said: "It seems inconceivable that we should refrain from taking action on this matter, for we owe it not only to humanity but to our own national self-respect.

"This represents not merely piracy, but piracy on a vaster scale of murder than any oldtime pirate ever practiced. This is the warfare which destroyed Louvain and Dinant and hundreds of men, women and children in Belgium; warfare to innocent men, women and children travelling on the ocean, to our own fellow country men and country women who are among the sufferers."

ACT OF BARBARITY, SAYS F. R. COUDERT

Lawyer Insists Sinking of the Lusitania Is Without Justification.

FIRST SURVIVORS' NAMES RECEIVED

THE LUSITANIA, SUNK BY GERMAN TORPEDO, WITH HEAVY LOSS OF LIFE.

Dying and Injured Brought in with Other Survivors to Queenstown—Some Landed at Kinsale and Clonakilty.

TWO TORPEDOES FIRED, SAYS STEWARD

Attack Made About Eight Miles from Irish Coast in Broad Daylight and in Fine Weather—Survivor Tells of Bravery of Cunard Officers.

[By Cable to The Tribune.]

London, May 8, 3 a. m.—At least 900 lives were lost when the Lusitania was torpedoed without warning in broad daylight yesterday afternoon by a German submarine, according to estimates by survivors. The estimate of First Officer Jones puts the total nearer 1,500.

Of the dead, more than two hundred are supposed to be Americans, as it is believed there were about 400 on board.

A dispatch from Queenstown sent out at midnight says:

"Up to the present 520 passengers from the Lusitania had been landed here from boats. Ten or eleven boatloads came ashore, and others are expected."

ADMIRALTY GIVES OUT NEWS.

PASSENGERS WERE AT LUNCHEON.

WENT DOWN BY BOW.

MANY NOTED NEW YORKERS ON LUSITANIA

Alfred G. Vanderbilt Was on Way to England on Business Trip.

N. J. REPRESENTED ON FIRST CABIN LIST

Charles Frohman, Lindon Bates, Jr., Charles Klein and Justus Miles Forman Aboard.

SOUTH COAST OF IRELAND.

Showing where the Lusitania was attacked and the points where survivors of the passengers and crew were landed.

INDEPENDENCE DAY.

Thursday, 4th July, 1918.

At Noon, the "Star Spangled Banner" will be sung in honour of our American Allies. To be followed by "God Save the King."

LLOYD'S,
3rd July, 1918.

Above: *notice of a comradely event in the last year of the First World War.*

Opposite: *the report in the* New York Tribune *of the torpedoing of the liner* Lusitania *by a German U-boat off the coast of Ireland in 1915.*

with munitions; that she was, in effect, an armed cruiser. The debate, which continues more than half a century after, cannot obscure the fact that the U-20's torpedoes were fired without warning of any kind and that the majority of passengers aboard could not be classified by any definition as combatants (thirty-five of the total 1,197 casualties were babes in arms).

The *Lusitania* has since been described as "the ship that won the war" – an extravagant judgement, but one that contains more than a germ of truth. Certainly the loss of more than 100 American passengers shocked the United States out of her determined isolation into a state of armed "preparedness". But equally important, in Britain the tragedy prompted massive public concern over the efficiency of the Admiralty's intelligence and warning procedures (an alert of generalised U-boat activity off Kinsale had been sent to the *Lusitania*, but only in the most equivocal terms), and over the absence of any organised convoy system. It is to be doubted if a convoy could have saved the *Lusitania* in the circumstances, but there were many at Lloyd's who were troubled that convoying was not seriously considered until 1917. The lack of possible escort vessels, the absence of experienced merchant marine signallers, the difficulties of keeping ships of varying speeds in station were all argued strenuously: but when the system was properly tried in the North Atlantic in May 1917 its merits were immediately self-evident.

The war brought in its train a new form of risk, which had not previously been considered seriously in Britain if only because the very thought of it was preposterous. Not since the Dutch had sailed flagrantly up the Medway had British property on British soil appeared in any danger. To be sure, there had been alarms but even Napoleon's hordes had been obliged to sit it out disconsolately on the far side of the Channel. In December 1914 this cosy insular feeling was rudely dispelled by the disgraceful bombardment of East Coast ports under cover of a convenient fog. The fate of West Hartlepool (impudent though it was) was not sufficient to panic London property-owners into stampeding for war-cover – but the shadow of Count Zeppelin's monstrous airships certainly was. It is related by Gibb that the rate for the first bomb-damage policy was fixed by Sidney Boulton at two shillings per £100 more in jest than in earnest – but it should be recorded that by the end of the war the Government's own rate for this risk was virtually the same as Boulton had quoted four years earlier. The fact was that the zeppelins were a dramatic flop, and bomb-damage insurance proved to be highly lucrative (in the final year of the war the Government itself made an overall profit of over £10 million) though subject, of course, to an 80 percent excess-profits tax which took the gilt off the gingerbread to some extent.

Lloyd's reacted to the unconventional problems and pressures of total war as it always had done in the past – with ingenuity and adaptability. The acute staff shortage led to the formation of the Policy Signing Bureau in 1916, which after early teething troubles proved its value and dispensed with the time-honoured but inconvenient handing round of dog-eared slips. Lloyd's own contribution to the nation's war-effort – apart from the thousands of members and subscribers who joined up and the immense amounts of money which were distributed to soldiers' dependants and the Red Cross during the conflict – was recalled years later by George V. The state, he said, had relied heavily on Lloyd's Intelligence network: agents, signal stations, the whole complex web of the Corporation's communications played a vital part in the war at sea, not least in curtailing the ancient abuse of trading with the enemy under a neutral flag and in maintaining cordial relations with neutral countries even as the Royal Navy searched their ships.

FRAUDS

"Nov 30 1663 . . . To the Coffee-house, where I heard the best story of a cheate intended by a master of a ship, who had borrowed twice his money upon the bottomry, and as much more insured upon his ship and goods as they were worth, and then would have cast her away upon the coast of France, and there left her, refusing any pilot which was offered him; and so the Governor of the place took her and sent her over hither to find an owner, and so the ship is come safe, and goods and all; they are all worth £500, and he had one way or other taken £3,000 . . . Her cargo, vessels of tallow daubed over with butter, instead of all butter."

Thus wrote Pepys in 1663, and over the centuries, by hard experience, underwriters have got to know the crooked game from A to Z – ships insured after the owners are already aware of their loss; ships scuttled with dummy cargoes aboard; forged bills of lading and invoices; antedated letters – the whole accretia of insurance frauds is no novelty to them.

So hoary, indeed, is the old scuttling ploy that it dates back to the ancient world. In his oration against Zenothemis, Demosthenes tells how that shipowner conspired with Hegastratus to scuttle a ship between Syracuse and Marseilles and collect the insurance money. And until quite recently the Greeks still had the record for faked claims (although admittedly the Spaniards ran them pretty close). Under the headline "Ships that do not come home", the *Daily Express* on 28 July 1921 revealed that twenty-nine Greek ships had gone down between September 1920 and February 1921. "Their insurable value was £2,360,000. This number has

now been increased to 50 ships insured for a total of £3,500,000", the article added.

In every instance, the facts were suspicious: sudden and violent leaks occurred in calm weather; vessels were damaged by mines where no mines existed; ships ran ashore for no apparent reason.

Yet the reason, in fact, was not hard to find. Ship values had rocketed after the 1914–18 war, and when cargoes began to fall off, some owners were faced with bankruptcy – unless, of course, they could lose the vessel they had bought at peak prices, and collect a heavy insurance claim.

Nor were the British entirely above reproach: until the loadline law came in, unscrupulous ship-owners would cram a ship up to the scuppers and send her to sea not just overloaded, but under-manned and over-insured as well. If she reached her destination, well and good. If she sank, the owner simply pocketed the insurance and a larger profit than if she had arrived safely.

Marine frauds come in all shapes and sizes. There was the case of a Turkish ship reportedly carrying £75,000 of gold from Port Said to Beirut for trans-shipment to Marseilles. The ink on the policy form was barely dry when a report came in that she had sunk outside Beirut, and that the crew had only with difficulty been saved. When the claim adjuster reached Beirut he was unable, even with the help of divers, to find any trace of wreckage in the shallow water. But he did locate a Lebanese carter who had filched a gold ingot from a case that had "broken" during trans-shipment and had been disgusted to find that it was made of iron; he also discovered that the crew which had been "saved" with such difficulty comprised the swimming champions of Beirut.

Another case centred around a gang who shipped horses to the United States and South Africa, and had them poisoned in transit. By being clever enough to claim only for a reasonable number each voyage, they avoided detection for some years, until underwriters discovered that the value of three horses insured for £1,400 was not more than £10 each.

A more complicated fraud, practised in the United States, involved buying a ship on credit; persuading a third party to advance money on her and to take out an insurance policy for 50 percent more than her real value; buying cargo with the cash, and when this was insured as well, scuttling the lot and collecting the claim-money.

But for sheer affrontery, Lloyd's prize exhibit – which Angerstein mentioned in the 1810 Parliamentary enquiry and Marryat had on risk – was Captain Codling. Carrying a cargo of cutlery, watches, musical instruments and other goods insured for around £5,000, the brig *Adventure* left London under his command in 1802 bound for Gibraltar and Livorno. But first Codling sailed up to Yarmouth, where he took some further merchandise on board; called at Deal and Aldeburgh; and then anchored in the Downs (where he seems to have collected a keg of rum). Finally, a month after leaving the Thames, he turned up off Brighton. It was a fine calm day, and to the surprise of the promenaders, the brig began slowly to sink before their eyes. Some fishing boats which had hastened out to help were ordered away with a barrage of salty oaths, and when the brig finally went under (in such shallow water that her masts still showed) Captain Codling and the crew rowed ashore in a dinghy and headed straight for the Old Ship Inn. There they lived it up for some weeks while the Lloyd's representatives had the brig salvaged, and only when a large hole in the hull was discovered, with the tools which had made it, did he finally take to his heels. He was eventually found hiding under a pile of blankets in a packet heading for the Continent, and was brought back for trial, together with the owners, for "wilfully and feloniously casting away a vessel". Even so, it would not have been an open and shut case had the crew not turned "King's evidence" with a vivid description of how they had been ordered to make holes "as near to the bottom as possible" by Codling – who was sentenced and hanged.

Above: *the memorial to* The Times, *for its part in uncovering an international mercantile fraud in 1840.*

Not all marine frauds, however, have been so brazen. In 1840 it was only through the diligence of the Brussels correspondent of *The Times* that a spurious company in Holland (with which several impecunious French aristocrats and one Member of Parliament were connected) was uncovered before it was able to perpetrate a million-pound swindle. A plaque of gratitude from the mercantile community to the newspaper stood until recently in Lloyd's, but at Printing House Square such exposés, it seems, are all in a day's work, for the official History of *The Times* makes no reference to the incident.

THE EGYPT'S GOLD

WHEN THE P & O liner *Egypt* was launched in 1897 she was the most handsome vessel in the entire fleet. Twenty-five years later, of course, she was no match for the transatlantic monsters which had since been constructed, but she was a dependable ship and had served honourably in the war. Now, in May 1922, refitted and repainted she was back in service on her old familiar Mediterranean routes. She sailed from the Thames on 19 May and by the evening of the 20th she was altering course to cross the Bay of Biscay. At 6.45 p.m. the banks of fog descended into one impenetrable sheet, obliging Captain Collyer to give the order to "stop engines". In the distance he thought he heard a faint whistle.

Stopping engines does not stop a ship: it would have taken the *Egypt* perhaps thirty minutes to slow to a halt, so that when out of the grey the French ship *Seine* loomed ahead on a direct course for the liner, there was nothing to diminish the fierce impact of the other ship's ice-strengthened prow. It sliced into the port side, and within eight minutes the *Egypt* was listing helplessly at thirty degrees, and within twenty she had foundered. Happily there were but forty-four passengers aboard – those were still the days when travellers considered it "correct" and prudent to join ships at Marseilles – yet only fifteen of them were saved, partly because of the panic which ensued among the predominantly Asian crew.

That was tragedy enough, but on that voyage the *Egypt* was also carrying well in excess of one million pounds in gold and silver in her bullion room – the bulk of it insured at Lloyd's. The melancholy in the Room, when the news was posted on the 21st, contrasted strongly with the bright spring sunshine outside. No one held out much hope of recovering a single bar from the depths of nearly 400 feet, further down than any diver had ever descended. Two subsequent salvage expeditions, one British and one French, served only to confirm this gloomy prognostication. The gold was given up for lost.

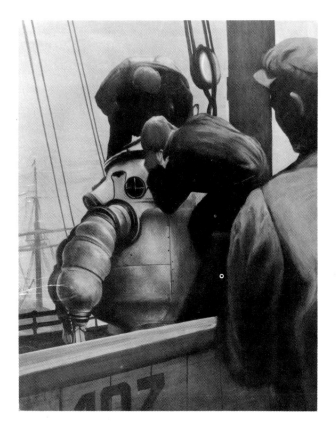

Above and left: *the P & O liner* Egypt, *which sank with over £1 million worth of gold and silver on board, and the curious diving-bell which was invented to accomplish its salvage.*

In 1929, however, an Italian crew under the direction of Commander Quaglia came forward armed with a German diving-chamber that looked like something out of Jules Verne. It took Quaglia a year even to locate the wreck of the *Egypt* with his sweep nets, while the sceptics still maintained that no diver could survive at such a depth. But he did; lowered to sixty-six fathoms, he telephoned to the surface that they had indeed found the *Egypt*. Patiently, week after week, explosives were lowered by mechanical grabs and placed with directions from the diving-chamber. Slowly the ship was blown apart, until at last the captain's cabin was accessible and the first reward – the ship's safe containing Government papers – was landed on the deck of the salvage vessel. It took another fortnight to detonate a way into the strongroom, precious time – for the weather was breaking. Just at the moment of triumph, the expedition had to be called off until the following year.

For Quaglia the delay was disastrous: his crew moved on in December to detonate a sunken munitions ship for the French Government. Something went wrong, and the salvage ship with every single person aboard was blown to pieces. Quaglia himself was not present but, distracted, he was on the point of giving up any further attempt on the *Egypt*. The following year, nevertheless, he was persuaded to try again with a new crew and spent the summer in a futile race against the Western gales. It was June 1932 before another grab – this time a curious umbrella-shaped contraption – could be lowered. It was hauled up and, as the ringing of the Lutine bell one hour later announced to Lloyd's, was found to contain two gold bars. Within twenty-four hours, more than £80,000 had been recovered.

It was another three years before the whole operation was completed. Thirteen years after the liner had sunk in the fog, one man's courage and patience had recovered more than one million pounds' worth of bullion.

THE TRANSATLANTIC LINERS

IN ONE YEAR, 1907, alone more than a million and a quarter emigrants from Europe sailed across the Atlantic, from Liverpool, Hamburg and Naples, tempering the hardships of the steerage with Hope. For a few pounds the ten- or twelve-day voyage would carry them to a new life and, who knew, perhaps a change of luck. For that kind of money, of course, the steerage conditions could hardly compare with the Palladian domes and Ionic columns of the first-class smoking-rooms. Nor did they: it was counted fortunate if the water supply did not fail two days out from port. To quote one investigator in 1906 "the steerage of the modern

Above: *the last moments of the Italian liner* Andrea Doria *after a collision with the* Stockholm.

Above: *fire sweeps through the French liner* L'Atlantique *in 1933.*

Left: *the end of the* Queen Elizabeth, *as she was being refitted in Hong Kong to become a floating university.*

ship ought to be condemned as unfit for the transportation of human beings".

But in that year a new kind of transatlantic liner entered service, Cunard's *Mauretania* – not only the fastest and most advanced (32,000 tons) but decidedly more dignified below-decks. Maybe the incessant chorus of condemnation from successive inquiries over the last few years was taking effect, or maybe there was now an edge of competition for the ever-swelling immigrant trade. For there seemed no end to the one-way tide towards that distant magnet, New York. Ever greater giants were called for, and built – the *Lusitania*, the *Olympic*, the *Aquitania* and the biggest of the lot, the *Imperator*, as well as supposedly the safest of them all, the *Titanic*. Only the outbreak of the First War staunched the optimistic tide, while predatory U-boats lurked along the seaways and took a dreadful toll of the great liners – whether they had been pressed into honourable service as troop carriers or continued to ply an innocent trade as passenger ships. Cunard alone lost nine ships, among them the *Lusitania* torpedoed off the coast of Ireland (see page 148), Canadian Pacific eight, and White Star the *Arabic*, the *Laurentic* and its brand-new *Britannic* among others.

After the war the shipping lines gathered up the remnants of their fleets, and embarked on a frantic rebuilding programme to recapture the lost immigrants once more. It was not to be. America in the future was to be for the Americans, and strict national quotas were imposed. No more alien "reds" or "anarchists"; no more solving of Europe's problems. Moreover, if anyone in the great shipping offices had cared to ponder on the significance of it, the Atlantic had shrunk on 14 June 1919 to a mere sixteen hours, which was the time it had taken Alcock and Brown to fly it.

The companies looked around for a new market and detected it heading in the opposite direction, the beginnings of the tourist boom. Now what mattered was prestige, greater luxury, efficiency and of course speed. The coveted Blue Ribband, which for twenty years had been the undisputed property of the *Mauretania*, was first wrenched away in 1929 by the great German ship *Bremen* which dashed across the Atlantic on its maiden voyage at the record average of 27.83 knots. The following year it was pipped by its stablemate the *Europa*; in 1933 the pride of the Italia Line, the *Rex*, made the westbound crossing at an average of 28.92 knots, a record which stood for only two years until the intense rivalry between the great leviathans of France and Britain, the *Normandie* and the *Queen Mary*, dwarfed all other contenders. Between 1935 and 1938 these two conducted their own private battle, each losing and then regaining the trophy time and again.

When the second war broke out, the *Queen Mary* was in possession of both the eastbound and the westbound records. In 1940 she enlisted for a gallant wartime career as a troopship, and emerged from the war battered (after a tragic collision with one of her escort cruisers) but unbowed. In 1952 she saw her Atlantic titles swept away by the incomparable *United States*, but her pride remained undented. The *Queen Mary* now basks in the sun at Long Beach, California, pensioned off as a floating hotel and museum. But her rival, the *Normandie*, was not so fortunate: in 1942 she caught fire in dock at New York and sank under the weight of water poured into her by firemen – no amount of herculean salvage efforts could ever put her back into service. The *Queen Mary*'s sister-ship, the *Queen Elizabeth*, came to an untimely end too, gutted by fire in Hongkong before she could matriculate as a floating university (and at the time of writing Lloyd's is still involved in the complicated claims arising from the fire).

Sadly, today there are few remnants of the proud Atlantic fleets. Most have disappeared, broken up to the last rivet in a far-distant port. And some have tragically entered the annals of Lloyd's: the White Star Line's *Republic* which foundered under tow in January 1909, after a collision with the *Florida*. No passengers or crew were lost, since for the first time in history a distress signal from sea was picked up at one of Marconi's land stations. Then only two years after the *Titanic* disaster, Canadian Pacific's *Empress of Ireland* was rammed in fog in the St Lawrence River and sank in the incredibly fast time of 15 minutes. Most passengers were asleep and the death toll was over 1,000 (the mother of one of the authors was aboard at the time but mercifully escaped – up a funnel). To these famous names must be added *L'Atlantique*, burnt-out beyond recovery in mid-Atlantic in 1933, the *Lancastria* sunk in 1940 by German dive-bombers with the appalling loss of an estimated 4,500 troops, the *Laconia* gutted to extinction just before Christmas 1963 after a fire had broken out in the hairdressing salon, and the Italian Line's *Andrea Doria* in 1956. This liner, which offered "the sea traveller as safe and comfortable transportation as is justly expected in this atomic age", collided in fog with the *Stockholm* just off Nantucket Light. It was a total write-off, costing underwriters over $13,000,000 – and Lloyd's in particular nearly $6,000,000.

THE AIRSHIP DECADE

TO BE SURE, there were plenty of people after the end of the Great War who still doubted there was any future in commercial transport by air. The best of their arguments, such as they were, revolved around the vast sums of money being expended on aeronautical development by a country whose

Above and right: *the wreckage of the US airship* Shenandoah *after it had been broken in two during a windstorm near Cambridge Ohio in September 1925.*

Above: *all that remained of the R.38 after disintegrating in flight in 1921.*

On page 158: *the German dirigible* Hindenburg *exploding at its moorings in Lakehurst, USA, May 1937.*

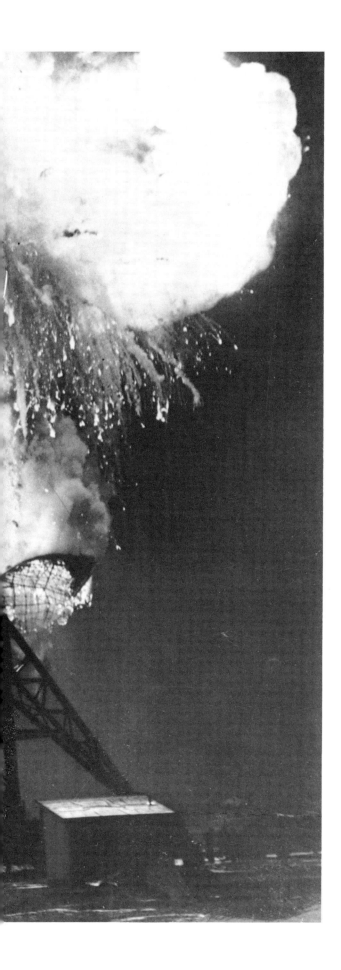

economy was patently unable to cope even with the army of unemployed which had trooped back from the trenches. It was, ironically, the same kind of debate which attended Britain's commitment to supersonic air travel half a century later. But the bitterest controversy, however, raged less over whether to scrap flying machines altogether, as what kind of flying machines to build.

There were those who had observed with awe Count Zeppelin's airships' brazen attacks during the war on London and were impressed by the ponderous majesty of these leviathans of the skies. Their cause was further advanced when Britain's own R.34 was the first airship to cross the Atlantic in July 1919. They argued that the aeroplane was rapidly approaching the frontiers of its weight-payload limit. The supporters of heavier-than-air machines, in turn, pointed out that the payload of a dirigible was in fact ludicrous (a mere eight to 10 tons) in relation to its sheer bulk, and that in spite of the R.34's achievement, the *Mauretania* could still cross the Atlantic faster and more comfortably. What was more, they said, a voyage in an airship was like carrying your own portable detonator.

In spite of such gloomy predictions Britain embarked in 1919 on a concentrated programme of airship construction. It proved to be a model of wasted and futile expenditure: the R.35, R.37 and R.39 never even took to the air. Of those that did, the R.34 was a total write-off in 1921, and the R.38 split in two in flight in 1921 with the loss of 44 persons. The American experience proved to be no happier. In 1922 the US airship *Roma* burst into flames killing thirty-four, and three years later the *Shenandoah* took its fourteen-man crew to their deaths. If confidence in the States was not yet profoundly shaken (a consortium of businessmen, even in the 'thirties, were planning to establish an airship mooring station at the top of the Empire State Building to service the transatlantic and transpacific passenger services they were certain would come along), it most certainly was in Britain.

It took the spectacular round-the-world flight of the *Graf Zeppelin* in 1929 (at an average speed of 78 miles an hour) to restore any sort of public enthusiasm for gasbags. All hopes were pinned on the magnificent R.101, by the beginning of 1930 proudly flying at its mast at Cardington. The trial runs were not encouraging (to be truthful, they were disastrous) but such was the pressure to refurbish British prestige in the air that a swanky inaugural flight to India and back was arranged with indecent haste, for October. The Secretary for Air, Lord Thomson, himself was to make the trip to prove the airworthiness of Britain's floating palace ("I've promised the PM to be back on 20 October" were his final joking words before he embarked).

He was back a great deal sooner, together with forty-five other victims of a tragic and horrifying

THE WEATHER
To-day: Generally fair; moderate southeast winds
To-morrow: Fair
Yesterday's temperatures: Max. 66; min. 53
Detailed weather report on Page 23

NEW YORK
Herald Tribune

LATE CITY EDITION

VOL. LXXXVII No. 29,407 (Copyright, 1927, New York Tribune Inc.) SUNDAY, MAY 22, 1927—196 PAGES—Section One * * * * FIVE CENTS In Manhattan, Brooklyn and The Bronx | TEN CENTS Elsewhere

Lindbergh Lands Safely in Paris at 5:21 P.M.; 3,800-Mile Flight in 33½ Hours Thrills World

New York Millions Hail His Triumph

Throngs Crowding Streets Cheer as 'Greatest Sporting Event in History' Ends Brilliantly

Showers of Paper Flood Streets as Goal Is Won

Women, Gripped in Dramatic Tension, Weep; Planes Fly Over City in Toast to Victor; Dirigible Joins in Fete

The hearts of New York's millions were thrilled yesterday afternoon when an American boy of twenty-five, 3,800 miles away in Paris, brought the greatest sporting event in history to a gloriously successful close.

Thousands of men and women choked the main streets in all the five boroughs to hear the news, but it was on Broadway between Thirty-fourth Street and Columbus Circle that the most dense throngs yelled themselves hoarse for Charlie Lindbergh, the young flyer.

Paper Showers Throngs in Streets

The crowds began to gather early in the afternoon, thousands of office workers foregoing home and even luncheon to mingle before the many bulletin boards erected throughout the city. Scores returned to their lofty offices in the Broadway and Forty-second Street section and passed the long, fretful hours tearing up telephone books and sending the torn leaves out over the square in billows of paper snow.

Each time a news bulletin described the Lindbergh plane nearer the goal fresh storms of paper swept down out of the sunny sky and covered the cheering thousands below. The New York which had welcomed Dewey, Roosevelt, the 27th and 77th Divisions, Marshal Foch, the Prince of Wales, the Crown Prince of Sweden and Gertrude Ederle, the girl conqueror of the Channel, prayed and wept yesterday and was thrilled as perhaps it had not been thrilled since the Armistice.

First Waking Thoughts of Flyer

Churches throughout the morning and until late in the afternoon were crowded with men and women down on their knees praying fervently for the success of the flying youth who backed his nerve and flying sense against every discouragement and attempt to dissuade him from what seemed until noon a hopeless but heroic feat.

There was hardly a nook of New York that did not hold a knot of speculating, wondering, but hoping persons. The hordes of New York went to sleep Friday night with a picture of Lindbergh winging alone across the dark ocean in their minds, and they awakened yesterday morning to inquire his whereabouts.

Finance, barter and trade, all the humdrum workaday and habitual acts of the typical New Yorker sank far into the discard, while subways tunneled clerks and bosses to work. On every swaying, crowded subway car a white

(Continued on page twelve)

Sections in To-day's Paper

'I'm Grateful,' Says Mother As Son Wins

'No Words to Express My Happiness,' Mrs. Lindbergh Smiles Through Tears as Word Ends Vigil

Guarded by Police As Crowds Gather

'All Credit Belongs to Him,' Says Teacher at News Ending Sleepless Ordeal

Special to The Herald Tribune

DETROIT, May 21.—A smile showed through the lines of care that marked the face of a stout-hearted mother as she discussed the feat of her famous son who accomplished to-day that which no man had ever accomplished before.

This mother was Mrs. Evangeline Lindbergh, teacher of science at Technical High School. An obscure teacher until a few days ago, she had the congratulations of millions to-day, due to the New York to Paris flight of her boy, Charles A. Lindbergh.

No Sleep Since Friday

There were tears in her eyes, but the smile that showed through the tears was not a forced one. She was happy, happier than she had ever been before.

This mother had not slept since Friday morning. She could not sleep, for, while she believed that he would win, she was also cognizant of the fate which befell the two French flyers on the venture less than two weeks ago. How many times the news of their disaster flashed through her mind as she saw visions of her boy winging his way across the sea alone she cannot remember.

Her Fears Quieted

But she had received the news that quieted all her fears. She knew her big boy had won in the greatest triumph in the air that had ever been attempted. She did not care to bask in her reflected glory, she made no pretense that she had encouraged him in aviation. When he started to fly he did so on his own initiative and this proud mother was

(Continued on page three)

Summary of To-day's News

"Well, I Did It"

"When I enter the cockpit it's like going into the death chamber. When I step out at Paris it will be like getting a pardon from the Governor."—CHARLES A. LINDBERGH

Money Offers Of $1,000,000 For Lindbergh

$25,000 Orteig Prize Is Small Item Beside Film and Theater Bids and Opportunities in Business

Charles Lindbergh, bashful, blushing, do-or-die son of the Middle West, who burst on the scene of aeronautics like a fiery comet out of nowhere ten days ago, rated yesterday as a very likely millionaire. Very likely is used advisedly, for the unaccountable youth may, like as not, turn down all money offers and revel in the glory of his adventure. But if he heeds the fabulous offers cabled and wirelessed him, he will garner $1,000,000 the first year and several hundred thousand dollars a year thereafter for fully four or five years.

Theaters to Bid for Him

The $25,000 prize which Raymond Orteig, owner of the Brevoort and Lafayette hotels, awards the New York-to-Paris flyer is as a drop in the bucket. S. L. Rothafel, better known as "Roxy," has offered him $25,000 to appear at the Roxy Theater for one week.

The Publix Theaters, which had Gertrude Ederle appear in its circuit for twenty weeks at $6,000 a week, will pay Lindbergh more than that if he will accept a contract. The Keith-Albee Circuit of vaudeville houses will match that offer, of necessity, to get "Lucky." The Loew chain of theaters will strain every effort to get him.

His Writings Worth $50,000

A motion picture concern, which asked that its name be withheld, wants him to do a picture for $100,000. If it proves successful, he can do more for them.

Mark Luescher, representative of the Keith-Albee theaters, complained

(Continued on page twelve)

Capt. Lindbergh's Story Of Bold Atlantic Flight

Landed Ready to Go 1,000 Miles More; Not Sleepy, but Slightly "Stiff"; Flew Within Ten Feet of the Water at Times

From the Herald Tribune Paris Bureau
Copyright, 1927, New York Tribune Inc.

PARIS, May 22 (Sunday).—"The thing I can't get over is how short a time it took to cross the ocean," said Captain Charles A. Lindbergh, as he sat on the edge of a bed in the American Embassy here this morning—the first bed he had seen in more than fifty hours—and told his story of his daring non-stop flight from New York to Paris.

"No, I am not sleepy at all," he insisted. "Only a little stiff.

"The weather was better than I had anticipated over Nova Scotia and Newfoundland—better than the Weather Bureau had expected. And then out on the open sea I ran into fog. I had to drive through a thousand miles of it. I couldn't get up over it and couldn't get below it, so had to go right through it a good deal of the time.

Near Water at Times

"Sometimes I was within ten feet of the water, just skimming above the surface. Sometimes I was 10,000 feet above it. I saw the lights of one ship at night on the open ocean. That was all. I didn't sight a single ship in the daytime. I understand, though, that one liner sighted me.

"At one time there was considerable sleet and ice on the bow of the plane, and I was a little concerned. But it cleared up."

"And you didn't feel in the least exhausted when you finished at Le Bourget?"

Willing to Go Further

"Not in the least," Lindbergh replied. "I would be willing to go half as far again."

The flyer was still awake at 3 o'clock this mornnig, clad in white pajamas and a light bathrobe.

"What about the kitten?"

"Well, now, I really didn't have any intention of taking that cat along," Lindbergh responded. "Yes,

(Continued on page three)

Mr. Coolidge Tells Of Nation's Pride

Message to Flyer Congratulates Him and Expresses Anxiety for Nungesser

From the Herald Tribune Washington Bureau

WASHINGTON, May 21.—President Coolidge cabled the nation's congratulations to Captain Charles A. Lindbergh this afternoon as soon as he had received word of his arrival in Paris. The message sent to the American Embassy there said:

"'The American people rejoice with me at the brilliant termination of your heroic flight. The first non-stop flight of a lone aviator across the Atlantic Ocean crowns the record of American aviation, and in bringing the greetings of the American people to France you likewise carry the assurance of our admiration of those intrepid Frenchmen, Nungesser and Coli, whose bold spirits first ventured on your exploit, and likewise a message of our continued anxiety concerning their fate.

"'CALVIN COOLIDGE.'"

Paris Goes Wild; Flyer Only Tired

20,000 Break Police Lines to Seize Triumphant American Airman in Joyous Welcome

'Well, I Did It,' First Words As Throng Shouts Acclaim

Young Sea Conqueror, First to Hop From America to Europe, Smiles Thanks for Ovation

By Wilbur Forrest
From the Herald Tribune Paris Bureau
Copyright, 1927, New York Tribune Inc.

PARIS, May 21.—Captain Charles A. Lindbergh landed at Le Bourget air field, outside Paris, at 10:21 o'clock to-night (5:21 p. m. New York daylight saving time) in his monoplane, the Spirit of St. Louis, in which he had flown alone from New York in the first non-stop flight ever made between New York and Paris.

With the shouts of 20,000 persons greeting him, Lindbergh twice circled the field and then made a perfect landing to finish the most hazardous and epochal air flight yet made by man. At midnight the American Viking was sleeping peacefully in an automobile which with thousands of other cars four abreast was jammed in the traffic over the distance of two miles leading out to the air field from Paris.

Barely Escapes Mobbing in Frenzied Welcome

Lindbergh covered the approximately 3,800 miles of his flight in thirty-three hours and thirty minutes, faster than he had expected. He left New York at 7:51 a. m. on Friday and arrived here at 5:21 p. m. to-day, New York time. His average time was thus about 113 miles an hour.

The twenty-five-year-old American flyer narrowly escaped being mobbed by his frenzied admirers by an accident when a part of the surging crowd mistook Harry Wheeler, a tall blonde from New York, for the hero of the hour and, despite his protestations, bore him triumphantly on its shoulders to the administration building of the air field.

Meanwhile, ten men were carrying Lindbergh towards a hangar on the other side of the field. The flyer was so exhausted that he lay back flat on their shoulders, head downward and eyes closed. This fact alone saved him from the mad attentions of the mob. Thousands who could not see him swarmed toward the other end of the field.

Flyer Smiles Happily Though Near Collapse

Lindbergh was so near collapse that he could not speak but occasionally opened his eyes and smiled happily, then fell back again. Before the airman, who was being carried feet foremost, walked a little bald-headed man flapping his elbows and yelling, "Clear the way!"

The crowd, realizing that the Atlantic had been bridged from continent to continent for the first time, broke all the police lines and surrounded the plane. Borne into the offices of the airport, Lindbergh was greeted by the American Ambassador Myron T. Herrick, and among the flyer's first words were:

"Well, I did it."

Two reporters of The Paris Herald were among the first to reach the side of Lindbergh's plane as it came to a stop on the field. As the machine came to a halt they clambered to the flyer's side. His face was drawn and he seemed deafened by the incessant roar of the motor. He tried to lift himself and fell back in semi-collapse. But still his unfailing love for his airplane was first in his thoughts. After his first greeting, the only words that came from the exhausted airman's parched lips were "Are there any mechanics here?" That was all.

Souvenirs Torn From His Machine

The newspaper men grasped his arms and helped lift him from the cockpit to carry him toward the Le Bourget administration building, where Dr. Charles Bove, of the American Hospital, gave him immediate attention. And as this was being done, crazed hundreds were tearing great sheets of solid aluminum from the wings of The Spirit of St. Louis and twisting them into bits for souvenirs of the greatest one-man achievement centuries have known.

Meanwhile Wheeler was carried in triumph to the pavilion, vainly protesting that he was not Lindbergh. But the great throng was unmanageable and stormed after him, smashing down the wooden fences and trampling policemen and government officials. They bore Wheeler into the building, the mob crashing through the door behind him.

When he finally reached Ambassador Herrick, Wheeler explained the mistake. As the Ambassador on the balco

holocaust: only eight people miraculously survived. The R.101 had travelled barely as far as Beauvais in northern France, before a gust of wind clutched at the sadly dipping nose and dashed it to the ground. The post mortem weeks later showed conclusively that the airship should never have been given a certificate of airworthiness in the first place. Virtually untested, over-heavy and riddled with actual or potential leaks, the thing was a death-trap. It was the end of dirigibles, so far as Britain was concerned. Others persevered, the Germans and the Americans with hopes of establishing regular cross-Atlantic flights. The splendid *Hindenburg* appeared all set to triumph in 1937, until one evening in May it nosed down to its mast at Lakehurst airfield at the end of a long voyage and exploded into a sheet of flame, which lit up the sky like a funeral pyre – which it was more than metaphorically: thirty-six people died, and so did the future of the airship that evening.

Meanwhile, aeroplanes had been performing heroically since Alcock and Brown's sixteen-hour Atlantic crossing in 1919. Ross Smith without so much as a wireless aboard had flown from London to Australia inside a month in the same year. In 1925 the Marquese de Pinedo took a leisurely six months to fly from Italy to Japan and back. In 1926 Lieut-Commander Byrd made the hazardous hop from Spitzbergen to the North Pole, and returned safely to the relief of all America. But the achievement which captured the heart of the whole world was Charles Lindbergh's solo flight from New York to Paris in May 1927. He looked so *young*, more vulnerable even than his machine *The Spirit of St Louis*, as it lurched, sputtered and eventually dragged itself into the air from Long Island. Even as he was flying his marathon solo, 40,000 hard-bitten boxing fans were praying publicly and devoutly at the Yankee Stadium for his safety. When he landed at Paris to the tumultuous welcome of 100,000 Frenchmen, those commercial firms that had been struggling against public apathy (indeed opposition) to scheduled flying took heart.

By the 1930s underwriters were having to insure bigger and more expensive machines than they would have dreamed of in the twenties, and it soon became clear that the small group at Lloyd's which had combined with certain companies to corner a virtual monopoly of aviation business would not be able to cope; very quickly large syndicates were assembled to deal with nothing except aviation risks. And, since it was only a brave – and wealthy – man who committed himself to a commercial flight in those days, there was a rapidly accelerating demand for passenger accident cover (not from the airlines themselves, but from their passengers) up to as much as £100,000 in many cases. Aviation was developing faster than any previous known means of transport, and Lloyd's was grasping the opportunities in both hands.

UNUSUAL INSURANCE

IT IS SAID that there exists no insurable risk on earth that cannot be insured with Lloyd's. In any event, it is true that any risk that cannot be placed in the Room may be considered uninsurable virtually anywhere in the world. Inevitably, since Lloyd's have branched out beyond the confines of purely marine insurance, underwriters have been presented with many weird and wonderful risks to consider. Some of course have been unashamedly for the purposes of publicity and others have been frivolous in the extreme (which may or may not account for the discernible traces of embarrassment earlier chroniclers of Lloyd's have displayed when arriving at this aspect of underwriters' activity). But a great many of them have been perfectly serious, and offer an intriguing insight into the ever-expanding spectrum of human fears in an age of anxiety.

Undeniably some people's bodies (or component parts thereof) may be considered their most important, often extremely valuable, asset and it is to be expected that they should look to Lime Street for protection. Marlene Dietrich's legs have been insured at Lloyd's – as have Rudolph Nureyev's for £190,000, though presumably for different reasons. Schnozzle Durante's nose, Bette Davis's waistline, Paderewski's fingers and Olivia de Havilland's jaw (before being socked by Ray Milland in a film shot) all required cover at one time or another. An eminent professional Fat Lady in the 1920s found it prudent to insure against growing thin; other thinner ladies have found it harder but not impossible to insure against the dreaded fat. One film company even took out a million-dollar policy with Lloyd's against the possibility of one of their actresses falling in love and getting married during her contract of service.

There was a time when saloon-keepers in America insured themselves against the injuries their customers might inflict on bystanders (which soon turned into a racket when the bystander agreed to let himself be slugged and split the claim), but latterly American preparedness has exceeded even these bounds: recently the litigants in a court case insured the life of the presiding judge at Lloyd's. Had the judge died during the hearing, they argued, considerable expense would have resulted through having to start the trial all over again. For rather less high-minded motives a cinema owner has been known to insure his audience against dying of excessive laughter – presumably the underwriter was confident that the film in question certainly wasn't that funny.

Underwriters at Lloyd's would be the last people

Some of the more unusual risks that have been accepted at Lloyd's in recent years.

Opposite: *the legs of Marlene Dietrich and Rudolph Nureyev; and the well-being of the Loch Ness Monster.*

This page: *the English World Cup football team, the nose of Schnozzle Durante, the diamonds of Elizabeth Taylor and (below) the life of Namu, the Killer Whale.*

to be surprised at the astonishing range of man's pessimism (or optimism). Hole-in-one insurances are regularly placed in the Room, sometimes for as much as $50,000 a time. The Shah of Persia's coach-builder had a special life insurance because, it turned out, he was the only man in the world who could have completed the building of the Shah's coronation coach. The author of a book entitled "July 14 Assassination" judiciously took out an insurance against the death of President de Gaulle before the publication of the book. Forty members of the "Whiskers Club" in Derbyshire each insured their beard for £20 against fire and theft, while Elizabeth Taylor's rather more famous adornment, her Cartier diamond, would cost underwriters $1,200,000 in similar circumstances. Even a grain of rice with a portrait of the Queen and the Duke of Edinburgh engraved on it has its own price at Lloyd's – in this case $20,000.

When a killer whale called "Namu" was captured off the Canadian Pacific coast and towed to Seattle for display in an aquarium, it was insured at Lloyd's for $8,000 against various contingencies, including rescue attempts by other whales. Even the Loch Ness monster, which has so far escaped Namu's fate, has a premium on his head. Cutty Sark Whisky recently offered a one million pound prize (like Bertram Mills Circus some years previously) to anyone who could capture Nessie alive – an eventuality which, needless to say, would have cost underwriters dearly but as the policy stipulated that it should be brought to London and identified by a qualified zoologist, the risk was minimal.

It is no less astonishing what people conceive to be occupational hazards. Lloyd's has insured a professional dance team against injuries "while doing the twist", and the owner of a chinchilla farm against the death of his animals due to noise from low-flying aircraft. A composer, Richard Stockler, has insured his ears, and a whisky distiller his nose. Numerous parents have obtained cover against the danger of multiple births increasing household expenditure (a couple in Michigan had twins and collected; insured again at a higher rate and promptly had twins for the second time). The British Trans-Arctic expedition took out a £30,000 indemnity policy for the duration of their trek across the North Pole, and the English World Cup football squad received cover for their trip to Mexico for the 1970 World Cup (which in view of the riots which preceded it was money well spent). As a percentage of any syndicate's premium income such policies as these are negligible. But even if they are scarcely going to affect the results at the end of the year they bring a touch of light relief to the often serious atmosphere in the Box. And they confirm Lloyd's reputation as the most receptive insurance market anywhere in the world.

LLOYD'S SINCE THE FIRST WAR

BY THE OUTBREAK of the war, the general pattern of modern Lloyd's was already formed and the ground rules established. Since then the story has been one of consolidation – of its internal structure by amendments to the 1871 Act in 1925 and 1951 – of retrenchment with the momentous 1982 Lloyd's Act which provided the framework for proper self-regulation, and of rapid technological development to keep pace with the increasingly complex commitments of the nuclear, post-industrial age. At Lloyd's, as elsewhere, the inexorable trend has been towards bigness: in 1928 during the last days at the Royal Exchange its overall premium income was £22 million; in the early sixties it was some £300 million. Twenty-five years later it is approaching £10 billion accruing from some 160 countries, a highly significant contribution to the country's invisible earnings.

All this has highlighted a recurring problem at Lloyd's, that of increasing pressure on the available space. Life at the Royal Exchange had become intolerable even before the war, notwithstanding the annexing of additional offices and the ditching of redundant statues to create more space for underwriting. It could get so hot sometimes in the Room that huge pans filled with blocks of ice had to be placed in the alleyways! In 1923 the Committee bowed to the inevitable and decided to build its own freehold property. An arrangement with the Royal Mail Group was made to jointly purchase the site of the old East India House (where was discovered in the course of excavations for the new building the fragment of skull of a Neanderthal lady – thus eclipsing by several millenia the youthful shades of Clive and Hastings). The commission to design a building for both parties went to Sir Edwin Cooper, an architect already noted for his monumental style as exemplified by his earlier design for the Port of London Authority headquarters. Lloyd's section was completed first and formally opened by King George V in 1928. It proved to be a worthy testament to the solidity of Lloyd's in the commercial order of things: outside a facade unadorned and megalithic, inside marble halls, vaulted ceilings, cast bronze gates and neo-classic mouldings. It had an area of 16,000 square feet and its ratio of seating to walkways of 1:2 suggested that at last the need to devour more floor-space was over. Yet by 1937 a brokers' annexe had to be opened next door and by 1948 the overcrowding was chronic.

Fortunately across the road the Luftwaffe had provided a possible alternative, a group of bomb sites that were gradually being bought up to form a large area. Here it was in 1952 that the Queen laid the foundation stone of Lloyd's second freehold building, Terence Heysham's stripped-down clas-

Above: *the Queen in the Underwriting Room at Lloyd's, on the occasion of laying the foundation stone of the new building in Lime Street, November 6 1952, from the painting by Terence Cuneo.*

Right: *Poy in the* Evening News.

sical design that curved subtly along the length of Fenchurch Avenue, a modern, five-story building with 44,250 square feet of underwriting space (making Lloyd's in fact the largest City landowner after the Bank of England). If hardly beautiful, it was at least functional. The Caller sat in the raised rostrum, wearing his traditional red robe with black collar, calling out the names of brokers wanted by their colleagues at the rate of anything up to sixty a minute. Above him stood the venerable Lutine bell, side by side with an indicating system which enabled itinerant brokers to signal their whereabouts automatically on a screen.

Upstairs was the Committee Room, where traditionally every Wednesday morning the Committee of Lloyd's met to discuss the problems of the day, and it is the sum of these deliberations, week after week and year after year, that has built up the mosaic of contemporary Lloyd's, at once archaic – after all it is six years senior to the Bank of England – yet curiously modern.

The Committee's agenda is sometimes parochial, but often far-reaching. A crisis, for instance, occurred in 1923 when an underwriter named Harrison turned up in the Committee room and broke the news that his syndicate was completely insolvent, with between £200,000 and £300,000 of claims to be met. Arthur Sturge, the incumbent Chairman of the day, called an extraordinary meeting of underwriters and there made a statement that in retrospect was historic. If Harrison's claims were not settled, he told them, the good name of Lloyd's would be seriously prejudiced. He put it to the meeting that in some way or other the money must be found. Every underwriter contributed, and the debts were paid off. "Harrison's Folly" as it came to be known touched a point of principle which is fundamental to Lloyd's. Whatever the cost, the policy-holder must be looked after. From this conception grew the Lloyd's Central Fund, which levies a small sum from each Member every year. Its value is never disclosed, but it serves today as an ultimate safeguard to the assured, should the total wealth of all the members of a syndicate at any time prove insufficient.

Internal crises of this nature are notably rare, but, although it is axiomatic that Lloyd's never involves itself in politics, political crises cannot be prevented from intruding from time to time upon Lloyd's. Such a crisis blew up in April 1936 when it became patently obvious to the City – followed closely by the press – that details of the Budget had been prematurely leaked. Massive insurances against an increase in income tax had been placed at the eleventh hour: some newspapers quoted underwriters' liabilities to be "at least £100,000, more than ten times the normal sum" (the normal sum, however, was very much an unknown quantity, for several people had made large sums of

Above: *headlines of 1936 on the Budget leak scandal.*

money on budget insurance in 1934). In due course J.H. Thomas, a Cabinet Minister, resigned and a Budget Tribunal was set up to inquire into the "leak". The Committee of Lloyd's presented a schedule of the relevant insurances to the Tribunal, which included the intriguing information that £30,000 worth of insurance at that time remained unclaimed.

Foreign legislation is also a question which frequently crops up. Under the guise of security, the governments of many countries bring in laws that are designed to protect their own national insurance

Above: *an impression of the Underwriting Room in 1927 by George Belcher of* Punch.

Below left: *The new building in Lime Street and (below) Sydney Jones' drawing of it in 1956.*

companies and keep the foreigners out. Many require that insurers put up a local deposit to guarantee their business. For companies who are a corporate entity and (theoretically at least) not mortal, this is by no means an insoluble difficulty. But for Lloyd's, made up of individual underwriters who lack this continuity, it has at times been a serious problem. Nothing like Lloyd's, made up of one-man businesses, exists elsewhere and insurance legislation abroad is not designed for it. Eventually, after years of discussion, the Committee decided that a finance company, quite separate from the normal workings of the Room but controlled by the Corporation, should be founded for the sole purpose of providing deposits abroad. In 1936 Neville Dixey finally brought this scheme to fruition.

The new company, known as Additional Securities Ltd, was to be managed by the Committee but owned by the underwriters, drawing its revenue from an annual levy of a quarter percent on the income of non-marine underwriters. Put this way, it sounds quite simple of course. But in fact it took ten years to devise, and enabled Lloyd's underwriters to extend their international operations in many areas which would otherwise be closed to them. (In the Communist world, of course, as in many newly emerging nations, insurance like most other things is nationalised, which often results in far higher premiums – though even the strictest ideological considerations do not seem to prevent a considerable slice of nationalised foreign business from returning to Lloyd's in the shape of re-insurance cover.)

Another troublesome matter for the Committee has been the problem of currency control. So long as the pound was paramount (and an Englishman's sovereign as good as his word) all transactions were easily negotiated in sterling. But once it had ceased to be the sheet anchor of commerce, settlement of claims had to be paid out in a bewildering catalogue of currencies, each subject to its own controlled idiosyncracies – the managers of the Policy Signing Office might be forgiven for wondering sometimes if they have not strayed into a new scenario for Alice Through the Looking-Glass. Whereas before the war they had only to deal with sterling rates, in the last three decades they have issued policies in over 150 different currencies – including, quite recently, roubles. Gosstrakh and Ingosstrakh, the Soviet State insurance, frequently place business in London, and some of the satellite countries prefer to deal with Lloyd's rather than with Big Brother's organisations.

During the Second World War the Government was given a monopoly on the insurance of private property, which was covered by the Board of Trade. By a gentleman's agreement, the Government also underwrote the war risks on shipping and cargo to and from the British Isles, but (since foreigners

Above: 'The underwriter who missed the total loss'. *Cartoon by H.M. Bateman from a specially commissioned series on Lloyd's.*

could not be obliged to insure with the British Government) the London market was permitted to cover the risks on cross-voyages between overseas countries. In spite of heavy losses through submarine activity, particularly during 1942, Lloyd's underwriters continued to write war risks and emerged at the end of hostilities generally unscathed. The chief problem of the war, as it turned out, proved to be that of keeping up the flow of necessary shipping intelligence without giving information to the enemy. The authorities in Washington, especially, suspected that news about ships' movements could be harmful to security. As it happened, all this information was routed through the Admiralty and Lloyd's own security arrangements were highly efficient. Nevertheless the Administration put its foot down and prohibited any insurance order to be sent abroad which mentioned either a ship or its destination.

They were equally drastic about domestic non-marine matters: neither for fire cover nor even reinsurance could the name of the insurer nor a description of the risk be given to underwriters. After nearly fifty years of covering fire and burglary risks in the States, Lloyd's were suddenly cut off from the entire American market. But for prompt action by Sir Eustace Pulbrook, indeed the American connection would most definitely have been snapped. For the first time the Chairman of Lloyd's flew over the Atlantic (at considerable personal risk and discomfort) to seek a solution through long and tedious negotiations with the military bureaucracy. The problem was ultimately ironed out by the setting up of a Lloyd's liaison office in New York, which would act as a sort of filter, receiving the details of non-marine risks to be covered and transmitting each risk back to London but without any details. Although quite in the dark about what he was covering, the Lloyd's underwriter would accept the risk and notify the New York office who would then issue the policy. For most of the war underwriting in the USA became a variation of Blind Man's Buff. But it enabled the ties between Lloyd's and America to continue.

LLOYD'S AT WORK

THERE ARE ASPECTS of the business conducted at Lloyd's which no amount of words are entirely adequate to explain – the imponderables, like what constitutes the right rate for a risk, or what distinguishes a good from a bad risk? In such matters underwriters have only their own experience and instinct to guide them. When asked how he set about assessing any particular risk, one notable underwriter in the Room today pondered the question for a moment, then observed that he just "felt it in his water". Little help to the outsider, but probably as accurate as you can get.

For nearly a century now, underwriting members have been grouped into syndicates managed by an agent, who appoints a professional underwriter to accept business on its behalf – and each member is responsible for his proportion of the liability of the syndicate's share of the risk. Because of this, members are called upon to provide a substantial deposit as security for their liabilities (which may be invested so that they still receive the dividends from it). The amount of premium that each underwriting member may earn is proportional to this deposit: the larger the deposit, the greater the premium income permitted. All premium income derived by the syndicate has to be paid into a trust fund from which claims are paid; it is retained in the fund for three years, after which, when the necessary reserves for late claims have been put aside, any profit may be released to the members. And, of course, as a further protection of solvency, the member's underwriting affairs are subject to an annual audit.

The underwriter's job remains what it always has been: to determine the rates and conditions for any particular risk and to decide what share of the risk he will take – nowadays not for himself, but for his syndicate. There are in the Room about seventy marine underwriters, over fifty non-marine and thirty motor. In the newer, but rapidly expanding, aviation market there are now more than twenty specialists.

Only Lloyd's brokers (that is, brokers approved by the Committee) are allowed to place business with underwriters in the Room. The general public cannot deal direct, and their insurances must be placed through an accredited brokerage firm. It is

Below: *the office of the Lloyd's agent in Amsterdam —there are now over 1,300 agents and sub-agents all round the world.*

this, in effect, which represents one of the big differences between Lloyd's and the insurance companies. The Lloyd's broker can place business with a company, of course, but whereas a company can do business direct with the public, the Lloyd's underwriter is completely dependent on the Lloyd's broker. Moreover Lloyd's is a competitive market that competes not only with the companies, but within itself. Underwriters may co-operate with each other over the provision of services (a central accounting system, for instance, a policy-signing office and claims-settlement arrangements) but they compete for business – and there are often many differing views within the market about the same risk.

The broker, when he receives an enquiry or an order from a client, prepares what is called a "slip" – a sheet of cardboard or thick paper on which the broker will put down details of the risk against which he requires cover. His job is to approach those underwriters whom he knows will be interested in that type of business, and to find the underwriter who will give him the best terms. Once the underwriter has agreed a rate and conditions, he will then write his "line" (*i.e.* share of the risk) on the slip and initial it. The broker will then move on to other underwriters and persuade them to contribute further lines until he has covered the whole risk.

At busy times there may be as many as 4,000 people on the floor of the Room – underwriters and their staffs and the brokers placing business with them. Addressing the Association of Business Graduates recently, Mr Paul Dixey remarked "I still find it fascinating to look down and watch where various brokers are placing their business. One may be placing a fleet of Greek ships, big tankers and ore carriers. The total value of the fleet may be $100 million. Perhaps the previous record of the fleet has been bad, the owner has not been too particular in his choice of officers and engineers, and there have been heavy claims for crew negligence. Underwriters will almost certainly be insisting that the owner has a large "deductible" (*i.e.* the part of the risk he bears himself) and has also to pay a large percentage of any crew-negligence claims himself.

"Another broker may be trying to cover a national airline against hi-jacking (a risk, incidentally, which commercially at least only Lloyd's underwriters have been prepared to insure). A third may be insuring a racehorse that has suddenly become valuable on winning a big race. A fourth is trying to arrange cover for all the shipments overseas of a famous distillery, while at the same time his colleague is endeavouring to insure the loss of profits that would result if the distillery was burnt down."

Paul Dixey summed it all up: "The whole world

Above: *Sidney Boulton, Chairman of Lloyd's from 1920 to 1921.*

Above: *Neville Dixey, who was Chairman of Lloyd's in 1931, 1933 and 1936.*

Above: *Peter Miller, the present chairman of Lloyd's.*

Left: *The underwriting room in Terence Heysham's 1958 building.*

Above: *Captain Carlsen's brave effort to stay aboard the stricken ship* Flying Enterprise *in January 1952. taken only twenty-four hours before the boat sank.*

does business at Lloyd's, and a great part of our strength is that we know what is going on all over the world. We don't always draw the right conclusions, but the rest of the insurance world looks to us to give them a lead, to show them the way to solve their difficulties. In the marine market especially, the whole world looks to London and Lloyd's in particular."

It is thanks to the experience, gained from writing business from all parts of the world, that the men of Lloyd's wield such an influence. There are leaders in the market who, from specialist knowledge, are generally accepted as experts whom the rest of the market will follow – critically of course, rather than blindly, for they keep records too, and a leader in a particular type of business will soon lose his authority if he were to lead the market astray. Equally, if the leaders are too rigid in their approach, other underwriters will cut their rates, even at the expense of market agreements. There are always rebels at Lloyd's, ready to show the "big boys" how to underwrite, and others who will flock to their standard. If the rates are too low, there will be market meetings and private talks, and eventually rates will be forced up to economic levels. Working in one Room, having coffee or lunch together, produces a collective wisdom, a Lloyd's view which the whole world is prepared to listen to.

TWENTIETH CENTURY HAZARDS

IN THE PREAMBLE of an Act passed in the reign of the first Elizabeth, the benefits of insurance were summed up thus: "upon the loss or perishing of any ship there followeth not the undoing of any man, but the loss lighteth rather more easily upon many than heavily upon few". Underwriters in the age of the second Elizabeth may be concerned with rather more than the loss or perishing of a ship, but the hazards they are called upon to anticipate and assess have not fundamentally changed.

Arbitrary Kings and Princes may no longer be able to detain vessels as the spirit moves them, but Governments and Presidents can be as fickle – as Lloyd's discovered in 1958 when the Indonesians seized forty ships from a Dutch shipping company, so exposing underwriters to a huge claim if the ships were not released by a certain date. Roy Merrett, a prominent marine underwriter, Harold Hopwood, the then chairman of the Institute of London Underwriters, and Paul Dixey (the present Chairman of Lloyd's) who had contacts in Indonesia, flew out to Djakarta to see what could be done. The Indonesians were well disposed towards Britain but they found it difficult to believe that the loss would fall on Lloyd's rather than the Dutch, and they kept the Lloyd's delegation hanging about in frustration. Meanwhile the deadline was approaching and the obligation to pay out £11 million in cash for ships, whose salvage and recovery value was uncertain, drew perilously close. Finally, Paul Dixey, remembering that he had once met the Indonesian Foreign Minister when he was Ambassador in London, put a call through to his wife and was invited to their home. In this informal setting he was able to explain Lloyd's predicament. The Minister was won round. "Mr Dixey" he said, "we're going to give you back those ships". And so, in the nick of time, the ships were released.

Equally, Greek corsairs and Barbary pirates no longer roam the Mediterranean preying on unarmed merchantmen; but modern guerillas and terrorists are more unpredictable in their targets and more sophisticated in their methods. They may strike at a crowded airport or an isolated pipeline with equal effect. It may even be the sad fate of an underwriter today to watch his risk going up in smoke on television in the evening – as several did when Arab terrorists blew up three airliners at Dawsons Field recently and had the whole spectacle filmed.

Nor have the savage forces of nature noticeably abated over the centuries, or man found a way to predict their fury. In 1954 a series of decidedly unfeminine hurricanes, perversely designated Carol, Edna and Hazel, swept through the Americas leaving a trail of claims in their wake amounting to some $75 million. But all these are hazards which have been recognised and enumerated in Lloyd's policies from the days of the coffee-house. What has changed – and changed with dizzying speed in the last two decades – is the magnitude and scope of the risks involved. The urge – sometimes the necessity – to travel farther and faster, to transport cargoes in larger quantities, to explore the once unattainable reaches of space, to protect our vulnerable environment from the calamities of our new technology, to build bigger and more ambitiously – all these have had to be reflected and safeguarded at Lloyd's. And, as always, the lessons have had to be learnt the hard way.

*   *   *   *   *

The immediate post-war period at Lloyd's showed highly profitable results, which lasted more or less through the fifties. But in the peacetime retrenchment (which paradoxically brought only a diminishing stature for the victors) underwriters, like the nation itself, seemed exhausted in spirit. The dead hand of egalitarianism appeared to crumble individual initiative at a time when historically speaking a new technological age was upon us. Underwriting became both constipated and careless. A scramble for premiums and marginal rates, aggravated by miscalculation of the effects of inflation, coincided with a series of catastrophic

disasters, and in the sixties Lloyd's was faced with one of the most serious crises of its history. Three or four bad years, of which 1965 was the worst, brought many syndicates almost to their knees and caused some financial experts to question, as they had periodically in the past, whether Lloyd's could indeed survive. For just as the accountants were revealing that, even without exceptional calamities, the current underwriting was unprofitable, the claims for Hurricane Betsy came in. Some individual Names found themselves faced with a call for anything up to £50,000 each.

Lloyd's as a whole went down tens of millions in 1965, and an average loss per member was up to £10,000 a head. In the face of such rivers of red ink, numerous members resigned, and even some of the moneymen were suddenly disenchanted with the Corporation. "I wouldn't touch Lloyd's with the wrong end of Kew Gardens flagpole" said a disillusioned banker. He was wrong, of course. The English spirit flourishes best in adversity and underwriters rose splendidly to the challenge.

Having recovered its equilibrium after the ravages incurred by Hurricane Betsy in 1965, the Lloyd's market was seemingly set to enjoy something of a profitable hiatus: earnings were quietly pushing upwards, every year the market was absorbing comfortably an increasing influx of new underwriting names and the financial commentators of the day had quite enough on their hands, what with the collapse of insurance groups like Vehicle and General and the property collapse and secondary banking crisis of 1974, to become too involved with goings-on in Lime Street. But this was to prove to be the calm before the storm: a storm from which Lloyd's today may have emerged fitter, stronger, more professional than ever before, but nonetheless painful to endure for all that.

Significantly the problems of the 1970s did not centre on profitability. True, the financial sums involved in world insurance business were increasing all the time, with bigger jets, bigger tankers and new technology bringing with it what underwriters refer to as "greater concentration of risk." But underwriters' inherent flexibility enabled the market to steer a sound enough course through such potential minefields and invariably still end up with a profit at the end of the day.

The problems were more of a moral nature. The resurgence of Lloyd's international reputation as an insurer of last resort – when the risks were too big or complicated for less flexible markets to handle – and the massive influx of new underwriting names brought with them some of the harsher realities of the commercial world outside.

Before the decade was through even Lloyd's traditionalists were reluctantly to concede that the market's by-words *Uberrema Fides* – utmost good faith – were not in themselves sufficient to maintain the standards of fair play and integrity on which the market's modern reputation was founded. Among Lloyd's new breed of technologically minded, utterly professional underwriters and brokers were a few who proved to be less than gentlemen. Now Lloyd's would never claim that its ranks had not been infiltrated by rogues before. But whereas in the past a wink and perhaps a shove from the guardians of propriety might have nipped malpractices in the bud, the litigious nature of modern society seemed to work against a Lloyd's whose laws in the main were drawn up in the previous century.

Many people operating in the market as underwriters or brokers found their loyalties torn between Lloyd's and outside interests, sometimes shareholders in public companies. A few were prepared to exploit the situation; rules were bent, sometimes broken; disputes occurred and parties involved were increasingly prepared to seek redress outside the market place rather than accept the decisions of the 'club' committee.

Against this troubled background Lloyd's found itself on the horns of an embarrassing dilemma as a result of developments in the world of insurance broking. Some American broking firms who channelled much of their business to Lloyd's were unhappy about market rules which refused them direct access to the underwriting room. Instead they had to pass the business to accredited Lloyd's broking firms and of course share the commission with them. However, a far more significant factor was the desire to acquire the international business accounts held by Lloyd's brokers in so many parts of the world outside the United States.

To get round the problem the Americans came up with a simple enough solution. They would takeover Lloyd's brokers through bids on the stockmarket. Several takeover moves duly went ahead, including one for one of Lloyd's most famous firms, C.T. Bowring. Lloyd's officials were plunged into confusion. Their rules prevented unapproved groups from placing business direct in the marketplace – to ensure the market was able to retain some measure of control – but at the same time it was clear that such a stance could be deeply offensive to major – and highly respectable – American groups who, after all, provided a large chunk of the market's total premiums.

While this debate was continuing an even more potentially damaging storm was brewing. Now referred to widely as the "Sasse affair", the trouble centred on one of Lloyd's smaller underwriting syndicates, the 110-member Syndicate 762 headed by Mr Frederick Sasse. By 1977 it had become apparent that the syndicate was running into heavy weather on a mass of US and Canadian claims, mainly from fire insurances on ghetto properties, introduced to Lloyd's via a "binding authority" agreement. Binding authorities enabled underwriters like Sasse to appoint representatives to undertake business on behalf of a syndicate without having it signed in the Lime Street "room".

Clearly in this case, however, something had got out of hand. Some of the policies involved were highly suspect and what's more it was clear that the syndicate's premium limits had been wildly exceeded. By the time Lloyd's was able to get a grip on the syndicate's affairs it faced losses of over £21 million, not a colossal sum when compared with the market's overall profits but one which spelt severe financial hardship, even bankruptcy for some of the 110 names.

There followed an unprecedented development. Many of the syndicate members came together to sue in the courts not only the syndicate's head and the insurance broker chiefly responsible for producing much of the business but Lloyd's itself. Against Lloyd's they claimed that proper controls had not been exercised over the running of the Sasse Syndicate and that under Lloyd's antiquated statutes "binding authorities" were not legal anyway. All business must be done in the Lime Street underwriting room, they declared, and Lloyd's had a duty to ensure that if not it should at least be rigorously controlled.

In the end, after much dispute and a host of writs and counter-writs, the committee of Lloyd's conceded that it would be unfair for the "armchair" underwriting members of the Sasse Syndicate to shoulder all the losses. A compromise was reached in which the syndicate members' losses would be limited to just over £6 million. Anything above that would be met by all 18,500 members of the Lloyd's market in 1980.

By that date, however, the Lloyd's committee, then chaired by Mr Ian Findlay, had become aware of certain disputes between underwriters and brokers and one of these, known in the market as the "Butter Mountain" following a fire which destroyed a butter warehouse in Holland, spurred the Lloyd's committee to take a brave step, a calculated gamble, in fact, in keeping with the risk-taking ethos of the market itself. They would appoint a working party to look into every aspect of the way the market conducted its affairs, and more significantly they promised to publish its findings. The inner workings of Lloyd's were to be exposed warts and all.

The committee under the chairmanship of Sir Henry Fisher, President of Wolfson College, Oxford, and a former High Court judge, who had no previous links with Lloyd's, duly set to work investigating every aspect of the market's affairs with particular regard to the way it regulated its members. After 18 months and 79 rounds of discussion, Sir Henry's seven-man committee came up in June 1980 with what Lloyd's existing chairman, Mr Peter Green, was to describe as "a blueprint for change."

It had quickly become apparent to the committee that Lloyd's needed to go through a similar transformation to that endured by another great British institution, the London Stock Exchange, some two decades before. As the Stock Exchange had discovered then, Lloyd's self-regulatory powers, as bestowed by Royal Charter, were out of step with the modern world. Its rule book was unwieldly, its statutes were firmly rooted in the previous century and its bye-laws so vague as to be easily flouted by erring members. Taking a leaf out of the Stock Exchange's book the Fisher Report declared that Lloyd's needed a new Council of Lloyd's. This would comprise the existing 16-man committee, which had previously controlled the market's affairs, but also six underwriting names, who did not work in the market and three completely independent outsiders, whose appointments would be vetted by none less than the Governor of the Bank of England.

This Council would have full powers to make new rules and by-laws to meet changing circumstances. The Fisher Report also proposed a whole series of procedures to tighten up the market's existing controls and a set of new disciplinary procedures, including fines, suspension and expulsion of members.

More controversially, as it was to turn out, the Fisher working party decided there should be a complete break in shareholding links between insurance brokers and managing agencies, the groups which look after the affairs of underwriting syndicates. These links should be terminated, the report suggested by divestment by the brokers concerned within the space of five years. The reasons Sir Henry gave for such a dramatic step were that the risks of abuses were sufficient to constitute a real threat to the good name of Lloyd's.

He pointed out that a Lloyd's broker could put pressure on an underwriter over which he had control, to write risks contrary to his better judgement, to offer preferential premium rates, to give higher commissions or to settle claims on terms which he would not otherwise agree.

On the other hand the broker could act against the interest of his client by giving business to his controlled syndicate although better terms might be available elsewhere.

Openly welcoming the majority of the Fisher Report's views, the existing committee immediately set to work drafting a new Act of Parliament, as required to set in motion the main body of proposals, including the formation of the new 25-man Council.

This in turn led to an historic event, for under Lloyd's existing constitution, the new Act required support by vote from more than half the market's members. On Monday, 4 November 1980 the Albert Hall was hired to enable the new Act to be debated by the full membership. Altogether more than 4,000 members turned out. Armed with 10,000 proxy votes in favour of the draft Bill being submitted to Parliament, Lloyd's chairman, Mr Peter Green was under no illusions as to which way the vote would go when he entered the hall. This, however, did not prevent a lively debate, nor indeed what some Lloyd's officials were to describe later with some bemusement as a "party atmosphere." The private Bill, mainly establishing and defining the functions and powers of the new Council was duly lodged on 26 November 1980 and is now continuing its Parliamentary passage.

Ironically on the very day the Bill was lodged another development in the affairs of Lloyd's was gaining publicity. The market announced that the total losses that underwriters could face on computer leasing insurance policies had been estimated by an American bank at $400 million. In a decade in which Jumbo jets collided and supertankers sank, seemingly by the dozen, there was something unique and almost quaintly typical of Lloyd's that the market should be facing the biggest stream of losses in its history from something as esoteric as "computer leasing insurance."

Computer leasing, the underwriters now readily admit was one of those classic cases, where the risk-takers at Lloyd's got their calculations wrong. The loss stemmed from developments in the computer market in the early 1970s. Computer leasing firms in the US were doing brisk business hiring out machines to a growing list of firms anxious to take advantage of new technological aids.

But the lesser firms had one big worry despite the booming growth of their profits. What if new advancements in technology rendered the computers they were renting out obsolete? Customers would cancel their contracts and they would be left high and dry holding near useless machines, which in many cases had been purchased through huge borrowings. The answer to their problems, of course, was insurance, but who outside the flexible underwriters at Lloyd's would consider such a novel venture.

Below: *the Broker's slip on the largest tanker afloat in 1973 showing the amount of risk accepted by each Syndicate and their reference numbers.*

Background: *the blowing-up of three commercial airliners, hi-jacked by Arab terrorists and taken to Dawson's Field.*

Insets: *other modern hazards that face a Lloyd's Underwriter: (top left) riot damage, during the Detroit race riots of 1967; (bottom left) hurricanes, here the fury of Hurricane Betsy vented on Fort Lauderdale, Florida in September 1965; (top right) floods, as at Rapid City, South Dakota October 1972; and (bottom right) space adventure, the splashdown of Apollo 15.*

Lloyd's reacted characteristically and soon policies covering the eventuality were streaming into the market. Then what can be seen, only in retrospect, as the inevitable, happened. IBM, the international leader in computer technology brought out a new series of machines, which were not only more efficient and smaller than previous models but in many cases a good deal cheaper as well. Leasing customers began cancelling their contracts by the hundred and the claims poured into Lloyd's. Many more claims are still to pour in as break clauses in contracts continue to occur.

The whole affair has of course caused many a red face among underwriters who led the risks in Lloyd's, but the market as a whole has not emerged too badly. Underwriters involved in computer leasing were ordered by the committee to provide for virtually all the anticipated losses against their 1977 profits.

Despite these provisions overall profits for that year – declared in September 1980, under the market's three-year accounting policy – still showed a rise to £131.3 million, the second best result in Lloyd's history. Announcing the result, Mr Peter Green, whose own syndicate, Janson Green, was involved in the computer leasing business, declared wryly: "many people with the benefit of hindsight have suggested that this was a class of business that underwriters had got badly wrong and I would not venture to disagree."

That, however, was only one symptom of an ailing industry which was having to operate in a context of world-wide recession, very high interest rates and market over-capacity. With an ever-growing insurance capacity chasing a declining market, underwriters were finding themselves having to quote totally uneconomic rates for business and hope to offset the almost inevitable underwriting losses with profits from investment of their premium income. Which is not, of course, insurance so much as financial manipulation over which the ever-present spectre of insolvency looms. In addition to this there were other new classes of business, apart from computer leasing, which were alarmingly defying all the best-calculated predictions. 'Longtail' business, where claims can come in many years after the insurance is first placed, was proving especially vulnerable: claims for asbestosis (for example), the disease contracted by prolonged contact with asbestos, were found to be mounting inordinately, inflated in the United States by often staggeringly large court settlements. Many such claims – not to mention the vexed question of the effect that such meteoric compensation under the present American tort system is having on insurance – remain even yet unresolved.

Another growing sector of the market, pioneered by Lloyd's aviation underwriters but still studded with risks, was spaceflight insurance. As the US shuttle started to ferry regular payloads into space and increasing amounts of priceless hardware were

put into orbit the demand for cover grew more pressing. From 1974 to 1982 Lloyd's insured numerous satellites for up to $100 million each and earned gross premiums of $120 million. But the harsh realities to date are that the losses paid out by the international insurance market have amounted to over $200 million. Yet the challenges of this type of business have also brought out that pioneering spirit which has always been a characteristic of Lloyd's. Having paid out more than $70 million when two satellites, Westar 6 and Palapa 12 launched in February 1984, failed to reach their intended orbits, underwriters led by Stephen Merrett determined to undertake an unprecedented salvage mission. They hired the shuttle Discovery to return to space and retrieve the rogue satellites, an operation that was carried out by five astronauts with brilliant success and which won them all the coveted Lloyd's silver medal. It was the first time the medal had been awarded for anything other than marine salvage and only the second occasion it had gone to a woman – Anne Lee Fisher, one of the crew.

This triumph, however, could not disguise the fact that on satellite insurance, as in so many other areas, premiums had for a number of years been too low. When the balance sheet for 1983 was presented (after the statutory three-year interval) in 1986, it recorded that Lloyd's had made an overall profit of just £36 million on a gross income of £6.1bn. What gave the greatest cause for concern was that virtually all the 1983 underwriting losses were incurred by the liability class of insurance, even though it constituted just 12 per cent of all premium income. Also behind these figures lay another disturbing problem.

Out of that sum provision had had to be made for £143 million underwriting losses on a group of syndicates formerly managed by Peter Cameron-Webb and better known by then – even to the most casual reader of the financial columns – as PCW. To unravel the tangled web of this company's activities it is necessary to go back at least to the early months of 1982, when an American firm Alexander & Alexander made a firm bid to take over the Alexander Howden Group, which was a broking and underwriting group owning amongst other things some of the fastest-growing syndicates at Lloyd's. When their auditors, as required by US law, began making the necessary review of Howden's affairs, they became suspicious of the activities of a number of the company's executives – later to be known as 'the gang of four' – which included the chairman, Kenneth Grob, board member Ron Comery, accountant Allan Page and underwriter Jack Carpenter.

What emerged from this investigation, painfully and slowly, was that the gang had used investors' money to buy a Swiss bank and to place reinsur-

Right and below: *The salvage of the century: US astronauts rescuing the errant satellites Westar and Palapa, after underwriters had paid out more than $70 million when they failed to reach their intended orbit.*

Above: *Historic meeting: Members assembled at the Albert Hall on 4 November 1980 to consider, and vote on, the proposals for the new Lloyd's Act.*

Above: *Another bastion falls: in the 1970s ladies – underwriting members and brokers – were permitted to take a full part in the proceedings at Lloyd's: here a vanguard of female brokers is welcomed on their first day.*

ance in offshore companies of which they were the principal beneficiaries. All this had been conducted through an almost impenetrable labyrinth of offshore companies. Almost impenetrable but not quite as it turned out, for the upshot of the affair which rumbled on for several years was the banning of all four principals from ever operating at Lloyd's again.

The Cameron-Webb affair came to light as a result of his complicity with the reinsurance activities of the gang of four. He was deeply involved, with his partner Peter Dixon, in similar schemes of his own which resulted in huge amounts of syndicate funds being misappropriated in offshore reinsurance schemes. Although some £38 million was subsequently recovered, worse was still to come for the dismayed members of the PCW syndicates. In the middle of 1985 they were informed by the agency that had taken over PCW's affairs to try to sort them out (Richard Beckett Underwriting Agency) that additional trading losses were as much as £130 million, for which they of course had collective and unlimited liability. These were, they learned, the result of legitimate underwriting losses, mainly from the placing of disastrous longtail insurances. There were many who doubted that there could be such a thing as 'legitimate' losses in the context of PCW, and positively refused to accept unlimited liability for the acts of fraudulent underwriters. The threat of litigation, both in Britain and the US, between Names and Lloyd's loomed ominously. Even now the threat has not been dispelled, but efforts towards what is hoped to be an acceptable and

Above: *Environmental risks: the 1960s and 1970s brought new and significant problems to the underwriting room, such as wholesale pollution of ocean and beaches by oil slicks, in the wake of supertanker disasters like the breaking-up of the Amoco Cadiz.*

honourable settlement have been continuing with a certain urgency.

The tribulations of PCW have taken us rather ahead of our story, but it was clear that when the Lloyd's Act became law in August 1982 it was not a moment too soon. Although the cases in question pre-dated the passage of the Act, the facts and implications of them inevitably took some time to filter through to the public consciousness. In a climate of nervousness and upheaval in the City – which was itself going through a traumatic period of assorted bank scandals and insider dealing prosecutions, not to mention a mania for mergers and an imminent revolution in the stock exchange – it was sometimes difficult to persuade the press and certain factions in Parliament that Lloyd's own crises were being so publicly aired *because* of the Act not in spite of it. Vociferous voices were heard insisting that Lloyd's should be brought within the scope of the Financial Services Bill (an instrument to provide statutory regulation on City institutions). But the reality was that after three years in business the new Council of Lloyd's was proving to be the best advertisement for self-regulation.

The newly-elected Council first met in January 1983 and one of its first acts was to appoint as chief executive Ian Hay Davison, a distinguished accountant who had already served on a Lloyd's working party. His primary task (and that of his successor in 1986 Alan Lord, former chairman of Dunlop) was to oversee the necessary moves towards effective self-regulation. In partnership with the new chairman of Lloyd's Peter Miller (who took

office in 1984) they have seen a veritable torrent of byelaws emerge from the Council, some forty-five in three years. The groundwork for much of the required internal legislation had already been done by a number of working-parties, and byelaws have now been enacted embracing a whole spectrum of issues, including disciplinary procedures and penalties, disclosure, divestment, and the banning of 'preferred' syndicates. As Peter Miller put it recently, 'Lloyd's has put more on its statute book in the last two and a half years than probably could and would have been achieved by any outside body in ten years'. And as an indication of its determination to put its house in order charges against more than 30 defendants have been determined and penalties imposed ranging from reprimands to expulsion and fines of up to £1 million.

In January 1987 the Neill Committee, set up the previous year by the Minister for Trade and Industry, reported that investigatory and disciplinary measures had been applied by the Council with 'integrity and effectiveness'. At the same time they identified a number of internal reforms that Lloyd's still needed to make (in particular for the protection of Names in the light of the PCW affair) and they recommended a greater participation in the Council by nominated members, that is members from outside the market itself. But the Committee's ultimate conclusion was that Lloyd's itself, rather than an imposed statutory body, was still the best instrument to regulate the market.

The response to this has undoubtedly been renewed confidence in Lloyd's future by investors. Membership of Lloyd's numbers some 31,500 since the beginning of 1987, an increase of almost 200 per cent over the past ten years, and its capacity has trebled, no less, over the past three years.

As if a tangible symbol of renaissance – even as the fledgling Council was spreading its wings – a new headquarters for Lloyd's in the 21st century was beginning to rise on the other side of Lime Street. Although the Society had only been trading in Terence Heysham's new building for 20 years, it was becoming increasingly clear as the market expanded dramatically throughout the 1970s that it could not be accommodated much longer in the inflexible confines of the 1958 building. In 1978 a competition was launched to find a new design-concept for the market-place, which in the event was won by Richard Rogers with a startlingly original answer to the problem. Underlying his design was the inescapable conclusion that since the Room could not expand horizontally then it should have the opportunity to expand vertically. The new Room now occupies four floors interconnected by a system of escalators, and has the capacity to grow in the forseeable future by at least another three floors.

However his solution, given the restraints of

Below and left: *Views of Richard Rogers' new Lloyd's headquarters, showing the famous atrium, the interior of the Room with its banks of escalators and old rostrum, and one of Lloyd's red-coated 'waiters'.*

Right: *Her Majesty the Queen formally declares the new building open on November 18, then signs her name in the distinguished visitors' book.*

the site, is a most striking piece of modern architecture, which has evoked comments ranging from 'oil refinery' to 'modern masterpiece', but which undoubtedly stands in dramatic contrast to the conformist architecture that surrounds it. Twelve stories high with a ribbed atrium as its central feature, it is to all intents and purposes an inside-out kind of building: clean, uncluttered almost austere inside, but with an exterior that unashamedly makes a feature of all the service facilities. Six satellite towers housings lifts, loos and other services, plus cascades of pipework virtually dictate the shape of the outer shell. It is certainly a building that cannot be ignored.

It was designed to accommodate the latest in computer technology as part of its infrastructure and Lloyd's aim to operate a paper-free market in the foreseeable future is coming to fruition as many underwriters now keep their records on computer film, and the market looks forward to conducting its routine business electronically. But in spite of this hi-tech leap forward Lloyd's has by no means jettisoned its traditions. The time-honoured boxes may be of a new design but they are still recognisable descendants of the stalls in Mr. Lloyd's original coffee-house, nor have the waiters lost their 18th century livery. The panelled

library and elegant Adam room have been transplanted intact from their previous home, and Sir Edwin Cooper's vast mahogany rostrum (for which there was no room in the 1958 building) has been restored to its place of honour in the centre of the Room, where it stands in incongruous yet strangely effective contrast to its surroundings.

For Lloyd's it has been an inspired, and at £167 million an expensive, act of patronage, and only time will tell if its flexibility will indeed meet the expanding demands of the market. But it is without doubt a token of Lloyd's confidence in its own future. When, in November 1986, Her Majesty the Queen came to open the building formally, the chairman Peter Miller welcomed her to 'the New Lloyd's' thus echoing an earlier move 200 years earlier by the Society from its crowded coffee-house into more spacious and substantial surroundings at the Royal Exchange. That migration, inspired by the 'Father of Lloyd's' John Julius Angerstein proved to be more than just a move into new premises: it was also an embarkation on a new era of development and prosperity. With its new corporate structure, its new premises, its new technology and its new spirit of realistic optimism Lloyd's may indeed – on the eve of its tercentenary – be on the threshold of another new era.

IMPORTANT DATES IN LLOYD'S HISTORY

1648 Birth of Edward Lloyd (d. 1713).

1688 First known reference to Edward Lloyd's Coffee-House in Tower Street.

1691 Transfer of Coffee-House to 16 Lombard Street.

1696 First publication of *Lloyd's News*. Published thrice weekly and discontinued after 76th issue dated 23 February 1697.

1701 Date of Edward Lloyd's earliest surviving shipping list. (Forerunners of *Lloyd's List*.)

1720 Royal Charters granted to Royal Exchange Assurance and London Assurance Companies, but underwriting by the private insurer (e.g. frequenters of Lloyd's Coffee-House) not prohibited.

1734 *Lloyd's List* established as a regular weekly publication.

1760 *Lloyd's Registry of Shipping* founded by a Society of Underwriters at Lloyd's Coffee-House.

1769 Establishment of *New Lloyd's Coffee-House* in Pope's Head Alley and production of rival newspaper *New Lloyd's List*.

1771 Seventy-nine underwriters and brokers each subscribed £100 for the purpose of "building or removing to another House for the more Commodious Reception of the Gentlemen Underwriters" &c. *First Committee of Lloyd's,* consisting of nine Subscribers, elected. Lloyd's thus became property of the subscribers and not of the Master, although official recognition of this does not appear until March 1774.

1774 Subscribers of New Lloyd's Coffee-House rent new rooms in *Royal Exchange* through intervention of John Julius Angerstein.

1775 First use of term A1 ("A" referred to hull, "1" to equipment, hence an A1 vessel was a ship of the highest class).

1778 Restriction on entry to Lloyd's New Coffee-House. Subscribers and their connections only allowed within the Room.

1779 Subscribers agreed on standard form of *Lloyd's marine insurance policy* - almost identical with that of today.

1785 Estimated end of original Lloyd's Coffee-House, together with original Lloyd's List.

1799 Loss of HMS *Lutine*.

1803 Patriotic Fund inaugurated with the purposes of:
1) giving financial aid to those people injured in the defence of the Country or providing assistance for the relatives of people killed in action; and
2) making presentations to those people distinguishing themselves in battle.

1804 Appointment of *first Secretary* to Lloyd's – John Bennett Jnr.

1811 *Trust Deed* signed by Subscribers. Appointment of *first Lloyd's Agencies*.

1824 Repeal Bill allowing existence of insurance companies other than Royal Exchange and London Assurance.

1834 Lloyd's Register becomes separate society.

1838 *Royal Exchange destroyed by fire.* Lloyd's temporarily accommodated in South Sea House. First appearance of *Lloyd's Shipping Index*.

1844 Lloyd's returns to rebuilt Royal Exchange. Title of Lloyd's premises changed to *Lloyd's Subscription Rooms*.

1857 *First Deposit* for Security made with Committee by an Underwriting Member.

1850/1859 *Lutine* salvage operations produce bell, rudder (now made into table) and £25,000 in specie.

1871 *Lloyd's* incorporated by Act of Parliament.

1871/1890 Money salvaged from *Lutine* used for setting up Signal Stations and telegraphic communications with Lloyd's.

ABOUT 1887 *First Non-Marine Policies* written at Lloyd's by *Cuthbert Heath,* founder of today's Non-Marine market.

LATE 1880s C. E. Heath wrote first Lloyd's reinsurance policy on *American Risks* for an English Company doing business in the United States.

1906 *San Francisco earthquake* claims met by Lloyd's Underwriters. Great credit to Non-Marine market.

ABOUT 1906/1907 As a result of heavy claims arising from San Francisco earthquake, C. E. Heath devised *Excess Loss Reinsurance* – an insurance paying no regard to ordinary claims but to operate only when ceding company had to meet unusually heavy claims.

1908 Introduction of *Annual Audit* and *Premium Trust Fund*.

1928 Lloyd's transferred to building in Leadenhall Street opened by HM King George V and HM Queen Mary.

1937 Additional Securities Limited formed to meet US state legislation requirements came into operation.

1939 Foundation of Lloyd's *American Trust Fund* for US dollar premiums.

1957 Building *opened officially* by HM Queen Mother on 14 November.

1958 Underwriting Room moved to new building on April 8.

1969 Foreign nationals admitted to underwriting membership of Lloyd's.

1970 Women admitted to underwriting membership.

1972 Lloyd's Life Ltd formed to allow Lloyd's Members to profit from long-term life business

1973 Women members of Lloyd's allowed to work in Underwriting Room.

1973 Lloyd's of London Press Ltd formed.

1980 Publication of the Fisher Report.

1982 Loyd's Act becomes law, providing for an elected Council (first meets Jan. 1983).

1986 H.M. The Queen opens Lloyd's new building by Richard Rogers.

1987 Neill Report published.

INDEX